# Phase II in Review
*The Price Commission Experience*

STUDIES IN WAGE-PRICE POLICY

# Phase II in Review
## *The Price Commission Experience*

ROBERT F. LANZILLOTTI

MARY T. HAMILTON

R. BLAINE ROBERTS

THE BROOKINGS INSTITUTION
*Washington, D.C.*

*Library of Congress Cataloging in Publication Data:*

Lanzillotti, Robert Franklin, 1921–
  Phase II in review.

  (Studies in wage-price policy)
  Includes bibliographical references.
  1. United States. Price Commission.  2. Wage-
price policy—United States.  3. United States—
Economic policy—1971–  I. Hamilton, Mary T.,
joint author.  II. Roberts, Blaine, 1944–
joint author.  III. Title.  IV. Series.
HC110.W24L35     338.5′26′0973     75-5164
ISBN  0-8157-5144-3
ISBN  0-8157-5143-5  pbk.


9 8 7 6 5 4 3 2 1

THE BROOKINGS INSTITUTION is an independent organization devoted to nonpartisan research, education, and publication in economics, government, foreign policy, and the social sciences generally. Its principal purposes are to aid in the development of sound public policies and to promote public understanding of issues of national importance.

The Institution was founded on December 8, 1927, to merge the activities of the Institute for Government Research, founded in 1916, the Institute of Economics, founded in 1922, and the Robert Brookings Graduate School of Economics and Government, founded in 1924.

The Board of Trustees is responsible for the general administration of the Institution, while the immediate direction of the policies, program, and staff is vested in the President, assisted by an advisory committee of the officers and staff. The by-laws of the Institution state: "It is the function of the Trustees to make possible the conduct of scientific research, and publication, under the most favorable conditions, and to safeguard the independence of the research staff in the pursuit of their studies and in the publication of the results of such studies. It is not a part of their function to determine, control, or influence the conduct of particular investigations or the conclusions reached."

The President bears final responsibility for the decision to publish a manuscript as a Brookings book. In reaching his judgment on the competence, accuracy, and objectivity of each study, the President is advised by the director of the appropriate research program and weighs the views of a panel of expert outside readers who report to him in confidence on the quality of the work. Publication of a work signifies that it is deemed a competent treatment worthy of public consideration but does not imply endorsement of conclusions or recommendations.

The Institution maintains its position of neutrality on issues of public policy in order to safeguard the intellectual freedom of the staff. Hence interpretations or conclusions in Brookings publications should be understood to be solely those of the authors and should not be attributed to the Institution, to its trustees, officers, or other staff members, or to the organizations that support its research.

# Foreword

Recent high rates of inflation in many industrialized countries have severely tested traditional stabilization policies and induced governments to experiment with various direct controls on wages and prices. Since the Second World War, Western European countries have been more inclined than the United States to intervene in private wage and price decisions. The United States avoided formal intervention from the time of the Korean War until August 1971, when President Richard M. Nixon invoked the Economic Stabilization Act of 1970 to impose a ninety-day freeze on wages, prices, and rents. The freeze was the prelude to a comprehensive structure of wage-price controls, which moved through Phases II, III, and IV in the period from November 1971 until April 1974.

The U.S. decision to impose price controls has been praised as a necessary and bold move, condemned as naive both in strategy and in execution, and dismissed as pure election-year politics. The control program no doubt can and will continue to be regarded as all these things and others as well. Nevertheless, it is important to understand how the program worked and to have a basis for judging its effectiveness. This volume reviews the basic strategy developed by the Price Commission during the Phase II period from November 1971 to the end of 1972, the issues faced in policy formulation and administration, and the economic lessons that can be drawn from the experience.

Research at the Brookings Institution has reflected a continuing interest in the evolution of wage-price policies in the United States since the publication of *The Wage-Price Guideposts,* by John Sheahan, in 1967. Arnold R. Weber's 1973 book, *In Pursuit of Price Stability: The Wage-Price Freeze of 1971,* dealt with Phase I of the control program. This book deals with the development, management, and effects of the price controls administered by the Price Commission during Phase II. A companion volume on the Pay Board experience with wage controls is in preparation. A final volume will trace and evaluate the development of wage-price policy in the United States since the Second World War. It is hoped that this series of studies will contribute to a better public understanding of the purposes, problems, effectiveness, and consequences of direct controls.

The authors of the volume, Robert F. Lanzillotti, Mary T. Hamilton, and R. Blaine Roberts are, respectively, Professor of Economics and Dean of the College of Business Administration at the University of Florida, Professor and Chairman of the Department of Finance at the Loyola University of Chicago, and Associate Professor of Economics at the University of Florida. Lanzillotti and Hamilton were members of the Price Commission; Roberts was a staff economist in the Office of Price Policy of the Commission during Phase II. All authors were members of the associated staff of the Brookings Economic Studies Program when the volume was being prepared. Since they were not of a single mind on some of the issues, final responsibility for reconciling differences of interpretation and recollection rested with Lanzillotti.

The authors acknowledge with gratitude the suggestions made by Barry Bosworth, David L. Grove, and Joseph A. Pechman on the original manuscript. Several of the econometric models used to assess the effects of the price control program were first developed by Ahmed Al-Samarrie, John Kraft, Bradley Askin, Charles Guy, and other members of the Price Commission staff. Anne Morrall and David Roberts assisted in various statistical calculations. The manuscript was edited by Goddard W. Winterbottom; its sources, data, and other factual content were checked by Evelyn P. Fisher; and the index was prepared by Annette H. Braver.

The views expressed in this volume are those of the authors and should not be ascribed to those named above or to the trustees, officers, or other staff members of the Brookings Institution.

KERMIT GORDON
*President*

*Washington, D.C.*
*April 1975*

# Contents

## Figure

# Phase II in Review
*The Price Commission Experience*

# The Evolution into Phase II Price Controls

President Nixon, in his announcement of a wage and price stabilization program on August 15, 1971, outlined two phases for controls. A freeze on wages and prices for a ninety-day period, which became known as Phase I, was to be followed by a longer-range program of controls that would be designed during the freeze and go into effect for an unspecified period of time after the ninety days. This latter program, announced to the nation on October 7 and to become effective November 14, was called Phase II. The President's initial action, which invoked the power authorized to him by the Economic Stabilization Act of 1970, was a complete reversal of his administration's economic "game plan" for 1971.

By the summer of 1971 there had come to prevail—widely outside the administration and reluctantly inside it—a growing impatience and lack of confidence in the efficacy of fiscal-monetary measures alone to control inflation at acceptable rates of unemployment. Such perceptions may have been naive or faulty or both in their comprehension of economic processes; and the correctness of the points of view held by different groups probably will be reviewed and debated indefinitely. But whatever the case, the game plan for 1971 was no longer tenable.

Viewed from the longer perspective of economic policy development and discounting fully the political aspects of the decision, Phases I and II represented a further drift toward an incomes policy in the United States,[1] especially when they are measured against the voluntary wage and price guideposts used by the Kennedy and Johnson administrations during the 1960s and against the events that followed their demise. The economic

1. Price and wage stabilization measures have not been incomes policy in the true sense of the concept. No direct attempts have been made to influence income distribution, and the institutional background for collective bargaining has been distinctly different from the one which has prevailed in Europe. Phase II incorporated a "voluntary" guideline on dividends, so the total effort was designed to give the appearance of some degree of influence on incomes, imprecise though it was.

significance of the announced program was that it institutionalized a
broad peacetime experiment in direct controls—a kind of measure generally reserved for managing conditions of wartime inflation—as an adjunct
to continuing fiscal and monetary actions. The purpose of this study is to
examine the nature and the effects of the program in the area of price
controls. Companion studies focus on the three-month wage-price freeze
of Phase I and on wage controls during Phase II.[2]

A number of questions can be asked about this experiment in peacetime controls. What was the economic situation preceding the freeze in
terms of the immediate outlook for inflation? Assuming the rate of inflation actually was beginning to reaccelerate, did the freeze and Phase II
constitute the proper economic policy? What economic theory underlay
Phase II, and what was Phase II designed to accomplish? Was Phase II
in fact a program of controls in form only, an economic sham designed
to satisfy public demands by interposing only minor interference with
usual pricing practices? How were the basic policies for price stabilization implemented, and what were the major problems? What were the
economic effects of Phase II, both generally and in specific industries?
Finally, what are the legacies and lessons of the experiment with price
controls?

Attempts will be made to answer these questions, some of them more
definitively than others, and some of them by means of inference and
informed conjecture. Attempts will be made also to pinpoint those areas
which will require more data, new developments in economic theory, or
other steps that can lead to a more rigorous analysis of Phase II price
controls.

The formulation and evolution of Phase II price controls is discussed
in the first three chapters, and Chapters 4 through 6 examine special
provisions that were made and problems that arose during the life of
Phase II, from November 14, 1971, through January 11, 1973. Some
purely economic aspects of controls are covered in Chapter 7, and
Chapters 8 through 11 contain empirical analyses of the effects, costs,
and benefits of the controls. In summation and retrospection, Chapter 12
suggests some of the lessons of this experiment and considers their implications for future economic policy and controls programs.

2. Arnold R. Weber, *In Pursuit of Price Stability: The Wage-Price Freeze of
1971* (Brookings Institution, 1973); and Arnold R. Weber and Daniel J. B. Mitchell,
manuscript in preparation.

## Price Movements in the 1960s

Historically, the most serious inflations in the U.S. economy have been associated with wars, but since the 1950s there has been concern with the recurring phenomenon of peacetime inflation concomitant with relatively high unemployment. The inflation of the mid-1950s originated with an economic boom that, in turn, generated an excess of demand in the economy. When the boom collapsed, however, prices continued to rise even though unemployment remained at a relatively high level from 1958 through 1961.[3] This behavior was contrary to traditional economic theory, or at the least it raised important questions—without good answers—about the lags implied in the process of adjustment to full employment and price stability. Although unemployment and excess capacity were substantial, policymakers were concerned that price increases might accelerate once unemployment began to decline.

But the early 1960s turned out to be a period of rather remarkable price stability. From 1960 to 1965, the consumer price index (CPI) increased at an annual rate of only 1.3 percent, with most of the rise occurring in the service sector—traditionally an area, taken as a whole, of notoriously slow growth in productivity. Wage increases also were moderate during this period: total compensation per man-hour rose at an average annual rate of 3.8 percent, or only slightly more than the rate of increase in output per man-hour. In late 1965 and in 1966, however, more rapid increases in prices and wages occurred, reflecting sharp increases in expenditures generally (the Vietnam war expenditures in 1965, coupled with massive outlays for welfare programs), expansion of the money supply, and the decline in the unemployment rate to around 4 percent. Price increases were large for some commodities, as well as for medical-care services—the latter induced by the introduction of the medicare program without a corresponding increase in resources. In addition, most major indexes of prices and wages showed significant acceleration by mid-1966, especially after the airline machinists' contract was settled at an estimated 4.9 percent a year wage increase, a figure that effectively crippled the Johnson administration's guidepost of 3.2 percent.[4]

3. For such figures and others in the following paragraphs, see the historical tables on unemployment, compensation, and prices and living conditions in U.S. Bureau of Labor Statistics, *Handbook of Labor Statistics, 1973* (1974).
4. *New York Times,* August 21, 1966.

Table 1-1. *First-Year Wage-Rate Changes in Collective-Bargaining Agreements Covering 1,000 Workers or More, for All Industries and Manufacturing, 1968 and 1970–72*

| Wage-rate action and related items | All industries | | | | Manufacturing | | | |
|---|---|---|---|---|---|---|---|---|
| | 1968 | 1970 | 1971 | 1972ᵃ | 1968 | 1970 | 1971 | 1972ᵃ |
| All wage actions | 100 | 100 | 100 | 100 | 100 | 100 | 100 | 100 |
| No wage increase | * | * | 1 | 2 | * | * | 1 | 1 |
| Increase in wagesᵇ | 100 | 100 | 99 | 98 | 100 | 100 | 99 | 99 |
| Under 1 percent | 0 | 0 | * | * | 0 | 0 | 1 | 0 |
| 1–2 percent | * | * | * | 1 | * | * | * | * |
| 2–3 percent | 2 | 1 | * | 2 | 2 | 1 | * | 2 |
| 3–4 percent | 2 | 1 | 1 | 4 | 2 | 1 | 1 | 2 |
| 4–5 percent | 7 | 1 | 1 | 7 | 8 | 1 | 2 | 6 |
| 5–6 percent | 12 | 3 | 3 | 20 | 11 | 6 | 4 | 23 |
| 6–7 percent | 19 | 17 | 9 | 20 | 27 | 33 | 16 | 24 |
| 7–8 percent | 34 | 11 | 5 | 16 | 25 | 18 | 7 | 19 |
| 8–9 percent | 6 | 8 | 7 | 7 | 7 | 10 | 9 | 16 |
| 9–10 percent | 6 | 5 | 10 | 8 | 8 | 6 | 6 | 2 |
| 10 percent and over | 12 | 54 | 61 | 12 | 9 | 24 | 53 | 4 |
| Not specified | 1 | 1 | 1 | 0 | 1 | * | * | 0 |
| Number of workers (thousands) | 4,589 | 4,675 | 3,978 | 2,092 | 2,277 | 2,184 | 1,913 | 792 |
| Mean adjustment (percent) | 7.4 | 11.9 | 11.6 | 7.0 | 7.0 | 8.1 | 10.9 | 6.6 |
| Median adjustment (percent) | 7.2 | 10.0 | 12.5 | 6.3 | 6.9 | 7.5 | 10.1 | 6.2 |

Percentage of workers affected

Source: *Economic Report of the President Together with the Annual Report of the Council of Economic Advisers, January 1973*, p. 62. Detail may not add to totals because of rounding.
* Less than 0.5 percent.
a. Preliminary.
b. The percentages of estimated average hourly wages, excluding overtime.

The rate of increase in both wages and prices was less rapid during the brief slowdown that occurred in 1967, but by late 1967 and 1968 it again accelerated in response to rapid growth in aggregate demand. Some response of this kind was to be expected, of course, but the surge in 1968 was disproportional to past experience.

A combination of monetary and fiscal restraints was introduced by the Nixon administration in 1969 in an effort to combat spiraling prices. By the end of the year, the measures had helped to push the economy into a recession, but the rate of inflation continued to rise across the board throughout 1969 and 1970. Despite a substantial increase in unemployment, acceleration was evident as well in hourly compensation and earnings. Although the CPI's rate of advance receded from 6 percent in 1970 to an annual pace of about 4.5 percent during the period from January to August 1971, a significant part of the retardation was attributable to the decline in mortgage-interest rates (responding to earlier monetary policy) and to the decline in used-car prices. After adjustment for these two developments, consumer items still were rising at an annual rate of nearly 5 percent.

The stubbornness of the unemployment rate, holding at around 6 percent, might have been expected to help slow wage increases. But the 6 percent overall figure must be interpreted in light of the changing structure of the labor force in the late 1960s. Large increases in the number of women workers, secondary workers, and teenagers—all of whom traditionally have had a rate of unemployment far above the aggregate—contributed significantly to the overall increase in the rate of unemployment. In contrast to the overall unemployment rate, the rate for married men stood at from 1.5 to 1.9 percent in the late 1960s and averaged about 3 percent during the period 1970–72, and it was declining through 1971 and 1972.

During 1970, the first-year adjustment in newly negotiated collective-bargaining contracts averaged 11.9 percent at an annual rate for all industries. Little relief was in sight: as other contracts expired, labor would attempt to stay ahead of the price-wage spiral (see Table 1-1). Thus, although there were a few signs of abatement in the inflation rate, pressures on costs remained strong, and the expectations of consumers, business, and labor were that the future rate of inflation would remain high.[5]

5. This was documented by various polls and surveys conducted in the summer of 1971. See, for example, various mid-1971 issues of *The Sindlinger Report on Consumer Confidence* (Sindlinger and Co.).

## Policy Considerations Leading to Controls

In its annual report issued in January 1972 the Council of Economic Advisers summarized its view of the policy dilemma that had pertained in August 1971:

1. The economy was rising, and a continued rise could be expected; but the rise was not as fast as was desirable, especially from the standpoint of reducing unemployment.
2. Although the rate of inflation had stopped rising and might have declined, the decline was not clear cut, and there was some danger that the rate might rise again.
3. The U.S. international balance-of-payments position was deteriorating sharply, and willingness abroad to hold dollars was ebbing.[6]

Policymakers in the summer of 1971 had to face the uncertainties associated with each of these three problems, as well as the fact that the interrelations of the three complicated the process of making choices. Among other things, a more rapid rate of expansion in the economy might have helped slow the inflation by speeding up productivity growth and attenuating the rise in unit labor costs. This seemed to be a plausible argument to the Council of Economic Advisers in early 1971, but by midsummer it had become less convincing amid a psychological atmosphere in which any action that appeared inflationary "tended to increase the expectations of inflation, even though the indication was superficial."[7] There was concern that action intended to be expansive— should such action intensify fears of inflation, force up interest rates, weaken confidence, and depress consumer and business spending— might become counterproductive. There was concern also that fiscal and monetary expansion might arouse fears of an acceleration of inflation and increase the flow of funds abroad, thus complicating the U.S. international financial problem. At the same time, restrictive monetary and fiscal policies were ruled out politically by the continued high rate of unemployment.

The political merit of controls also was debatable. Congress had approved presidential authority to impose controls in August 1970 over strong opposition from the administration itself, which asserted that such

6. *Economic Report of the President Together with the Annual Report of the Council of Economic Advisers, January 1972*, p. 65.
   7. Ibid., p. 67.

powers would not be utilized. But the lack of acceptable economic performance in mid-1971 elicited public advocacy of wage-price controls by many congressmen, as well as by labor leaders, and the question of imposing wage-price controls seemed likely to become one of the few domestic issues of the forthcoming presidential campaign. The institution of controls before that time might have taken some wind out of the fluttering sails of the opposition, but such a course was contrary to the ideological position of the Nixon administration.[8]

No one surefire device seemed to be in evidence to reduce all these difficulties without producing a number of undesirable side effects. The decision to institute a direct, temporary price and wage controls system, however, allowed more latitude for fiscal policy, because such controls would provide a degree of protection against the fact and expectation of inflation. Thus, the decision announced on August 15, 1971, really was part of an overall package of measures comprising (a) the direct-controls program covering both prices and wages, (b) changes in international financial arrangements, and (c) such fiscal actions as restoring the 7 percent investment credit, repealing the 7 percent excise tax on automobiles, advancing the effective date of previously legislated tax cuts, and deferring federal pay raises. The Council of Economic Advisers estimated that this package, in net, would increase expenditures for fiscal 1972 by $1.1 billion and raise the real gross national product for 1972 by about $15 billion.[9]

From the outset of Phase II, high-level administration officials stressed that the controls adopted were considered to be supplemental rather than fundamental to the mix of economic policy. The primary objective of Phase II was to allow the economy to recover and at the same time to appear to be doing something about inflation. If a controls program could temporarily calm public anxiety about inflation, and if economic output did pick up steam, a firm base for employment gains could be established and the pace of business activity stimulated further. Thus, controls were not considered to be a surrogate for responsible monetary and fiscal policy. It was assumed, however, that controls could have a significant, though marginal, impact on wages and prices, and that the benefits of

8. Despite this ideological opposition, the administration already had utilized the authority of the Economic Stabilization Act in establishing the Construction Industry Stabilization Committee in March 1971.

9. See *Economic Report of the President, January 1972*, pp. 69–72.

such controls would outweigh the economic costs of administering and complying with the program.

The secondary objective of Phase II was to alter expectations about the inflation rate. To the extent that the freeze was widely accepted among businessmen, political leaders, and (however grudgingly) organized labor, Phase II began amid a generally receptive attitude toward controls. The major restraint on both wages and prices during Phase II actually would reflect the changed environment within which decisions about wages (union and nonunion) and prices were made more than it would the specific regulations of the Pay Board and Price Commission.[10]

10. See Barry Bosworth, "Phase II: The U.S. Experiment with an Incomes Policy," *Brookings Papers on Economic Activity* (2:1972), p. 343; and the assessment presented here in Chapters 8–12.

# II

# Policy Formulation and
# Organizational Development

Atop the administrative ladder of the Economic Stabilization Program was the Cost of Living Council (CLC), which had responsibility for establishing broad stabilization goals, for overall coordination of the program, and for developing and recommending to the President policies, mechanisms, and procedures to maintain the stability of rents, wages, and prices.[1] The principal regulatory agencies under the CLC in the controls sector were the Price Commission, which had responsibility for establishing standards and implementation procedures to stabilize prices and rents; and the Pay Board, with analogous responsibility in the area of wages and salaries. To the Internal Revenue Service was mandated the operation of compliance centers to support the controls program, largely by disseminating information and investigating complaints about violations.

In addition to these principal agencies, four other bodies served in advisory capacities on matters of policy in their respective areas of concern: the Committee on Interest and Dividends, reporting exclusively to the CLC; the Construction Industry Stabilization Committee, serving the Pay Board; the Rent Advisory Board, serving the Price Commission; and the Committee on Health Services Industry, serving both regulatory agencies. Other federal agencies and departments inevitably interacted with the controls agencies.

Unlike the CLC, made up of high-level administration officials, and the Pay Board, originally a tripartite body with representatives from business, labor, and "the public," the Price Commission had an entirely

1. Executive Order 11640 (January 26, 1972), reaffirming Executive Order 11627 (October 15, 1971). By Executive Order 11615 (August 15, 1971), the CLC comprised the secretaries of the treasury, agriculture, commerce, labor, and housing and urban development (the latter was not named in Order 11615 but was included in an amending executive order, 11617, September 2, 1971); the director of the Office of Management and Budget; the chairman of the Council of Economic Advisers; the director of the Office of Emergency Preparedness; the special assistant to the President for consumer affairs; and, as adviser, the chairman of the Federal Reserve Board.

public membership. Its chairman was C. Jackson Grayson, dean of the
School of Business Administration of Southern Methodist University. The
six other original members were William T. Coleman, Jr., a partner in the
law firm of Dilworth, Paxson, Kalish, Levy and Coleman, in Philadelphia;
Robert F. Lanzillotti, dean of the College of Business Administration of
the University of Florida; J. Wilson Newman, former chairman of Dun
and Bradstreet, Inc.; John W. Queenan, former managing partner of the
accounting firm of Haskins and Sells; William W. Scranton, former governor of Pennsylvania; and Marina v.N. Whitman, professor of economics at the University of Pittsburgh. Marina Whitman resigned in February
1972, and was replaced, on May 16, by Mary T. Hamilton, professor of
finance at Loyola University, Chicago.

Despite the chairman's stated preference for deciding questions by
consensus, there emerged over time a clear tendency for the commissioners to split into two blocs on critical policy issues, with Newman,
Queenan, and Whitman forming one, and Coleman, Lanzillotti, and
Scranton the other.[2] More often than not, Grayson voted with the first
bloc when a tie had to be broken. This alignment assumed added significance after Whitman's resignation: despite his stated preference for
voting himself only to break a tie, Grayson tended then to vote with
Newman and Queenan, thereby creating a 3–3 standoff that for three
months prevented any modification of the basic regulations. After
Hamilton joined the commission, she tended to vote with her prede-
cessor's bloc.

The role and function of the Price Commission probably can be
examined best (a) in its relation to the CLC and other bodies involved
in the administration of the stabilization program, and (b) in the internal
organization, policy formation, and decisionmaking of the commission
itself. The role foreseen for the commission under (a) determined to a
considerable extent the machinery subsequently developed under (b).

## Administrative Jurisdiction of the Price Commission

From the very beginning, the commission operated with uncertainty
and limited information about general economic policies: about, for
example, monetary growth and the size of the federal deficit, as well as

2. This information, as well as many other examples of what might be considered "the inner workings" of the Price Commission, reflects the membership of
the senior author on the commission throughout its existence and the copious notes
that he kept.

agricultural and other highly relevant factors of policy. The commission rarely was consulted in the formulation of overall economic policy. Prior to and throughout Phase II, the commissioners held meetings with chairmen of the Council of Economic Advisers and of the Federal Reserve Board, the secretaries of the treasury and of agriculture, and other officials, but the purpose of these meetings was to obtain the views of these men about controls strategy rather than to allow the commission's views to have any impact on monetary, agricultural, or other policy. This kind of relation circumscribed the economic strategy employed by the commission in framing specific regulations and later in modifying them.[3]

In addition, the policymaking role of the commission, especially in relation to the CLC, was never spelled out with as great clarity as was that of the Pay Board. The clarity attained in the latter case resulted in some part from the tripartite character of the board but principally from the insistence of prospective labor members that their membership was conditional on an agreement in advance that the CLC could not overrule the board's decisions. Because the maximum cooperation and support of organized labor were regarded as vital to the success of the program, this assurance was granted by the CLC. But because the commission had public membership only, no such assurance about its role was regarded as necessary. Thus, the commission was forced to earn its independence early in the program.

### Interaction with the Cost of Living Council

At the first, organizational, meeting of October 26, 1971, Chairman Grayson advised the other commissioners that the CLC not only would monitor commission decisions but also might intervene in them. Further, certain questions about classification and exemptions had been predecided. The CLC made clear that it would determine the structure of the classification system for firms and unions for prenotification[4] and

3. Well into the program, in the summer of 1972, the commission did influence agricultural policy by triggering the lifting of import quotas on meat—but with the unfortunate consequence that the White House remained cool toward the commission for the remainder of its existence.

4. The controls regulations, described in detail in the following chapter, classified, or tiered, firms by size and required those above a certain size to prenotify the commission of price increases.

The CLC, however, did not entirely neglect the Price Commission in making decisions. For example, on November 9, 1971, CLC Director Donald Rumsfeld sent the commission a memorandum on some issues of price control coverage for its "consideration and advice," which were provided.

reporting purposes, as well as of exemptions for various products and services. The commission, however, had ample opportunity to comment upon the proposed tiering structure, and no disagreement arose over that decision.

The problems that did arise concerned policy determination for price regulations and the commission's degree of independence in making and announcing its policies and rulings. Several early issues served to demonstrate the CLC's belief that, on basic policies and, in particular, on sensitive issues, the commission was not expected to make decisions independently. The first indication of this attitude was the CLC decision to insert a section into the regulations—without notifying the commission—that exempted tier I firms from the prenotification requirement between November 14, 1971, and January 1, 1972. The CLC felt that it possessed not only the final authority to set policy in the price area, but also the authority to do so without consulting the commission.

Another indication of the notion of the commission's role and authority held by some CLC members emerged in connection with the negotiations with the United Mine Workers of America on the coal contract in 1971—pressure from the Labor Department to agree in advance to pass through whatever higher costs would result from the negotiations. On October 26, with the commission still in early stages of organization, the department made a proposal setting forth a formula by which the impasse in negotiations could be resolved. The proposal, in effect, was a draft statement to be issued by the council:

It is recognized that labor contract bargainers are currently faced with difficult circumstances. To clarify these circumstances to the extent possible for covered economic sectors under the post-freeze stabilization program the *Cost of Living Council* advises: Under the terms of the President's Executive Order:
1. The Pay Board will determine the acceptability of economic improvement agreed to in new labor contracts.
2. The Price Commission will determine the acceptability of proposed price increases.
3. The *Cost of Living Council* in its coordinating role will advise the Price Commission that labor cost increases approved by the Pay Board are proper as a relevant factor for full and concurrent Commission consideration of price increase proposals.

The commission's reaction was that if it were to yield to any such pressure from the CLC at the outset, all bargaining groups would attempt to use the same leverage. The commissioners would be forced as well to deal with specific increase requests, case by case, at the commission rather than the staff level, which seemed both an unwieldy and an unwise approach. Thus, the commission replied that it could not agree to the proposal.[5]

On November 22 and 23, 1971, the commission reached a consensus that a full pass-through of labor costs would not necessarily be allowed.[6] The CLC did not vote on endorsement of the commission's decision, but a report to the commission by the CLC's liaison indicated that had a vote been taken, the commission would have been supported 7 to 3, with Herbert Stein, James Hodgson, and Maurice Stans against.

In a meeting with the commission on December 6, 1971, Stein (the incoming chairman of the Council of Economic Advisers, succeeding Paul W. McCracken) stated (a) that the commission had "let go a real shocker" in its decision on coal; (b) that reconciling Pay Board and Price Commission decisions in relation to overall goals was the CLC's job; and (c) that the commission's role was "routine pass-on of Pay Board's actions." Finally, Stein expressed the view that the commission's main role was "to define and deal with windfall profits"—for example, windfalls that were a direct result of a rollback of a wage contract by the Pay Board. This commentary caused no small concern to the commission, which had proceeded on entirely different premises regarding its policymaking role.

The commission resolved to talk with Secretary of the Treasury John B. Connally about its role and policies, as well as about various comments that had been made publicly by Stein and others regarding "ending controls soon" or "before the 1972 elections." Meeting with the commission on January 18, 1972, Connally made these points: (a) overall, the commission was doing a good job; (b) the rent regulations were too complicated; (c) too many people in the administration were issuing statements about Price Commission business and about decontrol;

5. The case is an interesting parallel to the steel union negotiations in the late stages of World War II, during which the Wage Board awarded twice as large an increase as the War Production Board felt was necessary. President Truman attempted to seize the steel mills to keep them operating and eventually forced the higher settlement.

Other controversial cases involving the issue of limiting the pass-through of Pay Board–approved labor costs—for example, those of construction workers, stevedores, and building-service workers—are discussed in Chapter 10. The Pay Board's view of this issue is discussed in the companion study by Arnold R. Weber and Daniel J. B. Mitchell (manuscript in preparation).

6. See Price Commission Release 18, November 22, 1971.

and (d) the commission could not correct errors of the Pay Board, but instead it should "take the offensive" and should "not wait to be put on the defensive by decontrol talk from others." He wanted a moratorium on "decontrol talk," but expected it might "last all of two weeks." (Actually, decontrol talk ceased for many months following this meeting.)

On the question of decontrol strategy, Connally urged the commission to develop a plan and *not* wait for the council to do it; to "walk a thin tightrope" by relaxing the price regulations only so much as "to make the program believable" and to concentrate on those "firms and areas that have a big impact;" and to be "candid about decontrol plans [and not] overly influenced by political problems" in this regard. In short, "don't play politics with the program, since *confidence in the program depends on the commission maintaining such a stature.*"[7]

These episodes illustrate that the role of the Price Commission in policy formulation was established more by the stance that it asserted for itself than by any clear understanding set out in advance by the CLC. Connally's views were the most clear-cut, but they were not reflected in the statements and directives of CLC Director Rumsfeld. The latter were far more equivocal regarding the commission's role and authority—no doubt reflecting the real division of thinking within the administration about controls.

Actually, although there was some difference of opinion between the commission and the CLC on these issues, a good rapport existed until June 1972, when major disagreement arose over food prices. Of course, considerable early confusion existed about some of the regulations— about, for example, loss and low-profit firms, custom products, price posting, rents, utilities, and health services. But according to William Helmantoler (director of the Office of Public Affairs for the commission), as of early December 1971 the commission's handling of its part of the stabilization program had created a highly favorable public image. Such prominence was bound in time to become a liability.

In fact, policy development by the commission was effectively truncated beginning in March 1972; by the summer it had ceased to exist. On March 14, after several commissioners expressed concern about the need to consider various tightening (and loosening) modifications, the commission voted unanimously to contract with an outside group of economists to evaluate the commission's regulations. That same day,

7. Author's notes of the meeting (emphasis added).

Stein met with the commission and opposed the notion of an outside review. Instead, he suggested putting Marina Whitman, by that time a member of the CEA, in charge of an internal review.

Whitman presented an oral report to the commission on April 11. She stated that, based on econometric and judgmental models, the forecasts tended to point toward a figure in excess of the President's and the commission's target of 2.5 percent as an "acceptable" rate of inflation for 1972, but still there was no compelling evidence that the commission would fail to achieve its objective.[8]

On the same day, Stein and Rumsfeld urged no changes in the regulations; instead, they insisted, emphasis should be placed on ensuring closer compliance with existing regulations. Nonetheless, several commissioners felt tightening was necessary if the 2.5 percent target was to be met. A motion to limit manufacturers, wholesalers, and retailers to a dollar-and-cents pass-through of costs resulted in a 3–3 vote, with the chairman's vote creating the tie and defeating the motion. A second motion requiring a dollar-and-cents pass-through only for manufacturers produced the same vote. On May 16, Commissioner Mary T. Hamilton was sworn in, bringing the commission to full strength. A motion limiting manufacturers and service organizations to a dollar-for-dollar pass-through of allowable costs again was made and lost by a 4–3 vote.

From that date onward, proposals to tighten the regulations were deferred, with the chairman arguing that the commission wait for the next month's price indexes. In this atmosphere a touchy food-option memorandum to Rumsfeld was drafted on June 6. The memorandum in effect attempted to force his hand and that of the administration on lifting import quotas on meat.[9] After that episode, the signals from Rumsfeld through the chairman were for no changes until after the elections. In short, policy development was effectively halted by midsummer of 1972 by a split in the commission itself and by opposition from the CLC and the CEA.

8. Several outside evaluations finally were contracted. They pointed up the need for some tightening of the regulations if the target was to be met. The outside evaluators were Barry Bosworth (Brookings Institution), Edgar R. Fiedler (Treasury Department), John W. Kendrick (George Washington University), Robert L. Sansom (Environmental Protection Agency), and Jay N. Woodworth (Treasury Department). Charles L. Schultze (Brookings) and Michael V. DiSalle (attorney, director of price stabilization in 1950–52, and former governor of Ohio) also were consulted and confirmed the need for tightening.

9. See Chapter 5 for a fuller discussion.

*Coordination with Other Stabilization Agencies*

The nature and extent of coordination with other agencies within the Economic Stabilization Program varied considerably. On one level, communication was continuous, in the sense that liaison persons from the CLC, the commission, and the Pay Board regularly sat in on one another's meetings. The chairmen of the commission and of the board met once a week or so to exchange information, and with somewhat less frequency with the director of the CLC. These contacts were designed to keep one another informed and to minimize the number of surprise actions.

PAY BOARD–PRICE COMMISSION LIAISON. The commissioners and Pay Board members met as a group only three times during the whole of Phase II, and only the last joint session of the two groups, late in 1972, was intended for the discussion of policy. Despite this limited contact, each group continuously received the other's reports through their chairmen and liaison persons. Moreover, the commissioners felt, at least at the outset, that they should maintain a posture as a body of "public" members—that is, distinct from the tripartite character of the Pay Board, two-thirds of whose membership was by design representative of interest groups and, thus, a body in which compromises would be required if it were to function at all. The commission had no equivalent compositional problems, although differences often arose among its members about which decision was in the public interest.

Thus, the fact that the board and the commission did not meet formally to develop an agreed-upon strategy and policy did not mean that their efforts were uncoordinated. The two groups differed on the basic policy issue of full pass-through of board-approved wage increases, but that difference merely demonstrated the complexity of resolving equity in a context of price-wage controls. The independent stances adopted by the two groups represented a healthy characteristic in that each was forced to reconcile its decisions with its particular mission. That more equitable decisions all around would have been reached by some other relation between the two bodies—even by a formal consolidation of the two such as was discussed in the summer and fall of 1972—is not at all certain.

IRS–PRICE COMMISSION LIAISON. Because the Internal Revenue Service represented an essential component in the discharge of the commission's responsibilities—not only for all of its enforcement services but also as a valuable conduit for feedback from the field offices—extensive and thorough efforts at coordination were necessary. An IRS official, Raymond N. Snead, participated in discussions about the enforceability of various regulations, monitoring, litigation, audits, and other topics, thereby giving the IRS a direct input into deliberations and actions of the commission. Even when the commission did not follow the advice of the IRS, it was put on notice about the implications and potential trade-offs of policy alternatives.[10] In addition, inquiries from, or visits by, IRS agents on commission matters had the benefit of the great respect held by businesses for such authority.

On occasion, the IRS went beyond monitoring and enforcement—in effect, to the point of rewriting commission policy. This is not to say that the position of the IRS represented a power play or anything of the sort, but rather that this rewriting occurred almost by necessity, because of the great difficulty or virtual impossibility of determining compliance with the regulations. In retail trade, for example, firms were permitted to continue their customary practices in pricing products. For some firms, this meant pricing on a category-by-category basis; for others, on an item-by-item basis; and for still others, by a combination of both approaches. The IRS contended that the only effective way to determine compliance with the limits on customary initial percentage markup was to require firms to price item by item.

This placed the commission in a dilemma: it was committed, on the one hand, to the principle of not altering customary business practices and, on the other, to a strict enforcement program. As matters turned out, the IRS persuaded many firms to change to an item-by-item pricing, and the commission went along. At least some of the companies that changed their practice found that the shift, although troublesome and costly, actually produced useful detail on cost allocations and interproduct profitability. Firms even may have been pushed toward achieving more effective profit maximization than customary practices had produced.

Another administrative decision reached late in Phase II involved the "Texas Plan." Experimental in nature, the plan called for the IRS

10. For example, the IRS early made it quite clear that the posting of retail prices would be confusing to the public and that compliance by retailers would be difficult to check without an audit.

regional office in Texas to handle all Price Commission work for companies located in its region, including prenotification, reports, and other matters (though appeals still would be made to Washington). The Texas Plan as such died with Phase II, but Phase IV operations generalized its procedures for all firms across the country.

### Relations with the Committee on Interest and Dividends

The commission's relation with the Committee on Interest and Dividends (CID) was purely a liaison arrangement by which information was supplied to the commission. Nonetheless, the chairman of the CID, Arthur F. Burns (chairman of the Federal Reserve Board), met on several occasions with the commission, including brainstorming sessions on November 3, 1971, and January 12, 1972. Burns's initial suggestions in November were in line with the consensus already reached by the commissioners—that is, not to attempt to control everything, but to focus on certain industries and leave an area of freedom within which firms could operate.

In January, in the atmosphere of decontrol talk, Burns counseled that the commission should assume a time horizon of two to three years in sharpening regulations but hoped that its members would be "going home" after a year or even six months. (In short, lead a kind of double life, acting as though the commission might be in business indefinitely, but such that you can responsibly go home in six months.) He urged a larger "zone of freedom" for firms in pricing—along lines of the various exception arrangements that the commission eventually was forced to make by expediency and considerations of equity. He also analyzed the nature of the business recovery, indicating the implications of commission actions for various facets of the recovery process—for example, the unemployment level, consumer psychology, and business expectations. Finally, he indicated frankly that the planning of the structure of Phase III should be undertaken jointly by the Council of Economic Advisers, the Federal Reserve Board, and appropriate congressional committees. Burns, in short, provided timely, helpful advice on policy.

### Use of the Advisory Committees

The Rent Advisory Board and the Committee on Health Services Industry consisted of individuals experienced in the respective fields, and the majority of their recommendations were accepted and implemented by the commission. Each group met to deliberate and formulate its recommendations, which were presented to, and discussed with, the commission by the respective chairmen or their deputies. All in all, the liaison and relations with the advisory committees worked exceedingly well (a) in providing expert, in-depth feasibility studies for the development of regulations to cover these special problems; and (b) in facilitating industry and public acceptability. The Phase II experience with these bodies would commend the arrangement to any future programs of direct controls that involve these areas of concern.

## Liaison with Other Agencies

UTILITIES AND THE REGULATORY FUNCTION. The utility regulations generated additional liaison activity with other regulatory bodies. This was considered to be a low-cost trade-off against the alternative of assuming the regulatory burdens of the Federal Power Commission, the Interstate Commerce Commission, the Civil Aeronautics Board, and the Securities and Exchange Commission, not to mention the numerous state and other regulatory bodies. Before long, the principle of delegation of authority changed the relations from a liaison activity to more of a referral and compliance activity. The commission implemented its delegation of authority by certification of the various agencies as its surrogate.

The sweeping authority granted the commission over virtually all prices placed that body in the role of a superagency over other regulatory bodies; understandably, not all persons responded positively—to say nothing of enthusiastically—to this development. In January 1972, for example, the commission decided to freeze utility rates temporarily, pending hearings to determine more fully the issues and criteria that should be considered in bringing utilities into compliance with the letter and spirit of the stabilization program. All chairmen of federal regulatory agencies (as well as state commissioners and others) were invited to testify. One chairman chose not to "appear" before the commission. Certification of the Federal Power Commission became a rather long-drawn-out affair because of difficulties over the Price Commission's requirements that rate increases be reviewed annually.

THE DEPARTMENT OF AGRICULTURE. Some of the more difficult liaison issues arose with the Departments of Agriculture and of Justice. Because food prices constitute the bugbear of any price control program, the Agriculture Department provided the commission with forecasts and outlook papers on food and other agricultural commodities, and the commission regularly utilized the services of specialists from the department. Unfortunately, their analyses did not prove to be especially helpful in anticipating the problem of food prices, and in some instances the department's policies were actual obstacles to stabilization efforts. Over time, reports from the department became increasingly inaccurate and heavily influenced by departmental policy and "official outlook," and few persons on the commission placed much faith in them.

One of the positive values of the stabilization program was its highlighting of the perverse effects generated by restrictive agriculture policies. These were illustrated during the commission's meeting with Secretary Earl L. Butz on February 22, 1972, about food prices. To concern expressed by commissioners about restrictive policies on beef production and on the limitation on beef imports, Butz replied: "Farm prices definitely are going up further, and in this political atmosphere the Department of Agriculture is taking credit for the development. . . . Sure, steers hit a twenty-year high in Omaha recently; it's about time. Farm income is getting back to a reasonable figure. . . . The going price of beef in grocery stores is about right because it clears the market."[11]

These forecasts were on a par with others received from Agriculture. Butz said that he expected "the edge will be off the beef problem by the end of 1972" and that "there will be too many hogs in 1973 and hog prices will be down." He insisted that the restrictions on grain production were proper, because "corn had a phenomenal crop in 1971 and we'll have to bring that down in 1972." He characterized as proper the $2 billion for continued restricted production of corn, wheat, and other crops. His suggestion to the commission was to "look at packer margins, wholesaler margins, and retailer margins."

The only item of some help to the Economic Stabilization Program was the news that the President would authorize higher import quotas on meat—from 1.16 billion pounds to 1.24 billion, which was almost a minimum in impact on supply. The issue of food prices and the lifting of import quotas finally reached a kind of crisis in June 1972.

THE DEPARTMENT OF JUSTICE. Liaison with the Department of Justice was necessary because that department was responsible for legal actions involving noncompliance, as well as for support in suits against

11. Senior author's verbatim notes for this and following attributions to Butz.

## Evolution of TLP Policy

The basic rationale for the TLP policy arose out of administrative convenience rather than economic logic. When the freeze ended, the commission was deluged with requests for price increases. The 72-hour rule required a vast number of prompt decisions and severely strained the limited staff resources. Thus, any simplification of price-approval procedures for multiproduct firms would greatly reduce the administrative burden.

The TLP concept evolved from negotiations in December 1971 with two major companies, U.S. Steel and Dow Chemical. In the steel industry, wage increases of about 14 percent had gone into effect on August 1, 1971. In early August, U.S. Steel had raised prices of products that accounted for about 60 percent of its production, but the increases for other products scheduled for mid-August were precluded by the freeze. Under the general guidelines, steel companies thus had cost justification for price increases averaging 7 to 8 percent, and a number of other cost increases were imminent. Given the importance of steel prices in all price indexes and the attention that any increases unquestionably would receive in the press, the potential public reaction to an announcement of price-increase approvals of that magnitude caused considerable concern. The dilemma was resolved by approving a weighted-average price increase of 3.5 percent for product lines, with the understanding that the company would not file for further price increases for one year. In essence, this enabled the company to put into effect prices announced but not implemented prior to the freeze.

In the case of Dow, thousands of products and product lines were involved. To avoid filing a massive number of price-increase request forms (known as PC-1s) the firm had requested approval of a weighted-average price increase of 2.5 percent to cover all product lines. Recognizing the potential savings in paperwork and time for both parties, the commission directed the staff to explore the possibility of a 2 percent limit. This was accepted by the company and became the first TLP-type agreement, although the policy was not adopted formally until January 18, 1972.[3]

3. On December 22, 1971, the commission announced it would consider applications from tier I firms for twelve-month agreements limiting weighted-average price increases to 2 percent or less. (Price Commission News Release 37, December 22, 1971). All product lines were to be included, although in practice this was not always the case.

The TLP approach at first was labeled "term average pricing," but this designation was changed to emphasize the limited aspect of the pricing agreement.[4] As the commission gained more expertise in this area, it became clear that the original terms had been too liberal, and the limitations were made more stringent. Of the forty-four TLP agreements granted through January 13, 1972, only five were below 2 percent. Although a 2 percent weighted-average price increase was considered well within the goals of the program, it was overgenerous in high-productivity, volume-sensitive industries. In addition, although a Price Commission press release stated that "top limits will be set for price increases on individual products or product-lines,"[5] no specific rules existed for implementation of this policy. A firm requesting a TLP agreement was required to include proposed weighted-average price increases for individual product lines, but these were merely advisory. Procedurally, TLP requests were reviewed and negotiated by staff analysts, and the agreements were referred for final approval to a review committee composed of executive committee members.

A substantial number of TLP agreements were negotiated before the policy was fully developed, and consequently forty-eight of the agreements in existence in August 1972 included no individual maximums. In isolated instances, the early agreements did specify maximum increases for individual products. These were determined in negotiation with the commission staff and often were as high as 15 percent. Admittedly, there was a paucity of information about historical pricing policies of large multiproduct firms, but even what was available was not explored. Members of the commission expressed concern that staff implementation of TLP policy was too liberal; the 2 percent allowable WAPI seemed to be viewed as a standard rather than a maximum.

In March 1972 the commission reduced the maximum allowable WAPI to 1.8 percent and set a maximum of 8 percent for price increases of individual products.[6] Within these limits, TLP agreements were tailored to the individual firm, which tailoring resulted in differences in pricing flexibility among agreements and, therefore, among

4. In addition, one of the commissioners disliked the acronym TAP.
5. Price Commission News, December 22, 1971.
6. The reduction was little more than symbolic of a toughening attitude of the commission, which was the interpretation that the move received in the press. This move, however, was the sole result of an effort by part of the commission to adopt a much stricter overall policy, which was centered around the removal of the profit margin on allowable-cost increases.

firms. Differences usually were in the magnitude of the WAPI authorized for the firm; but in some instances, an agreement with a firm excluded critical products or stipulated a maximum price increase for these products of less than 8 percent. Generally, this occurred when the price increase of a product or product line would have a significant effect on inflation or inflationary expectations.[7] For example, crude oil and home heating oil, considered critical products, were excluded from the TLP agreements with petroleum companies so that the products could be regulated more closely.

## Impact on Price Stability

At the end of 1972, 185 TLP agreements were in effect.[8] With few exceptions, the participating firms were large manufacturers, because TLPs generally were unattractive to service-oriented or labor-intensive firms. This, as well as the high concentration in chemicals, machinery, and petroleum, is reflected in the distribution of TLP firms by industry, as shown below, by two-digit standard industrial classification:

| Standard industrial classification | Industry | Number of TLP firms | Percent of total |
|---|---|---|---|
| 12 | Coal | 1 | 0.6 |
| 13 and 29 | Petroleum | 21 | 11.6 |
| 19 | Ordnance | 2 | 1.1 |
| 20 | Food | 15 | 8.3 |
| 21 | Tobacco | 2 | 1.1 |
| 22 | Textiles | 1 | 0.6 |
| 24 | Lumber | 3 | 1.7 |
| 26 | Paper | 6 | 3.3 |
| 27 | Printing and publishing | 2 | 1.1 |
| 28 | Chemicals | 48 | 26.5 |
| 30 | Rubber | 8 | 4.4 |
| 31 | Leather | 1 | 0.6 |

continued

7. The criteria used to identify critical products were (a) the impact on price levels, as measured by contributions to the major price indexes; (b) the ability of the firm to control market prices through price leadership or concentration of production; and (c) the potential impact on the prices of other products or of intermediate or finished goods.

8. A total of 187 were negotiated during Phase II.

Table 4-1. Simulations of the 1967–71 and 1970–71 Periods Showing Impact of Term Limit Pricing Agreements

| Average price change due to TLPs[a] (percent) | Firms covered by term limit pricing agreements | | | | | | | |
| | 1967–71 simulation | | | | 1970–71 simulation | | | |
| | Number | Percent of total | Sales (millions of dollars) | Percent of total sales | Number | Percent of total | Sales (millions of dollars) | Percent of total sales |
|---|---|---|---|---|---|---|---|---|
| Above 1.9 | 25 | 13.4 | 18.6 | 15.1 | 12 | 6.5 | 5.4 | 4.4 |
| 1.5 to 1.9 | 11 | 5.9 | 8.0 | 6.5 | 8 | 4.3 | 5.3 | 4.3 |
| 1.0 to 1.4 | 23 | 12.4 | 22.0 | 17.8 | 7 | 3.8 | 6.2 | 5.0 |
| 0.5 to 0.9 | 16 | 8.6 | 15.3 | 12.4 | 18 | 9.7 | 18.9 | 15.4 |
| 0.0 to 0.4 | 11 | 5.9 | 6.3 | 5.2 | 16 | 8.6 | 10.6 | 8.6 |
| −0.4 to 0.0 | 18 | 9.7 | 9.1 | 7.4 | 17 | 9.1 | 13.5 | 10.9 |
| −0.9 to −0.5 | 18 | 9.7 | 9.2 | 7.5 | 21 | 11.3 | 11.1 | 9.0 |
| −1.4 to −1.0 | 22 | 11.8 | 10.2 | 8.3 | 21 | 11.3 | 14.7 | 11.9 |
| −1.9 to −1.5 | 20 | 10.8 | 13.5 | 11.0 | 18 | 9.7 | 14.8 | 12.0 |
| Below −1.9 | 22 | 11.8 | 10.9 | 8.9 | 48 | 25.8 | 22.6 | 18.4 |
| Total firms | 186 | 100.0 | 123.1 | 100.0 | 186[b] | 100.0 | 123.1 | 100.0 |

Sources: Simulations by Price Commission, Office of Price Policy, Price Analysis Division. The simulated prefreeze price indicators were calculated by multiplying the sales of each company covered by Price Commission decisions by the corresponding annual rates of prefreeze price increases for each of the 4-digit standard industrial classification industries in which it produced. Gross national product deflators were used to calculate prefreeze price changes. Figures are rounded and may not add to totals.

a. Average price increase approved under TLP minus simulated prefreeze price increase. Negative differences indicate that the term limit pricing award was less than the historical price change.

b. Rockwell Manufacturing Company is not included in the simulation.

| Standard industrial classification | Industry | Number of TLP firms | Percent of total |
|---|---|---|---|
| 32 | Stone, clay, glass, and concrete products | 8 | 4.4 |
| 33 | Primary metals | 5 | 2.8 |
| 34 | Fabricated metals | 5 | 2.8 |
| 35 | Nonelectrical machinery | 15 | 8.3 |
| 36 | Electrical machinery | 21 | 11.6 |
| 37 | Transportation equipment | 3 | 1.7 |
| 38 | Instruments | 8 | 4.4 |
| 48 | Communication | 1 | 0.6 |
| 50 | Wholesale trade | 3 | 1.7 |
| 58 | Restaurants | 1 | 0.6 |
| 67 | Holding and investment offices | 1 | 0.6 |

Six firms having TLP arrangements were not classified.

Sales covered by TLP agreements were about $124 billion, or 38 percent of total applicable sales of tier I firms.[9] The weighted-average price increase approval for TLP firms was 1.92 percent; in contrast, the average approval for other firms in the prenotification category was 5.44 percent. This comparison, however, may be misleading. Firms that could cost-justify price increases well above the levels authorized by the TLP policy would not be expected to enter into an agreement of this kind unless market conditions were such that cost-justified price increases could not be put into effect. Evaluation of the contribution of the policy to price stability depends upon what the price performance of TLP firms would have been under the alternative procedure of filing for increases on a product-by-product basis. This, of course, cannot be known, but some insight is provided by a staff simulation study of price behavior of TLP firms prior to controls. For each firm, a precontrols weighted average of price changes was estimated for the industries in which the firm operated. The weights were the sales of the firm in each industry, so the average reflects both industry price movements and company structure. Two precontrols periods were used, 1970–71 and 1967–71. The differences between TLP approvals and the changes characteristic of the precontrols periods give a rough indication of the stabilizing impact of TLPs. In Table 4-1, a negative difference in the

9. Applicable sales are those covered by Price Commission decisions. These data relate to the 185 agreements in effect at the end of 1972.

first column implies that the agreement exerted downward, or stabilizing, pressure on prices, assuming that the overall rate of inflation in 1972 was comparable to that in either or both of the precontrols periods.

For all firms, the weighted-average price increase for both precontrols periods was larger than under the system of TLP approval. TLP approvals for 86 out of 186 firms, however, were in excess of the 1967–71 simulated increases, and these 86 TLPs accounted for 57 percent of all TLP applicable sales. The 1970–71 comparison is more favorable, but still it indicates that TLP agreements had no downward pressure on price changes for 61 firms, which accounted for 38 percent of applicable sales.

Moreover, the TLP approvals understate the flexibility in the weighted average of price changes. The TLP weighted-average price increase was an approval for increases over base prices. Increases up to base, which could be tied to either May 1970 or the highest price charged in 10 percent of the transactions during the freeze, were not included. There were several instances, particularly in chemicals and aluminum, in which the prices of May 1970 were significantly above those during the freeze period. This increased the potential for price increases not included in the TLP authorization. In addition, price decreases could be included in determining compliance with the agreement. Therefore, if a TLP firm reduced prices for some products because of competitive conditions, it became better able to increase prices of other products.

Although the findings of the simulation study are subject to many qualifications, they support the view generally held by the commissioners and the staff that TLPs were too generous. For a number of important reasons, however, it would be incorrect to infer that greater price stability would have been achieved under the regular procedure of filing PC-1 forms. In many instances, the individual price-increase maximums were below those which were cost justified. Thus, the commission did gain to some extent by reducing the administrative red tape for the firm in return for a lower average price increase and lower increases on specific products—although the gain for the commission may have been below the potential.

More important, quarterly reports filed with the commission indicated that nearly half of the TLP firms were unable to implement fully the weighted-average price increase that had been approved. This was particularly true for firms in chemicals, petroleum refining, and electrical machinery, in which sales covered under TLPs represented a substantial portion of total industry sales. From this, it might be concluded that the major downward pressures on prices of TLP firms were market forces. The special 0 percent TLPs granted to major broadcasting networks did reduce average price increases below the levels that would have been implemented by the broadcasting industry.[10] These unique TLPs allowed advertising rates to be raised or lowered without limits, so long as the weighted average of all changes were less than, or equal to, zero.

## Assessment of the Policy

Evaluating the TLP policy is difficult; seen in retrospect, nearly every feature of the policy shows both positive and negative aspects. Available data suggest that the quantitative impact was minimal; an agreement actually may have had the effect of decontrolling prices. On the other hand, the administrative simplicity reduced demands on commission resources and, on balance, was beneficial to both parties. Estimates by the commission staff indicated a saving of 30 to 35 man-years, or 25 to 35 percent, in operational resources. This estimate is based on the average time required to process a TLP agreement relative to that required for a prenotification of a price increase (PC-1) and the average number of PC-1s for a non-TLP firm.

Between January 1, 1972, and December 7, 1972, 1,577 tier I firms submitted for processing a total of 9,847 PC-1 forms and 187 TLP requests. If firms in industries with a relatively small number of PC-1 requests (trade and utilities) are excluded, an average of eleven requests were processed for each non-TLP firm. A PC-1 request required about three man-days to process; a TLP, about seven to eight man-days. (The total time required for preparation, submission, and approval of the PC-1 form could well amount to sixty days for a large firm.) That the prenotification procedure allowed for repeated interchange between the commission and the firm is a factor that partially offsets this saving: such interchange is likely to encourage compliance— or, alternatively, to discourage noncompliance.

The major administrative problems for the commission resulted from inconsistencies among the different types of TLP agreements, inconsistencies that were inevitable because agreements were negotiated on a

10. This was a necessary variant of the TLP agreement, divorced from cost justification, because of broad and changing differences in the popularity of programs.

firm-by-firm basis. More than half of these negotiations were carried on with no clear set of rules determining the policy. Monitoring also created significant problems. In the words of the staff, TLPs "left a cloudy audit trail."

Participating firms responding to a questionnaire in the fall of 1972 gave overwhelming endorsement to the TLP policy. The administrative advantages of filing a single TLP request rather than numerous PC-1s were no doubt substantial, but such cost savings were offset in part by monitoring expenses. One firm estimated monitoring costs of more than $50,000.[11] The policy endorsement was related more directly to the flexibility afforded in relative pricing and to a firm's ability to implement price decisions without delay.

The flexibility in pricing related products minimized interference with resource allocation. Individual prices could respond to demand as well as to cost pressures, because price increases did not have to be cost justified on a product-by-product basis. The inherent risk of such a policy is that firms may exploit market conditions.[12] Price increases may be concentrated on products with inelastic demand or on those over which a firm can exercise monopolistic power. If these products have a significant weight in the price indexes, stabilization efforts will be impeded.

These risks were the rationale for the March 1972 decision to place an 8 percent ceiling on the allowable price increase for individual products covered by a TLP agreement. The new policy, although often effective in preventing firms from imposing large, highly visible price increases, created new problems. In some instances, production of a particular item was curtailed if a firm found itself unable to recover valid costs. Inequities also developed between TLP and non-TLP firms. Many of the latter had a weighted-average price increase for a particular product line approved under the PC-1 prenotification procedure. These PC-1 approvals for product lines were more liberal than TLPs in that many exceeded 2 percent, often there were no individual product maximums, and additional increases could be requested when costs increased. On the other hand, under a TLP agreement, the burden of allowable-cost increases could be shifted across as well as within product lines.

11. Given the state of computerized information flow within the firm, this estimate probably is high in describing marginal cost to the firm.

12. A theoretical distinction may exist between interference with resource allocation and exploitation of demand; practically speaking, however, the difference is ideological.

These issues are not easily resolved. In some respects, the commission limited its options by the March 1972 decision on maximum allowable increases for individual products. The decision precluded the opportunity to relax individual maximums in return for a commitment by the firm to a lower overall price increase. On the other hand, a policy tailored to individual firms is difficult to administer and may impair the impartiality of a controls program.

The legacy of term limit pricing is clearly evident in the overall controls strategies adopted in Phases III and IV. The general standard for price increases in Phase III was that a price could be increased above base to reflect increased costs, so long as the base-period profit margin was not exceeded.[13] Alternatively, a firm could limit price increases reflecting increased costs to a weighted annual average of 1.5 percent and not be subject to the profit-margin limitation. In essence, this freely extended the TLP option to all firms. It established a zone of freedom of 1.5 percent, and firms complying with this zone were exempted from the profit-margin limitation. No limits were set on increases for individual products.

In Phase IV, the "110 percent rule" combined the regulations—or experience—of Phases II and III. The regulations permitted a prenotification firm to apply a cost-justified price increase to a product or service line—but price increases for individual products were limited to 10 percent over and above the dollar-for-dollar cost-justified average price increase.

## Conclusions

The TLP policy represented a modification of the prenotification rules, with administrative convenience the overriding consideration in its adoption. The effectiveness and contribution of the policy to price stability in Phase II is difficult to assess. There were clearly administrative advantages, and interference with resource allocation was minimized. At the same time, actual decontrol would have saved more resources and interfered less with resource allocation.

13. Under Phase III regulations, the base price was that authorized on January 10, 1973, and the base period for profit-margin purposes was extended to include any fiscal year ending after August 15, 1971.

With hindsight, it might be argued that the weighted-average price increase should have been tied to standard industrial classification codes. This would have prevented some anomalies that arose when a firm operated in diverse industries. It might have been possible as well either to eliminate the individual maximums or to use these as a trade-off for a lower weighted-average price increase. Similarly, increases in the allowable profit margin could have been offered in return for a reduction in the weighted-average price increase.[14] Finally, the TLP policy could have been tightened by disallowing price reductions as offsets against price increases.

From an economic standpoint, the central feature of TLP as a controls strategy is the relative pricing flexibility that it produces. Conceivably, a TLP policy could be divorced completely from cost, focusing only on price adjustments. Early in 1972, Arthur Burns recommended that firms in manufacturing be permitted zones of freedom, or flexibility, within which they would be free to adjust prices without prenotification. The flexibility in weighted-average price increase would be uniform. If the limits were observed, the profit-margin rule would not apply. The rationale was that such a policy would stimulate—or at least not inhibit—investment. Although it was not adopted in this form during Phase II, the policy became an integral component of Phase III regulations.

14. This trade-off, discussed in Chapter 7, actually was requested by some firms.

# V

# Controls in the Trade Sector
# and Problems with Food

The decision to impose Phase II controls at the retail as well as the whole-sale level was in part a legacy of the Phase I freeze, which had been comprehensive. Some members of the commission argued that a significant reduction of coverage in Phase II could seriously undermine the credibility of the program at a time of need for public acceptance of stabilization goals in all sectors of the economy.

Several of the commissioners, however, strongly opposed inclusion of retail trade because of the generally recognized competitive nature of this sector and the severely limited resources available to the stabilization program. Such a view is appropriate if the inflationary problem is attributable to cost rather than demand pressures; controls in manufacturing, in which market imperfections may be present, together with the competitive nature of retailing, should provide adequate price restraint. But retail prices are highly visible, and the commission reluctantly adopted controls at the retail level on the premise that it was necessary for public credibility and support of the program. In other words, the justification was cosmetic rather than economic.

## Trade Controls in General

The regulations for wholesale and retail trade differed from those for manufacturing and services, but they incorporated the two basic policy precepts of Phase II controls: cost justification and profit-margin limitation. These precepts, particularly cost justification, had to be modified in order to conform with customary business practices in the trade area. Typically, prices at wholesale and retail are determined by applying a markup to the cost of goods sold. The markup is applied in some cases to an item (item-by-item pricing); in others, it is applied to a category or general line of merchandise (category pricing), with separate items within

51

the category varying in price in response to demand. Generally, the markup is set at a level that will provide a customary profit after coverage of overhead and other expenses.

Phase II regulations froze the percentage of markup that could be applied to the cost of goods sold, but because at least half of the commissioners preferred to limit allowable-cost pass-throughs to increases in direct costs, prices were allowed to reflect only increased costs of the goods and not increases in overhead or wages. These stipulations, although adopted for wholesale and retail trade, were rejected for manufacturers. As a result, if increases in indirect costs were greater than direct cost increases, the regulations represented a greater constraint on prices in trade than in manufacturing—which, in fact, became the case. The limitation on allowable-cost pass-through also provided an incentive for firms to hold down indirect cost increases.

In addition, retailers and wholesalers were subject to the base-period profit-margin limitation: price increases that caused a firm to exceed its base-period profit margin could not be put into effect. To the extent that profit margins were exceeded, firms were subject to price-reduction and refund orders from the commission.

### Development of Policy

In its early deliberations, the commission decided against the policy of ceiling prices used during World War II and the Korean war controls period. Ceilings, it was felt, not only eliminate flexibility of the marketplace, but also are more likely to create shortages, especially of meat. A ceiling policy also tends to encourage shifts from low- to high-profit items, which often discriminates against the poor. Moreover, previous experience with ceilings had shown the need for a large administrative bureaucracy.[1] A ceiling on price rises was rejected lest it encourage an immediate increase in all prices by the amount of the official ceiling—in anticipation, that is, of new freezes or of tougher rules that would prohibit the increase at a later date.

1. In World War II, the Office of Price Administration employed some 60,000 persons; the staff of the Office of Price Stabilization in the Korean war period numbered 15,000. In Phase II, the staff for the entire economic stabilization program was held to 1,000 plus about 3,000 man-years from the Internal Revenue Service. Cost of Living Council, *Economic Stabilization Program Quarterly Report Covering the Period July 1 through September 30, 1972*, p. 5.

The commission at first favored control of gross dollar-and-cents margins, with price adjustments made only on a quarterly basis. A gross-margin system would have controlled prices by limiting the wholesale-retail spread to a constant dollar-base margin. Because the gross margin is a net figure reflecting decreases as well as increases in price, gross margin control would have had a potentially more restrictive effect than the regulations finally adopted by the commission. Although recognizing the possible advantages of this gross-margin approach, the commission decided that a policy based on customary initial percentage markup (CIPM) would be more in line with traditional practice in the industry, with cost increases defined as the invoice cost paid by wholesaler or retailer, including transportation costs. This view was endorsed in consultations with representatives of retailing interests. (Over time, however, the problem of compliance forced the commission to depart from the policy of recognizing traditional pricing practices.)

A company qualifying as a category pricer was required to continue to apply its historical product-pricing procedure at the lowest applicable level for the firm. If the customary practice of a firm was item-by-item pricing, this practice could not be changed. No price increases were permissible, however, until after compliance with price posting—a requirement that proved to be of negative value in that it appeared to promise consumers more information than the regulations required about the legality of prices actually charged.

The initial base period for the markup was August 15 to November 13, 1971. A firm's base markup was redefined as the last CIPM applied before November 14, 1971, or, at the option of the firm, the markup during its last fiscal year ending before August 15. An item-by-item pricer choosing the fiscal-year option was allowed to use its highest CIPM within that year. Category pricers, on the other hand, were required to use the weighted-average markup applied during the fiscal year. These differences, which have no economic rationale, resulted in some inequities in the treatment of category pricers relative to item-by-item pricers—precisely the kind of problem that some commissioners wished to avoid by excluding trade from the controls program.

*Problems*

At first glance, the regulations for wholesalers and retailers appeared straightforward. Complexities developed in part because of a multiplicity

of base periods: base price, base profit margin, and base CIPM were defined by different calendar dates, and the base-period CIPMs allowable
for pricing purposes were not those required in various reports to the
commission. The last factor reflected a peculiarity of the reporting form
and contributed heavily to enforcement problems.

More basic, however, were commission regulations that had the effect
of disallowing customary business practices if these were in conflict with
the CIPM rule. Of course, the stringent definition of category pricing
made item pricers out of most firms even when they had a historical pattern
of category pricing. But other problems, the extent of which is difficult to
assess, included (a) inventory repricing; (b) recommended retail prices
by manufacturers; (c) preticketing practices; and (d) the use of rounding
off and price points. When merchandise costs increase, retailers and
wholesalers often revalue existing inventory. Under Price Commission
regulations, this was illegal if it increased the CIPM above base. Similarly,
commission regulations prohibited selling at a manufacturer's suggested
retail price or at a preticketed price if this resulted in a higher CIPM. One
instance of the rounding-off or price-point problem concerned vending
machines, in which prices must be increased in increments of 5 cents.
Because the price increase justified by application of a CIPM to an increase in the cost of a candy bar generally would be less than 5 cents,[2]
vending-machine operators often had to absorb increased costs in order
to remain in compliance with the program.

### Posting

The Price Commission regulations issued on November 13, 1971, contained a posting requirement, a holdover from Phase I. It required retailers
to display prominently at the place of sale their base prices for all nonexempt food items and for the forty items in each department having the
highest dollar sales volume or those items accounting for 50 percent of
total dollar sales. These were to be posted on or before January 1, 1972,
and no price increases could be put into effect until the requirement was

2. A firm with a base CIPM of 100 percent would charge 10 cents for a product
with an invoice cost of 5 cents. If the invoice cost increased to 6 cents, the allowable
price under Phase II regulations would be 12 cents. This kind of price is not com-
patible with vending machines, few of which are designed to return pennies. The
normal procedure, a price increase from 10 to 15 cents, was prohibited by Phase II
regulations.

met. On December 16, 1971, the regulations were amended to allow a retailer with total sales of $100,000 or less in the last fiscal year to treat the store as a single department.[3] In January 1972, the posting requirement was eliminated for retailers with annual revenues of $200,000 or less, but the information still had to be available upon request by a customer.

The original purpose of the posting requirement was to facilitate detection of violations. In practice, however, the posting of base-period prices was confusing to the consumer, generated many groundless complaints, and actually became counterproductive because some groups misinterpreted the posting as a sham. It is estimated that the IRS spent more than 15 percent of the time it devoted to the program in investigating unfounded complaints about food retailers.[4] A base price has little meaning to a consumer unless he knows the markup. In addition, because markups legally could vary from store to store, allowable prices of an identical item also could vary from store to store. Posting was burdensome to the retailer, and conceivably, if it had been eliminated, the cost saving could have been passed on to the consumer as price reductions. Options for changing the posting regulations, including unit pricing in retail food stores, were considered frequently; none was adopted other than those discussed above.

*Enforcement*

Because of the regulations themselves, as well as the nature of record keeping, price controls at the retail level were difficult to enforce, and compliance checks required an inordinate amount of time. To audit or check compliance of a firm choosing the fiscal-year option for a base CIPM, the IRS had to review virtually all transactions within an entire year—a job costly both for the IRS and for the firm. One retail food chain estimated the cost of organizing records for such an audit was 15,000 man-hours.[5] Elimination of the fiscal-year option would have lightened the burden for the IRS substantially, but it would have represented a major change in the regulations and would have caused extreme hardship for firms that already had made sizable investments in order to conform. In

---

3. The Cost of Living Council exempted retail firms with sales under $100,000 from all aspects of the stabilization program on February 4, 1972.
4. Price Commission Master Issue File No. 38C.
5. Price Commission Master Issue File No. 40i.

addition to bearing the dollar cost of instituting new and detailed record-keeping procedures, many firms had made significant changes in pricing practices.

The exemptions made by the Cost of Living Council for small businesses and retailers with annual sales under $100,000 resulted in decontrol of about 75 percent of all retail firms.[6] Decontrol of the remaining firms would have reduced the demands on IRS resources considerably, but those remaining firms accounted for 85 percent of total sales. In addition, the exemption of all retailers might have created problems in the area of wages, because the industry is highly unionized and would have been subject to wage controls. Had Phase II been continued beyond January 11, 1973, the commission would have made extensive changes in the wholesale-retail regulations, perhaps even to decontrol of retail trade. In addition to the problems encountered in Phase II, future problems were inevitable because of scheduled increases in social security taxes and pending legislation to increase minimum wages. The regulations in Phase III recognized this explicitly and allowed federally mandated cost increases to be added to the CIPM on a dollar-for-dollar basis.

## Controls on Food

The prediction of the group of economists who met on November 3, 1971, as well as those made by many others, were correct: the most troublesome problem at the retail level was food. Indeed, it was *le bête noir,* the biggest single bugbear, of the entire price-control program. The high visibility and erratic behavior of food prices were a concern throughout Phase II and a major factor in the demise of Phase III. Control was particularly difficult: demand is relatively inelastic and supplies are subject not only to weather and other seasonal phenomena, but also to the perverse effects of long-standing agricultural programs of price support and acreage diversion.

### General Policies

At the beginning of the stabilization program, all raw agricultural and seafood products were exempted from controls. The rationale was obvious: attempts to repress price increases might cause shortages and lead to

6. Price Commission Paper M-549, December 12, 1972.

black markets or rationing. But problems inherent in the exemption came to light quickly. Food processors purchasing these raw materials incurred widely fluctuating costs, and those in tier I, which were required to file prenotifications of price increases, found themselves in a particularly difficult and disadvantageous situation. Therefore, the commission approved a volatile-pricing rule in December 1971[7] to provide relief to a prenotifying firm that incurred frequent fluctuating costs in the prices of its raw materials or of its partially processed products. If its customary practice had been to increase its own prices in immediate and direct response to these market fluctuations, the firm was permitted to continue doing so, subject to the extent authorized by prior agreement with the Price Commission.[8]

The major change in policy occurred in June 1972, when the Cost of Living Council announced that all agricultural products sold in unprocessed form at the retail and wholesale levels would be placed under controls after the first sale. This in effect controlled margins in the distribution chain. But for the most part, actions taken in the food area were on the supply rather than the controls side, and as a result good economics emerged relatively unscathed.

### Food Price Behavior

The basic problems in the agricultural area were domestic supply shortages, perverse agricultural policies, and increased demand both at home and abroad. Domestic food production actually declined in 1972 as a result of adverse weather conditions and the impact of the 1970 corn blight on hog production. Crop failures in other countries—particularly in the Soviet Union, India, and mainland China—led to increased demand for U.S. exports of food grains. Relatively inelastic demand, together with relatively inelastic short-run supplies, resulted in price increases. The food component of the consumer price index rose at a seasonally adjusted annual rate of 6.5 percent during Phase II, accounting for about 40 percent of the total rise in the CPI in that period. At the wholesale level, the prices of farm products and processed foods and feeds rose at a seasonally adjusted annual rate of 16.1 percent during Phase II, accounting for about 65 percent of the overall rise in wholesale prices.

7. See Chapter 6.
8. Price Commission Regulation 300.51(f), in *Code of Federal Regulations,* Title 6 (January 1, 1972), pp. 26–27.

Typically, agricultural output is supplied by many small producers who individually have relatively little or no control over the market. Therefore, the industry is highly competitive and prices respond rapidly to changing market conditions. The data in Table 5-1 indicate that volatile price behavior was quite evident in the period from January 1969 to August 1971,

Table 5-1. *Rates of Change in Selected Consumer and Wholesale Price Indexes, Various Periods, 1969–73*

Seasonally adjusted annual rate in percent

| Item | 1969[a] | 1970[b] | 1971 before freeze[c] | Phase I[d] | Phase II[e] |
|---|---|---|---|---|---|
| *Consumer price index* | | | | | |
| All items | 6.1 | 5.5 | 3.8 | 2.0 | 3.6 |
| Food | 7.2 | 2.2 | 4.8 | 1.7 | 6.5 |
| Commodities less food | 4.5 | 4.8 | 2.9 | 0.3 | 2.4 |
| Services[f] | 7.4 | 8.2 | 4.5 | 3.1 | 3.5 |
| *Wholesale price index* | | | | | |
| All commodities | 4.8 | 2.2 | 5.0 | 0.3 | 6.9 |
| Industrial commodities | 3.9 | 3.6 | 4.5 | −0.1 | 3.5 |
| Farm products, processed foods and feeds | 7.5 | −1.4 | 6.5 | 1.1 | 16.1 |
| Consumer finished goods | 4.9 | 1.4 | 3.8 | 0.7 | 5.6 |
| Food | 8.2 | −2.5 | 6.7 | 2.1 | 10.6 |
| Finished goods, less food | 2.9 | 4.0 | 2.2 | 0.0 | 2.3 |

Sources: Derived from official consumer and wholesale price indexes of the U.S. Bureau of Labor Statistics.
a. December 1968–December 1969.
b. December 1969–December 1970.
c. December 1970–August 1971.
d. August 1971–November 1971.
e. November 1971–January 1973.
f. Not seasonally adjusted; data contain almost no seasonal movements.

as well as during Phase II. At the wholesale level, for example, an increase of 7.5 percent in the prices of farm products and processed foods and feeds in 1969 was followed by a decline of 1.4 percent in 1970. In 1971, a strong recovery occurred in farm prices: in the first eight months of the year, prices rose at a seasonally adjusted annual rate of 6.5 percent.

To some extent and with some lag, retail food prices usually mirror changes at the wholesale level. The food component of the CPI increased at a seasonally adjusted annual rate of 7.2 percent in 1969 and 2.2 percent in 1970. The rate of increase escalated in the first half of 1971, but a pronounced slowdown occurred in July and August. The seasonally adjusted annual rate of increase for the three months ending in August was 3.4 percent, compared with 7.4 percent for the three months ending in May. For the eight months of 1971 prior to the stabilization program, the rate of increase was 4.8 percent.

Price behavior during Phase II directly reflects changing supply conditions coupled with increasing demand caused by rising real incomes. In the first quarter of 1972, the index for food consumed at home—the major part of the CPI for food—increased at an annual rate of 7.3 percent. This reflected sharply higher prices for beef and pork and for fruits and vegetables during the latter part of the quarter. Reduced hog marketings resulted in a sharp rise in pork prices between November 1971 and February 1972. An expanded output in 1970 and early 1971 had depressed pork prices; this, together with high corn prices following the 1970 corn blight, led to a cutback in production plans. By the fourth quarter of 1971, per capita supplies were below the level of the preceding year. This, in turn, put pressure on beef prices, and the unadjusted CPI for selected beef cuts increased 4.1 percent between January and February 1972. Fruits and vegetables also were in seasonally short supply.

Prices eased in March 1972, and in the second quarter of the year the index for food at home declined at a seasonally adjusted annual rate of 1.3 percent. This was virtually unnoticed by the consumer, who tends to have a myopic view of price changes: decreases only rarely are perceived, particularly in a period of controls.

For the quarter ending in September, the index rose again at an annual rate of 7.9 percent as a result of a second explosion in meat prices and higher prices of fruits and vegetables, the latter caused by storm damage and generally unfavorable weather conditions.[9] The seasonally adjusted annual rates of increase for the quarter were 10.9 percent for meat, poultry, and fish and 21.4 percent for fruits and vegetables. In the last three months of 1972, an easing in the rate of increase of fruit and vegetable prices more than offset an acceleration of prices of all other major food groups; as a result, the rate of increase in the index for food at home slowed to 6.3 percent.

For 1972, the rates of price increases at wholesale exceeded those at retail for all major groups, as shown below (from Bureau of Labor Sta-

9. Ironically, the storm damage can be attributed to Hurricane Agnes and the ensuing rains. This prima donna arrived in the Washington area on June 21, a day of great import in Price Commission deliberations (see pp. 61–62).

tistics WPI and CPI reports released in February and April 1973, respectively):

|  | Percentage increase, 1972 | |
| --- | --- | --- |
|  | Consumer price index | Wholesale price index |
| Total food | 4.7 | 8.0 |
| Food at home | 5.0 | . . . |
| Cereal and bakery products | 1.8 | 7.6 |
| Meats, poultry, and fish | 10.3 | 13.2 |
| Dairy products | 1.9 | 4.8 |
| Fresh fruits and vegetables | 1.9 | 6.6 |
| Eggs | 15.8 | 25.8 |
| Food away from home | 4.2 | . . . |

Meats, poultry, and fish increased by 10.3 percent at the retail level and by 13.2 percent at the wholesale level. Except for dairy products, discrepancies between retail and wholesale prices were even larger for the other major categories, particularly for cereal and bakery products, whose wholesale prices reflected the increase in wheat and flour prices in late summer after the grain sale to the Soviet Union. The resulting increases in the price of bread were not reflected at the retail level until several months later.

### The Impact of Shortages on Public Policy

The first food crisis occurred in February 1972, when the seasonally adjusted one-month increase in the overall food component of the consumer price index was 1.8 percent; the increase for meat, poultry, and fish was 4.6 percent, and for fruits and vegetables, 2.7 percent. These large increases led to the decision to hold hearings on food prices in April to provide a forum for public opinion and to focus attention on the role of agricultural policy. Treasury Secretary John B. Connally also held a jawboning session with representatives of large food chains on March 29. On the following day, some of the chains announced a voluntary thirty-day freeze on retail meat prices. This action took the heat off the problem of food prices, but only temporarily.

The sharp rise in food prices in the first quarter was followed by declines in the second quarter for most food items other than fruits and vegetables. Nonetheless, consumer anger and frustration abated little: in the eyes of the public, the credibility of the program was severely strained. Moreover, substantial increases in May wholesale prices, particularly for livestock and live poultry, had yet to be reflected at the retail level. The anticipation of these new price increases at retail was a source of great concern to the commission; some dramatic action seemed necessary to parallel the effect of the earlier jawboning. The course the commission chose to pursue in dealing with this second food crisis had important consequences.

THE CLASH OVER SUPPLY. The commission gathered first on June 6 to consider its options on food prices, but it postponed action until the next meeting, on June 21. That food prices were a priority item on the agenda of that meeting had been well publicized in the news media. At the second meeting, the commissioners reviewed in detail fifteen controls options including control of all agricultural products, control of farm-retail price margins on items unprocessed at the retail level, a freeze on all prices, jawboning, and others. None of these options was adopted because of the commission's strong conviction that such action would only create new problems. Instead, the commission drafted a strong memorandum to Donald Rumsfeld, director of the Cost of Living Council, urging that immediate steps be taken to increase the supply of food. Specifically, it recommended the suspension of import quotas on meat, as well as any other action that might be effective. The letter also laid out several diverse controls strategies and implied that the commission would implement one or another of them if it seemed necessary.

Price Commission deliberations occasionally were subject to unintended leaks: with increasing frequency, proposed actions or actual decisions were being reported in the news media before official releases had been prepared. The meeting of June 21 was no exception: that same evening, while a public statement of the commission's action still was being drafted, radio and television news in Washington carried reports of a mandate from the Price Commission to the White House. Speculation about commission action was widespread. On the following morning, the *Wall Street Journal* ran an article with the headline "War on Rising Food Prices to Be Urged by Panel; Temporary Freeze, Curbs on Raw Farm Items Possible."[10] Much of this was conjecture; the public statement issued by the commission after its meeting was general:

10. *Wall Street Journal,* June 22, 1972.

The Price Commission today expressed increased concern about the continued rise of food and other agriculture products.

The Commission stated that its investigations show that high prices are apparently not the result of non-compliance with Price Commission regulations by any of the groups involved in the production and distribution of those products. In the case of food, for example, profit margins currently appear to be lower than normal.

Various measures are currently under active consideration by the Commission and further staff work is being conducted in coordination with other governmental agencies involved.[11]

On June 22, the President held an impromptu news conference in the White House. The *Wall Street Journal* reported: "President Nixon, grabbing the political hot potato of food-price controls handed to him by the Price Commission, said he is considering both controls and a move to increase meat supplies. . . . Less than 24 hours after disclosure of the Price Commission's decision to seek a broad federal effort to hold down food prices, Mr. Nixon said he had directed the Cost of Living Council 'to see what further action can be taken to deal specifically with food prices, but particularly with meat prices.' "[12] The President mentioned the possibility of a temporary lifting of the quotas on imported meat. The text of the memorandum from the commission to the White House was made public later on June 22, but the release was anticlimactic.

The commission met again in a special session on the following Sunday. Because the commission had succeeded in getting the President's attention on the seriousness of the food price problem, and some action on meat import quotas was likely, the meeting was concerned solely with a general appraisal of the entire stabilization program and with options for modifying the regulations. Nothing was decided other than to await the President's actions and then to appraise further steps.

On the following day, it was publicly announced through the chairman of the CLC that the President had ruled out a price freeze on meat and other foods, but that all quota restrictions on meat imports would be lifted for the remainder of 1972 to alleviate the immediate shortage.[13] The 1972 meat-import agreement allowed exporting nations to sell 1.24 billion pounds of meat (mainly beef) in the United States, or about 5 percent of total U.S. consumption. There was no expectation of any large impact from the lifting of the import quotas, because the major suppliers to the

11. Price Commission News Release 115, June 21, 1972.
12. *Wall Street Journal,* June 23, 1972.
13. *Wall Street Journal,* June 27, 1972.

United States—Australia, New Zealand, and Argentina—already were exporting in large volume to the countries of the European Economic Community. The action taken was appropriate, however: it attacked the supply problem directly rather than trying to fix prices below a level at which supply and demand would be in balance.

The entire episode probably was viewed as a source of embarrassment by the White House, and it resulted in strained relations between the Price Commission and the White House for the duration of Phase II. The *Chicago Daily News,* reporting the lifting of meat import quotas, stated: "There was some evidence that the Price Commission, which makes recommendations to the Cost of Living Council, had been silenced on the politically touchy issue of food prices. It met in an unusual closed session of more than four hours Sunday, but said nothing."[14] This interpretation is in part misleading. The purpose of the memorandum from the commission to Rumsfeld and the White House had been to urge the administration to take some drastic action, preferably on the supply side. Although it had troubled Rumsfeld, the memorandum appeared to have been effective, and the President was on the point of acting. Nonetheless, it is true that the commission in effect was instructed to take no further action on food. The commissioners had made their point, but at real cost in terms of rapport with the CLC.

On June 29, the CLC announced that the prices of all agricultural products sold in unprocessed form at the retail and wholesale levels would be subject to price controls after the first sale. In his statement Rumsfeld said that the new price-control action "cannot drive food prices down" but was designed to "exert discipline on markups and margins at each step of the food marketing chain."[15]

The explosion in meat prices that the commission had anticipated and tried to mitigate hit with full force in the consumer price index for July: selected beef cuts had increased by 2.9 percent from the previous month. Retail prices remained firm throughout August, despite declines in the price of meat at wholesale. The CLC had been monitoring beef prices closely, and on August 4, Rumsfeld warned large food retailers that "the carcass price of beef had begun to decline during the week ending July 15, and that the Cost of Living Council expected to see a corresponding reduction in retail beef prices as soon as possible."[16] The letter was followed on

14. *Chicago Daily News,* June 26, 1972.
15. *Chicago Tribune,* June 30, 1972.
16. *Cost of Living Council News,* CLC-142, September 7, 1972.

September 6 by a telegram stating: "Retail beef prices must be reduced. I have directed Stabilization Officials of the Internal Revenue Service to monitor approximately 100 of the larger food chains in the nation so that the Cost of Living Council will be in a position to make the public aware of those firms which have reduced their prices."[17]

The unadjusted index for selected beef cuts declined by 1.7 percent in September and 1 percent in October but resumed its rise in November. Increased prices for coffee and canned fruits and vegetables also contributed to an overall rise in the CPI in late summer and fall.

THE CONTRIBUTION OF TRADITIONAL AGRICULTURAL POLICY. During the latter part of 1972, the locus of the food crisis shifted, reflecting the sharp escalation of wholesale prices of grains and protein meal. The impact on domestic prices from the decline in world production of grain in 1972 was dramatic, as was the persistent shortage of protein meal. The index for farm products, processed foods, and feeds rose at a seasonally adjusted annual rate of 30.1 percent in the three months ending in December 1972 and at 45.1 percent in the three months ending in January 1973. The impact of this surge in prices was not felt fully at the retail level until 1973, when Phase II and the commission already had been laid to rest.

The shortage of protein meal reflected the growing worldwide demand for meat and poultry feeds. On the supply side, contributing factors were a reduced Peruvian anchovy catch, losses in peanut crops, and an inadequate expansion of soybean production in the United States. The acreage planted in 1971 remained substantially unchanged in spite of attractive prices. The set-aside policy authorized by the Agricultural Act of 1970 had encouraged the production of corn at the expense of soybeans.

The losses in grain crops in many countries resulted in a decline of 3.2 percent, or 36 million metric tons, in world grain production in 1972. In contrast, production had increased on average by 34 million metric tons in each of the ten preceding years.[18] The shortfall in 1972 was aggravated by the provisions of the Agriculture Department's wheat program for maximum set-aside of acreage for crops in 1973. Surprisingly, this was announced on July 17, 1972, shortly after the first purchase of wheat by the Soviet Union. The decision was not reviewed until much later, too late to affect fall plantings of wheat.

17. Ibid.
18. John A. Schnittker, "The 1972–73 Food Price Spiral," *Brookings Papers on Economic Activity* (2:1973), pp. 498–99.

The first wheat sale was made on July 5. On July 26, the *New York Times* reported that total sales would be in the neighborhood of 1 million tons. Between July 5 and July 31, the price of wheat rose from $1.50 to $1.60 per bushel. In August, it became apparent that Soviet wheat purchases already were close to 10 million tons. Although the Department of Agriculture had reduced Commodity Credit Corporation grain stocks by some 4 million tons since May 1 (the bulk of it in August) and on September 22 had eliminated subsidies on wheat exports, it seems clear that the department had failed to comprehend the severity of the grain shortage. The heavy demands for U.S. grains, coupled with the shortage of protein feeds, could have only ominous implications for the persistent rise in food prices.

REDIRECTION OF AGRICULTURAL POLICY. Despite the severe strain placed on the stabilization program by continued increases in food prices, the experience called attention to the need for substantial change in agricultural policy. For decades, much of this policy had been oriented around the belief that restrictions on supply were necessary to prevent market gluts in basic agricultural commodities. Unfortunately, dramatic and costly events were required to illuminate the reforms needed, and the expected shift in direction toward expanded production is more likely to affect prices in the long run than in the short.

Retail prices, especially food prices, have high visibility. And herein lies the anomaly: that food is the area in which price control options are most limited and consumer expectations the highest; and that it also is the area in which some observers measure the credibility of the program on an almost day-to-day basis. Under these circumstances, disenchantment with the program and with the commission was inevitable. The Price Commission tried hard from February through the early summer of 1972 to impress on Agriculture the importance of reevaluating agricultural policy, especially the acreage set-aside program. It received in return the impression that departmental policy was directed instead toward raising farm income and that, if higher food prices were the result, this was the commission's problem. As on many other questions about controls policy, such administration views prevailed, and actions relevant to increasing supply had to await the presidential election in November.

# VI

# Special Regulations

The regulations adopted by the Price Commission at the beginning of Phase II, deliberately general in nature, were intended to apply constraints to all sectors of the U.S. economy without creating distortions and inefficiencies. This approach was both necessary from an administrative standpoint and preferable from an ethical one. Rather than ruling on specific price increases, the commissioners attempted to develop administrative law. In many cases, however, the general strategy of passing through costs was too generous, as is revealed by some available data and by various theoretical considerations.[1] The general regulations also were inadequate in several areas. Resulting problems were alleviated to some extent by special provisions, including exception procedures, but they never were wholly resolved.

This chapter covers these special provisions and some of the problems to which they were addressed, as well as those basic conflicts which arose out of the attempt to comprehend so diverse an economy within a few pages of legal regulations.

## Problems Arising from General Regulations

Among the numerous difficulties encountered during Phase II were (a) establishment of base price; (b) recoverable costs and the date of last price increase; (c) allowance for volatile costs; (d) profit-margin limitation; and (e) treatment of loss and low-profit firms. In some instances, the difficulties were related to basic definitions in the regulations; in others, they reflected more substantive issues.

### Definition of Base Price

The general rule for price stabilization during Phase II allowed prices to be increased above base only with cost justification and subject to the

1. See, for example, the empirical analyses presented in Chapters 9 and 10 and the theoretical discussions in Chapter 7.

constraint on profit margins. Following the logic of the freeze, the appropriate base price for control purposes was the ceiling price authorized during Phase I. Accordingly, the regulations published on November 13, 1971, defined the base price as "the highest price charged . . . to a specific class of purchasers in a substantial number of transactions . . . during the freeze base period."[2] "A substantial number" of transactions was defined further as 10 percent or more of the total number of transactions by a particular firm during the freeze period. The regulations also permitted the base price, thus defined, to be adjusted upward to accommodate sellers trapped by temporary special deals, allowances, or long-term contracts entered into prior to the August 1971 freeze.

The definition of base prices was complicated further by language in the Economic Stabilization Act of 1970. Specifically, the President was delegated authority to stabilize prices "at levels not less than those prevailing on May 25, 1970."[3] The Price Commission regulations stipulated, therefore, that a seller was not required to establish any price lower than the average price received on May 25, 1970.[4] This was viewed as a limitation of the general rule prohibiting a price above base without cost justification. The May 25 price was a legal price, but it was not a legal base price under the first regulations promulgated by the commission.[5]

Needless to say, this created confusion, and in September 1972 an amendment to the commission's regulations permitted the use of the May 25 price as an optional base.[6] The amendment in effect increased the potential for inflation. If the May 25 price were above the price established by the rule on 10 percent of transactions, prices could be increased up to the May 25 level without prenotification, and allowable cost increases could be applied to the higher base.

Both the 10 percent rule and the May 25 optional base became of increasing concern to the commission. Generally, the 10 percent rule established a base price above the average or median price charged during the freeze. In addition, the May 25 price was in some instances significantly

2. Economic Stabilization Regulations, sec. 300.505(a), in *Federal Register*, vol. 36 (November 13, 1971), p. 21795.

3. Economic Stabilization Act of 1970, sec. 203(a)(1) (85 Stat. 744).

4. Economic Stabilization Regulations, sec. 300.403, in *Federal Register*, vol. 36 (December 16, 1971), p. 23979.

5. See Price Commission Ruling 1972-223 in ibid., vol. 37 (August 26, 1972), p. 17428.

6. Economic Stabilization Regulations, sec. 300.403(b), in ibid. (September 20, 1972), p. 19378.

above the price established by the 10 percent rule. This created unintended slack in the regulations because the commission had control over neither price increases up to base nor the May 25 price.[7]

The degree of slack varied by industries. The potential for uncontrolled price increases was substantial in primary and nonferrous metals and chemicals. In addition, a large proportion of chemical firms had term limit pricing (TLP) agreements. Because the weighted-average price increase granted in a TLP agreement did not include increases up to base, the monitoring of these TLP agreements was extremely difficult.[8]

In October 1972 the commission considered revising the base-price concept by eliminating the 10 percent rule, the May 25, 1970, rule, or both. Prices below base were presumed to reflect market conditions. Because the economy appeared to be moving into a period of stronger demand pressures, however, it seemed likely that competitive conditions would be less of a deterrent to charging authorized prices in the future. But no decision was made to change the base-price concept, in part because of additional complexities that would have been caused.[9] Most of the problems caused by a change could have been resolved, but the controlling consideration in retaining the status quo was that during the fall of 1972, the commission still was operating under an undefined time horizon for the controls program and the realities were difficult to assess. In any case, the commission not only was reluctant to make substantial changes in the rules of the game at that time, but also was discouraged from doing so by the Cost of Living Council.

7. The Division of Price Analysis estimated that in December 1971, 632 products included in the wholesale price index were selling below apparent ceilings. The ceiling was defined as the highest price in one of four months: May 1970, June 1970, July 1971, and August 1971. The estimated effect on the WPI of an increase in prices of these products to authorized levels was 1.89 percentage points. The estimated impact for the industrial commodities component was 1.82 percentage points. By August 1972, the total number of products selling below apparent ceilings was 545. An increase to ceilings would have had an estimated impact of 1.34 percentage points on the overall index and 1.50 percentage points on the industrial commodities index. (Price Commission Issue Paper MIF 73d, October 4, 1972.) Thus, little of the available freedom to raise industrial prices was allowed by market conditions.

8. See Chapter 4.

9. For example, if the freeze base price were $1.00, the May 25, 1970, price were $2.00, and the current price were $1.50, what should the new base price be? Would cost increases since the freeze be allowable? And so forth. In addition, tightening of the regulations to eliminate such slack would have punished the firm that had exercised price restraint—which may or may not have been equitable, depending on the reasons for the price restraint.

Associated with the base-price problem and the indefinite time horizon for Phase II was the pressing problem of renewal for TLP agreements, many of which expired in December 1972 and January 1973. Renewal of these agreements required specification of the appropriate base price for the new agreements. For those firms which did not renew, what was the new base price to be? The issue was resolved by making firms with expiring TLP agreements "an offer they couldn't refuse": either a ninety-day extension of the existing agreement or going back to base. Most firms saw the appeal of an extension.

## Price Increases and Cost Recovery

In general, prices could be increased over base in Phase II only to reflect increases in allowable costs. The first regulations issued by the commission stated that price increases could reflect "allowable cost increases in effect on or after November 14, 1971."[10] (This ambiguity was the product of the division of labor between the commission and the legal staff.) The commission subsequently qualified this to mean costs incurred since the date of the last price increase or January 1, 1971, whichever was later.[11] This qualification seemed straightforward, but some complications developed later on.

The problem is best illustrated by the requests made by the automobile manufacturers in August 1972 for price increases to cover only federally mandated costs. The companies had incurred other costs but were willing to postpone recovering these until early 1973. The postponement clearly was in the interest of the stabilization program.[12] If an authorized pass-through of federally mandated costs constituted a price increase, however, other cost increases (nonmandated) incurred earlier could not be used as justification for subsequent price increases. The commission decided that approval given for price increases based only on the federally mandated costs would not constitute a price increase for the purpose of subsequent filings under the procedure outlined in the PC-1 form. The decision on

10. Economic Stabilization Regulations, sec. 300.012, in *Federal Register,* vol. 36 (November 13, 1971), p. 21792.

11. Section 300.12 in ibid., vol. 37 (January 19, 1972), p. 775. This decision, admittedly arbitrary, was a compromise among several arguments as to the equitable date for cost reach-back. All arguments had some merit for specific situations; no practical solution was obvious.

12. See the discussion of the automobile case in Chapter 12.

the automobile case seemed well justified because the companies were requesting only a dollar-for-dollar pass-through.

The fact that the companies believed that commission rules disallowed a markup on mandated costs was revealed by testimony at the auto hearings. This was not the case. The commission previously had decided to disallow a markup on federally mandated costs, but the issue had been controversial and the commission was sharply divided. Three commissioners had felt strongly that a profit margin should not be allowed on mandated costs; others had questioned the equity of differentiating between mandated and other costs. One commissioner, who favored the proposal, suggested that the decision not be made public before consulting with the CLC. At the subsequent meeting, the chairman informed the commissioners that he had discussed the matter with the CLC director and now wished to change his vote, thus reversing the action of the previous meeting. The upshot was that the issue of mandated costs remained unresolved.

The "date-of-last-price-increase" issue arose in another context. Final approval of price-increase requests from the major firms in the container industry was suspended temporarily pending audit of their books by the IRS, but the can companies were granted an interim increase. The commission ruled that the date of the interim increase would not be considered as the date of the last price increase for purposes of subsequent cost justification.

### The Volatile-Price Rule

A separate but related issue was pricing in response to volatile costs. Processors of raw materials—especially firms processing raw agricultural products that were exempted from the controls program—often incurred costs that fluctuated widely over only short periods of time. The issue was first raised in November 1971 by meat packers that were prenotification firms. Because prices paid for live cattle account for about 75 percent of total costs for the average packer, profit margins are highly sensitive to cost fluctuations. Strict enforcement of the prenotification requirement would require frequent requests for price increases and might also force a processor to operate at a loss for up to thirty days while the commission was considering its request. On the other hand, a subsequent drop in the price of the raw agricultural product could result in windfall profits for the manufacturer. Such distortions clearly were not the intent of the regulations. Moreover, the prenotification requirement created an inequity between prenotification firms and smaller firms that were permitted to raise their prices without prenotification.

In its early discussions, the commission endorsed the view that when raw or partially processed agricultural products represented a major cost item, prenotification firms should be allowed to increase their prices without prenotification in response to increases in prices of the raw materials; price increases based on other costs still would require prenotification. But recognizing the inherent danger in allowing increases in prices of raw agricultural products to be passed through the entire chain without prenotification, the commission wanted to restrict any modification of policy to firms that would experience severe hardship if required to prenotify. This problem was intensified by the fact that although fluctuations in raw material prices are most common in agriculturally related industries, other industries have historically priced their products in response to price fluctuations of raw materials. If a firm were permitted to determine its own qualification for exemption in this manner, a serious erosion of the commission's authority would occur.

The volatile-price rule as finally adopted required a firm to obtain prior approval from the commission. To qualify, a firm had to demonstrate a historical policy of pricing "immediately and directly" in response to changes in the cost of a raw material. An immediate and direct response was interpreted as being a change in the selling price that corresponded closely to the change in the cost of the raw material and occurred within thirty days.

At first, the commission also considered adding the stipulation that the raw material cost must represent at least 30 percent of the selling price of the processed product before an increase would be allowed. This idea was abandoned as being too arbitrary, and the approval or disapproval of volatile-price agreements was based on internal guidelines. In return for elimination of the thirty-day prenotification of price increases, qualifying firms agreed to pass through increases in raw-material costs on a dollar-for-dollar basis,[13] and no change in profit margin was allowed. Downward adjustments reflecting reductions in market prices of raw materials also were required, but firms were not required to reduce a price below the level of May 25, 1970.

13. Price Commission Ruling 1972-15, in *Federal Register*, vol. 37 (January 18, 1972), p. 765.

Volatile-price agreements were signed with 180 firms. Most of the agreements related to agricultural or agriculturally related commodities, including meats, cattle hides, and coffee.

### Profit-Margin Limitation

Phase II regulations did not impose a ceiling on total dollar profits, but they did limit profit margins: allowable price increases could not be put into effect if doing so would result in a firm's exceeding its base-period profit margin. This rule was intended as an incentive to increase absolute profits through increased sales and gains in productivity rather than through increased prices.

Some of the problems associated with the profit-margin rule arose through complexities of definition, whereas others were more substantive. The profit-margin calculation excluded revenues from farming, public utilities, life insurance, and foreign subsidiaries. Revenues from domestic sales of other items (exempt as well as nonexempt) and from export sales were included. In that exports and some other items were exempted from price controls but not from profit controls, this treatment was inconsistent.[14]

EXPORT SALES. The commission considered excluding all export sales from both the base- and current-period profit margins. The issue arose because the Revenue Act of 1971 included several tax changes supported by the administration. One was the tax advantage afforded firms that qualified as domestic international sales corporations (DISCs), the purpose of which was to stimulate export sales. Price Commission regulations tended to negate this advantage: an increase in profits on exports or a shift from domestic sales to exports with a higher rate of profit could result in a firm's exceeding its overall base-period profit margin. To avoid rollbacks on domestic prices, a firm therefore might prefer to establish a foreign manufacturing or sales subsidiary rather than operating under the auspices of DISC. Conversely, a change in the regulations could have resulted in de facto violation for other exporters. If the rate of profit on foreign sales were below that in the base period, exclusion of foreign sales would raise the current profit margin, possibly above the base level. The

---

14. In fact, the commission's general counsel questioned the legal authority of the commission to include profit earned on export sales in the profit-margin test, but the issue was never litigated.

only recourse at that point would be a reduction in prices of products sold in the domestic market.

INTEREST DEDUCTIONS. A particularly serious problem in connection with the definition of the profit margin was the treatment of interest costs. The profit-margin rule promulgated by the commission originally defined the margin as net operating income before taxes and before extraordinary items. The commission rule did not differentiate between short- and long-term interest for purposes of deductibility. But the forms developed by the staff deviated from this concept: on them, short-term interest was deductible in calculating the profit margin, whereas long-term interest was not.[15] As a result, the profit-margin limitation distorted corporate financing by encouraging not only debt rather than equity financing but also shifts from long- to short-term debt.

In August 1972, the anomaly of this situation and its significance for money markets and interest rates was brought to the attention of the commission. A memorandum from the staff of the Federal Reserve Board indicated distortions were occurring in money markets because of these regulations. The commission felt strongly that its policy decision had not been implemented properly in the forms and changed the regulations to permit deductibility of long- as well as short-term interest. The regulations on interest deductibility were retained in this form during Phases III and IV.

DEFINING THE BASE PERIOD. The definition of the base period for profit-margin determination also created some problems. The base was defined as the weighted average of the best two out of three of the firm's fiscal years ending prior to August 15, 1971. Several other base-year options were considered, but none was clearly superior to the one chosen. The commissioners agreed, however, that a recent period was more appropriate for controls purposes. This logic argued for a subsequent rolling forward of the base. But because 1971 was a low-profit year and 1972 a year of controls on profit, a rolling forward of the base offered little prospect of relief to firms experiencing losses or low profits. It was necessary, therefore, for the commission to adopt a special rule, discussed in the following section, for loss and low-profit firms.

EVALUATION. The effectiveness of the profit-margin rule is open to question. In some instances, price increases were disapproved on this

15. This was clearly not the intent of the commission, and is another instance in which staff procedures or forms were allowed to become policy.

basis,[16] and in others, price rollbacks and refunds were required because of violations of the rule. Firms also were encouraged to make voluntary rollbacks to base prices in order to be relieved from the profit-margin constraint, or "repurified."[17] Finally, the profit-margin limitation had an indirect impact on prices in industries in which competitive pressures were strong. If some of the firms in the industry were prevented from increasing prices because of the profit-margin limitation, other firms also were restrained in their pricing behavior. This impact was significant in the automotive industry, when Ford and General Motors were denied increases and the requests from Chrysler and American Motors were subsequently granted.[18]

On the other hand, a number of criticisms have been made about the profit-margin limitation. The limitation freezes firms that are in fortuitous profit relations, and if it precludes normal returns to the firm, it may discourage corrective changes, including changes in management. In addition, competition may be diminished as a result of lowering the umbrella of price leaders, thereby eliminating firms of inefficient size.[19]

Many of the distortions that allegedly arose from the profit restrictions were related to the inability to attract investment capital because of low profits. The cement industry, for example, claimed that the shortage of cement was attributable to lack of capacity and to plants that had become marginal producers because of expenditures required to meet pollution and safety standards. The commission held hearings on the cement industry in the fall of 1972. Testimony indicated that the shortage of capacity had resulted in large part from lack of planning; the industry had a histori-

16. As of December 1972, seventy-one requests for price increases had been denied because of the profit-margin limitation. If approved, about $650 million of additional revenues would have been realized over the following year. Denials of price increases for General Motors and Ford alone accounted for about $500 million of these revenues. The commission staff estimated that about 10 percent of tier I and II firms were at or near the profit-margin limitation in December 1972.

17. Refunds and rollbacks from firms in violation of the profit-margin constraint, together with refunds and rollbacks from firms wishing to repurify, amounted to about $20 million.

18. Some of the witnesses at the auto hearings argued that the Price Commission had an obligation to grant increases to Ford and General Motors to avoid causing undue hardship in the market for Chrysler and American Motors.

19. This occurred in the baking industry. International Telephone and Telegraph, whose subsidiaries include several bakers, was not allowed to raise prices because of the profit-margin limitation. Thus unable to compete by means of lower prices, several local bakeries throughout the nation complained that bankruptcy was imminent.

cal record of swinging between undersupply and oversupply. Because these conditions existed before the commission came into existence, the basic causes of inadequate capacity did not seem attributable in this instance to commission regulations. Consequently, the industry's request for a class exception to the profit-margin constraint was denied.

The extent to which the profit-margin limitation was an important disincentive to investment in other industries is unknown. Clearly, however, profit-margin limitation does interfere with the normal cyclical expansion of profits.

### Loss and Low-Profit Firms

Because the first regulations had made no provision for firms incurring losses in the base period, such firms apparently were to be unable to increase prices during Phase II. A similar problem existed for firms with abnormally low profits during the base period. But these problems were complex, and the commission deferred a decision on specific policy.

Exempting low-profit firms from controls probably would have had no adverse effects on prices; such firms generally are not price leaders. But in December 1971 this did not seem to be a feasible policy alternative. The commission staff estimated that as many as 100,000 firms with sales of more than $1 million might have incurred losses or had profit margins well below industry averages during the base period.

A number of options were considered as means of granting relief to these firms. The options included (a) an adjustment of the base period for determining profit margins; (b) adjustments based on return on equity; and (c) adjustments based on return on investment. The option of extending the number of years permissible in calculating base margin was discarded because staff analysis indicated that this would provide relief for only a small percentage of firms. Also, other firms justifiably would have requested similar treatment.

As a temporary expedient, on December 14, 1971, the commission authorized a 3 percent minimum base-period profit margin for any firm with sales of less than $1 million. On December 21, the commission established an interim policy permitting any firm that incurred a loss in the base period to raise prices to achieve a breakeven point or a profit margin of 0 percent.

An important consideration in the development of a longer-run policy was that a normal after-tax return on business investment is on average about 10 percent, which corresponds to a pretax return on investment of between 15 and 20 percent. Regulatory agencies generally permit an after-tax return on investment of about 7 to 9 percent. Therefore, a pretax return of 10 percent would be well below the average for businesses in the United States. The commission did not want to prohibit a firm from earning a reasonable profit, but neither did it want to endorse a policy that could result in raising the profit margin for a loss or low-profit firm above the margin for firms not entitled to special treatment. Among the potential disadvantages of a pure return-on-capital guideline is the provision of incentives for a firm to alter its capital structure and of rewards for inefficient use of capital. The commission also felt that differences in asset turnover should be taken into account.

The loss–low-profit issue became acute in mid-January, when the Fertilizer Institute applied for a class exception to the base-period profit-margin constraint. Most fertilizer producers were low-profit firms and had losses during the base period. On January 25, the commission approved a loss–low-profit rule that compromised between a strict return-on-capital approach and a profit-margin-on-sales approach.

In trying to devise a policy or regulation to deal with this special problem arising from the profit-margin limitation, the commission resorted to a philosophy of controls that it had rejected previously. The compromise adopted was an adjustment in the profit margin, the criteria for adjustment being tied to capital-turnover ratios. The applicable profit margin increased on a sliding scale as the capital-turnover ratio decreased. This applied only to firms with annual sales of $1 million or more; the earlier rule for smaller firms was retained.

The loss–low-profit rule required a two-part procedure for increasing prices. First, a firm calculated price increases necessary to reach a break-even point. Second, it could increase prices even further if cost justification could be shown, but the latter increases could not exceed a weighted average of 2.5 percent, and an increase on any individual product could not exceed 5 percent. In addition, the firm was subject to the adjusted profit-margin limitation based on capital-turnover ratios.

The IRS had indicated, however, that administration of the commission's approved two-step rule was too complex. Furthermore, the limitation was difficult to justify because term limit pricing agreements in force at that time often included individual price-increase maximums as high as 15 to 25 percent. Consequently, in late February, prior to official publication of the regulations in the *Federal Register,* the 2.5 percent average maximum and the 5 percent individual maximum restrictions were deleted.

The regulations published in March defined a low-profit firm as any manufacturer, retailer, or wholesaler that during its most recently ended fiscal year or during its alternative fiscal year had either (a) net sales of less than $1 million and a profit margin of less than 3 percent or (b) net sales of $1 million or more and a profit margin below that indicated in a reference table based on capital-turnover ratios.[20]

In May, a rule was approved for loss and low-profit service organizations other than providers of health services, insurers, milk producers, public benefit corporations, cooperatives, and public utilities. This rule was not tied to capital turnover and was more stringent than the rule established for other sectors. Qualifying organizations were those with profit margins of less than 1 percent. Prices could be increased only to attain this margin.[21]

## Trade-Offs: Repurification and Price-Reduction Plans

The Phase II regulations pertaining to profit-margin limitation applied only to firms that increased prices. A firm filing a certification of no price increases was not in violation even if its profit margin rose above the base-period level. At the start of the program, about 300 companies filed letters indicating that they did not intend to raise prices. By October 1972, however, only 117 firms had filed actual certifications of no price increases. The motivation may have been to avoid the profit-margin constraint. Alternatively, this course of action may have been adopted because of competitive pressures or to avoid disclosure of any data to the Price Commission.

By August 1972, profits of most firms were increasing. The number of firms at or near the base-period profit margin probably was increasing also. On August 22 the commission issued a special regulation enabling firms that had increased prices to trade the profit-margin constraint for

20. This alternative fiscal year was the average of any two of the base-period years normally used in calculating the base-period profit margin. *Federal Register,* vol. 37 (March 9, 1972), pp. 5044–45.

21. Ibid. (June 1, 1972), p. 10944.

price reductions. Specifically, firms that lowered prices to or below base levels and made refunds—to customers when identifiable, or to the marketplace generally—of revenues attributable to the above-base prices would no longer be subject to profit-margin limitations. Companies with sales of $50 million or more required commission approval of their price-reduction plans sufficiently in advance to allow implementation by the end of their fiscal year.[22]

This special regulation was designed to attain substantial price decreases and refunds for customers. As Chairman Grayson put it at a Price Commission meeting, the regulation "is a way everybody gains. Consumers win because there are reductions in price or direct refunds. And the company comes out ahead because it is allowed flexibility in its profit margins."

Repurification, on the other hand, required that a firm reduce all of its prices to base levels. Some firms desiring to escape the profit-margin limitation were unwilling to do so; substantial input-cost increases for some of their products would have required that those products be sold at less than cost. One firm requested approval of a weighted-average price reduction in return for an increase in its allowable profit margin. This type of situation gave rise to a proposal for price-reduction plan (PRP) agreements, but none was adopted during Phase II because the commission was unable to agree on appropriate rules.

The proposal for a price-reduction plan amounted to a trade-off between profit-margin limitation and price reduction. Essentially, the proposal would have rewarded a firm for not fully implementing cost-justified price increases. For example, a weighted-average price reduction of 2 percent (a kind of negative TLP) might be required in return for a 1 percent increase in allowable profit margin. One disadvantage of such a policy was that it might have had to be implemented on a firm-by-firm basis, which was contrary to the commission's preference for general policies.

If any conclusion is to be drawn from this review of certain of the difficulties encountered with the Phase II regulations, it is that inconsistencies and inequities are inevitable. Fortunately, they were no more prevalent than they were, and the business community adapted quite well

22. Price Commission, Special Regulation 1, in ibid. (August 22, 1972), p. 16859.

to the general regulations. More critical and severe conflicts in the regulations may have been forestalled by the surging economy, but such an assessment must remain open to individual interpretation. On the other hand, many of the difficulties that did arise during Phase II could have been ameliorated, if not avoided, by different administrative and organizational procedures. Certain lessons to be drawn from these observations are developed in Chapter 12.

# VII

# Economic Implications of
# Price-Control Rules

Little economic analysis of alternative controls strategies, either theoretical or empirical, was made available to the Price Commission at the time of its formation. The only working document supplied was the report of the Certified Public Accountants Advisory Committee that analyzed various procedural and mechanical facets of price controls from an accounting point of view. Because of the time pressure and limited interest in economic analysis at the outset, the commission developed no conceptual economic framework for its regulations. As a result, decisions on economic questions were based on ad hoc economics without any particular or general theoretical analysis.

The major "conceptual" framework for directing the commission's work centered more on administrative procedures and regimen than on the economics of controls. Organizational development and efficiency focused principally on processing the flood of forms.[1] The commission

1. The decision to institute controls in August 1971 was not accompanied by an overall grand design outlining specific strategies to be employed by the price-control agency. Likewise, the economic literature offered only limited help in terms of providing a theoretical framework for controls, optimal control strategy, or even the pros and cons of different controls, and a review of the theories of inflation provided no role for price-wage controls. See, for example, Harry G. Johnson, *Essays in Monetary Economics* (Harvard University Press, 1967); David Fand, "Keynesian Monetary Theories, Stabilization Policy, and the Recent Inflation," *Journal of Money, Credit and Banking*, vol. 1 (August 1969), pp. 556–87; Warren L. Smith, "On Some Current Issues in Monetary Economics: An Interpretation," *Journal of Economic Literature*, vol. 8 (September 1970), pp. 767–82; Edmund S. Phelps and others, *Microeconomic Foundations of Employment and Inflation Theory* (Norton, 1970); Paul Davidson, "A Keynesian View of Friedman's Theoretical Framework for Monetary Policy," *Journal of Political Economy*, vol. 80 (September/October 1972), pp. 864–82; Karl Brunner and Allan H. Meltzer, "Money, Debt, and Economic Activity," ibid., pp. 951–77; Martin Bronfenbrenner and Franklyn D. Holzman, "Survey of Inflation Theory," *American Economic Review*, vol. 53 (September 1963), pp. 594–661; Milton Friedman, "The Role of Monetary Policy," *American Economic Review*, vol. 58 (March 1968), pp. 1–17; Robert J. Gordon, "The Recent Acceleration of Inflation and Its Lessons for the Future," *Brookings*

rarely brought economic analysis to bear on debate on central issues. Economic rationales for regulations were developed by the commissioners coincident with the promulgation of specific regulations and in the drafting of public speeches. One of the few issues that led the commission to concentrate seriously on the economics of the adopted strategy was the dollar-for-dollar limitation on cost pass-through.[2] Nevertheless, some commissioners, the staff, and the press often raised questions about the strategy and rules of the commission. Would the strategy of the basic regulations reduce the rate of inflation? How did the regulations affect the price-output decisions of firms? What would be the effects of the adopted price-control strategy in the longer run? Would the controls regulations cause inefficiencies as a result of price distortions, alter investment decisions, or encourage firms to incur unnecessary costs? Were the rules equitable for all firms? Would the regulations cause a shift in income shares? Would alternative strategies provide more satisfactory answers to some questions?

## Impact on Price-Output Decisions of Firms

The price regulations can be assessed by the price-output effect on firms, but determination of the aggregate economic consequences is more difficult. The logic behind a temporary and limited incomes policy implied that large firms in concentrated sectors be controlled, because in this area, the limited resources for controls presumably might have the greatest potential effectiveness.

As originally implemented, the allowable-cost strategy—the first line of defense—limited price increases to the percentage increase in unit

---

Papers on Economic Activity (1:1970), pp. 8–41; Charles C. Holt, "Improving the Labor Market Trade-off between Inflation and Unemployment," American Economic Association, Papers and Proceedings of the Eighty-first Annual Meeting, 1968 (American Economic Review, vol. 59, May 1969), pp. 135–46; Robert E. Lucas, Jr., and Leonard A. Rapping, "Price Expectations and the Phillips Curve," American Economic Review, vol. 59 (June 1969), pp. 342–50; George L. Perry, "Inflation versus Unemployment: The Worsening Trade-off," Monthly Labor Review, vol. 94 (February 1971), pp. 68–71; Albert Rees, "The Phillips Curve as a Menu for Policy Choice," Economica, vol. 37, n.s. (August 1970), pp. 227–38; and H. T. Shapiro, "The Efficacy of Monetary and Fiscal Policy," Journal of Money, Credit and Banking, vol. 3 (May 1971), pp. 550–54.

2. Commission controversy over the dollar-for-dollar issue is covered in Chapter 2.

costs. The rules were interpreted to include both nominal increases in price and implicit increases from a reduction in quality or quantity of the product. Several problems are readily apparent under such a rule: for example, joint costs of production, changes in the mix of products sold, inventory valuation, intercompany transfers, and the technique of measuring factor productivity.

The second line of defense was the profit-margin limitation, but both rules are similar in their effect. Assuming a single-product firm, a rule limiting a percentage price increase to the percentage increase in the average cost of the product is equivalent to a constant profit-margin limitation: namely, the profit margin of the firm prevailing just prior to cost increases.[3] Therefore, combining the two rules of the Price Commission's controls strategy, the single-product firm would have been constrained to the lesser of (a) its profit margin just prior to controls (more precisely, just prior to cost increases) or of (b) the profit margin of the best two of three fiscal years ending before August 15, 1971.

A complete appraisal of the effects of these two rules also must consider the limitations on permitted cost increases that were introduced during Phase II. Beginning with the decision on coal prices in December 1971, increases in labor costs in excess of the Pay Board basic standard were declared not allowable as a justification for price increases. A few weeks later, certain discretionary cost increases also were declared non-allowable: for example, write-off of goodwill and increases in the quantity of overhead not related to factor cost increases. Thus, if the single-product firm granted wage increases in excess of the Pay Board standard, its profit margin would have been squeezed under the Price Commission rules.

At first, firms were required to deduct projected productivity gains from cost increases, but later, they were required to measure only the productivity of labor for the past fiscal year. Finally, firms were required to use a productivity deduction calculated and published by the Price Commission for each four-digit standard industrial classification product line.

For purposes of estimating the price-output effects, it has been assumed that the single-product firm experiences the following:

---

3. A technical appendix to this chapter presents these propositions in more rigorous form.

1. A trend growth in output per man-hour equal to the offset required by the Price Commission;
2. No change in output per unit of other variable factors of production; and
3. A reduction in average fixed costs for any volume increases in excess of the trend rate of growth in labor productivity.

That all factor price increases were allowable is assumed as well.[4]

### The Profit-Maximizing Firm

The price-output effects of the general price regulations under the above assumptions vary according to the objectives of the firm. Under the constant profit-margin limitation of Phase II, the allowable price is constrained to a constant percentage above average costs, after all costs have changed. The profit-maximizing firm will not be limited by the rules of the Price Commission if the desired price (at which the marginal revenue equals marginal cost) is less than the allowable price.[5]

Some commissioners often pointed out during Phase II that the allowable-cost strategy provided an incentive for firms to incur increased costs, because an $x$ percent increase in unit costs entitled the firm to an equivalent $x$ percent increase in price. Thus, they argued, margins would remain constant but absolute profits would rise. But this incentive could exist only under a limited set of circumstances. First, assume the excess of cost expenditures (relative to those necessary for a given level of production) have no revenue-generating value for the firm. The firm will have an incentive to incur such costs if the allowable price is less than the desired price and demand is inelastic.[6] In such cases, the profit-maximizing firm will allow costs—and, hence, the allowable price—to increase until marginal revenue is zero. By letting average unit costs rise by $x$ percent, the firm is entitled to an $x$ percent increase in price. If demand is inelastic, the quantity demanded will fall by less than $x$ percent, giving a percentage increase in profit precisely equal to the

4. The extent to which these assumptions are realistic for conditions prevailing during Phase II is debatable, because in a number of cases the productivity figures obtained from unpublished Bureau of Labor Statistics data were inaccurate. However, the necessary alterations in such cases are obvious from this approach.
5. See proposition 1 in the appendix to this chapter.
6. See proposition 2 in the appendix to this chapter.

percentage increase in revenue. If demand is elastic, however, allowing costs to increase by $x$ percent will cause total revenue and profits to fall.

If the firm has no incentive to incur additional costs, there will be no distortion of the efficient capital-labor ratio.[7] When totally nonproductive costs are incurred, the kind of inefficiency would vary with the whims of the firm's management.

More likely, however, is the possibility that such costs will be incurred to speed modernization, thus generating future revenue. If such unnecessary cost increases were allowable under Phase II regulations, the constrained profit-maximizing firm would have an incentive to incur even greater costs,[8] the amount depending upon how much additional revenue is generated per dollar of unnecessary cost increases.[9]

### The Sales-Maximizing Single-Product Firm

If a firm's objective is to maximize sales, the price-output effects of the price regulations on the firm are quite different from the effects on the profit-maximizing firm.[10] Accounting profits are in part a necessary return to factors of production that are not measured in the accounting process. If all unmeasured costs in the accounting sense are fixed, then the allowable price may be (a) above the average total cost for all levels of production, (b) equal to average total costs at only one level of production, or (c) equal at two levels of production. Whichever, either the Price Commission controls strategy would be ineffective or the sales-maximizing firm would be forced to operate at a loss.[11]

---

7. By contrast, public utility regulation based on rate of return on capital causes an overinvestment in capital. See, for example, Harvey Averch and Leland L. Johnson, "Behavior of the Firm under the Regulatory Constraint," *American Economic Review*, vol. 52 (December 1962), pp. 1052–69; William J. Baumol and Alvin K. Klevorick, "Input Choices and Rate-of-Return Regulation: An Overview of the Discussion," *Bell Journal of Economics and Management Science*, vol. 1 (Autumn 1970), pp. 162–90; and Jerome L. Stein and George H. Borts, "Behavior of the Firm under Regulatory Constraint," *American Economic Review*, vol. 62 (December 1972), pp. 964–70.

8. See proposition 3 in the appendix to this chapter.

9. This would include the present value of future revenues created by these cost expenditures.

10. This refers to a firm that maximizes revenue subject to the condition that total revenue is greater than, or equal to, total costs.

11. See the appendix to this chapter.

### Target-Rate-of-Return Pricing

Under a target-rate-of-return pricing model,[12] a short-run repricing because of increased unit costs is equivalent to maintaining a constant dollar profit per unit of output when the firm is operating at its normal rate.[13] Because investment is constant, the same dollar profits would produce the target rate of return. It follows, therefore, that if the firm had no volume offset for fixed costs (because all accounting costs were variable or the firm projected no change in volume), the allowable price increase permitted by commission rules would be greater than the price increase required by a firm using target-rate-of-return pricing. If the firm experienced a volume increase and volume adjustment for allowable, variable-cost increases, then the allowed price increase could be greater than, equal to, or less than the desired price increase, depending upon the magnitude of the volume offset, the increase in allowable costs, and the profit margin of the firm.[14] Because the volume offset was entirely up to the firm during Phase II, the requested price increase would be "greater than or equal to," rather than "less than," for the firm using target-rate-of-return pricing.[15]

12. Target-rate-of-return pricing is construed to mean that the price is set so that if the firm produces at normal output (generally defined by management as 70 to 80 percent of capacity), the firm will earn its target rate of return on investment (net worth plus long-term debt). See, for example, A. D. H. Kaplan, Joel B. Dirlam, and Robert F. Lanzillotti, *Pricing in Big Business: A Case Approach* (Brookings Institution, 1958); and Robert F. Lanzillotti, "Pricing Objectives in Large Companies," *American Economic Review*, vol. 48 (December 1958), pp. 921–40.

13. Maintenance of a constant dollar profit per unit of normal output was referred to as a "dollar-for-dollar pass-through" of cost increases. See proposition 4 in the appendix to this chapter.

14. See proposition 5 in the appendix to this chapter.

15. This type of firm would have no incentive to incur unnecessary costs unless its projected volume increase was too high to allow it the target-rate-of-return price. In this latter event, if it did incur additional costs, the percentage increase in price would equal the percentage increase in costs, and the percentage increase in profits would be commensurate with both. Thus, if the volume projection were too high (which is unlikely), unnecessary costs could be incurred to raise profits at the normal level of output to achieve the target rate of return. This analysis does not consider current demand conditions, but in general the target-rate-of-return rule is not a profit-maximizing rule.

*The Multiproduct Firm*

In the case of a multiproduct firm with no interdependencies of demand for various products of the firm (or only a small interaction), application of the commission's allowable-cost strategy to each product or product line is equivalent to requiring a constant profit margin for that product or line. Analyzing the effects in terms of the single-product firm is valid for the multiproduct firm on a product-by-product basis, provided that joint cost increases were correctly reported to the commission. But because the profit margin reported by the firm was the weighted average of the profit margin for each product (the weights being the proportion of total sales for that product), the profit margin of the multiproduct firm could increase if sales of relatively high–profit-margin items increased more than its low-margin items.[16]

Because there are joint costs among various products and the allocation of joint costs is somewhat arbitrary, creative accounting can vitiate the implication of a constant profit margin for each product line. Thus, the allocation of joint cost increases only to those products for which the higher prices are attainable in the market also could cause an increase in the firm's overall profit margin.

The year 1972 was one of high productivity gains, substantially above the trend average required as an offset for the Price Commission regulations.[17] Although the trend productivity offset was not implemented by the Price Commission until May 1972, it represented a significant improvement over the estimates supplied by the firms.[18] Thus, the actual treatment of productivity by the Price Commission would allow some cyclical increase in profit margins because the allowable price increase would be greater than the percentage change in allowable unit costs.

The profit-margin limitation was adopted for these reasons and became the second line of defense. Because most firms were substan-

16. See proposition 6 in the appendix to this chapter.

17. The weighted average of the Price Commission productivity figures for manufacturing four-digit SIC codes (weighted on the basis of 1970 shipments) is 3.7 percent (Price Commission report DPAM-481). From the fourth quarter of 1971 to the same period in 1972, output per man-hour increased by 5.2 percent in the private nonfarm sector and 4.9 percent in the manufacturing sector (U.S. Bureau of Labor Statistics, *Monthly Labor Review*, vol. 96 [June 1973]).

18. Internal sampling of price-increase request forms indicated the average productivity offset prior to May 1972 to be less than 1.0 percent.

tially below their base-period profit margin when Phase II began, however, the profit-margin limitation fell significantly behind the first line, the allowable-cost strategy.

The incentives to incur unnecessary costs when the multiproduct firm was at its base-period margin are about the same as for the single-product firm.[19] For various reasons some firms were over their base-period profit margin at the beginning of Phase II. Those unable either to obtain an exception from the Internal Revenue Service or the Price Commission because of abnormalities or to qualify under the loss–low-profit rule could not raise prices until they had absorbed cost increases to the point at which their profit margin was equal to the base-period limitation. These firms had no incentive to incur any unit cost increases, let alone nonproductive costs.

Microeconomic theory does not disclose how many firms would become inefficient, nor does it consider the supply responses to situations in which the regulations were effective. For aggregate inefficiencies to result from the regulations, however, there must be some effect on the price-output decision of the firm. Theory indicates, however, a number of circumstances under which the regulations would be inconsequential to the price-output decisions of the firm.[20]

## Equity of Price Regulations

Although equity is a nebulous concept, it has powerful political ramifications and had to be given adequate consideration in the formulation of regulations. The question arose during Phase II as to whether the combined regulations of the Pay Board and Price Commission were unfair to business or unfair to labor. Was one sector being asked to do more than its fair share in the battle against inflation?

If "fair" is defined in this context as describing regulations that do not change the relative shares of income going to profits and wages from what they would have been without the controls program, then

---

19. A slight correction is necessary for the multiproduct firm if high-profit-margin items increase relatively more than low-margin items. Because this normally would raise margins, some product margins then would have to be reduced.

20. The prices of TLP firms, as discussed in Chapter 4, were affected little by the regulations.

requiring business to absorb costs must be labeled "unfair to business."[21] For example, assume income is divided between labor income and profits. Then, if the percentage increase in price is equal to the percentage increase in unit labor costs (percentage change in wages less percentage change in output per man-hour), the percentage change in profits will just equal the percentage change in labor income. In other words, relative shares will be constant.[22]

Therefore, to the extent that price increases allowed during Phase II corresponded to changes in standard unit labor costs (that is, wage increases adjusted for trend gains in output per man-hour), the controls would permit some cyclical shift in the relative share of income accruing to profits.

At a more detailed level, unusual circumstances did create inequities for specific firms. This was to be expected, of course, in the process of attempting to draft general regulations for such a complex and heterogeneous economy as that of the United States.[23]

## Proposed Alternative Price-Control Rules

Alternative price-control strategies proposed to the Price Commission throughout Phase II ranged from imposing ceiling prices on all items to controlling the level of profits for an industry. A dollar-for-dollar pass-through was applied to specific cost increases in lumber, hides, and meats, and, at several points during the life of Phase II, it was nearly

21. This point has been made by George L. Perry, "Controls and Income Shares," *Brookings Papers on Economic Activity* (1:1972), pp. 191–94.

22. To prove that statement, let

(1) $$PY = WL + \pi,$$

where $P$ = price, $Y$ = output, $W$ = wage rate, $L$ = quantity of labor, and $\pi$ = profit income. Then

(2) $$\% \Delta P + \% \Delta Y = f_1(\% \Delta W + \% \Delta L) + f_2 \% \Delta \pi,$$

where $f_1 = WL/PY$ and $f_2 = \pi/PY$.

If $\% \Delta P = \% \Delta W - \% \Delta(Y/L) = \% \Delta W - \% \Delta Y + \% \Delta L$, it follows from (2) that

$$\% \Delta W + \% \Delta L = \% \Delta \pi, \quad \text{or } \% \Delta(\pi/WL) = 0.$$

That is, no change occurs in relative shares.

23. Major problem areas, conflicts, and exception procedures are covered in Chapter 6.

adopted as the general price-control regulation. Other proposals actively considered by the commission included a controls strategy based upon direct cost increases only and a fractional pass-through of cost increases. Regulation based upon rate of return was proposed to the commission at various times, but it never was given serious consideration.

### Dollar-for-Dollar Pass-Through

As usually interpreted, the dollar-for-dollar pass-through meant a price increase that would maintain unit dollar profits. Thus, for a constant volume of production, dollar profits would be constant and the firm could increase dollar profits by expanding output instead of simply raising prices, as was the case under the general strategy.

A dollar-for-dollar pass-through of costs provides an allowable price that is a constant dollar amount above average costs. Under the dollar-for-dollar pass-through of cost, increases in volume that take advantage of economies of scale will increase profits more than will the same increase in volume under the constant profit-margin rule. Without a change in volume, the dollar-for-dollar pass-through keeps dollar profits constant, whereas the constant margin increases dollar profits. If the increase in volume were such that, even though factor prices increased, average costs of production were lower, then the firm would have greater profits under a constant-unit profit rule than a constant-margin rule.[24] For just as the full percentage pass-through of unit costs will increase profits with a constant volume, profits will be lowered if unit costs fall for a given volume under a constant profit-margin rule.

Under a rule stipulating constant dollar profit per unit, the firm using target-rate-of-return pricing would never have a profit incentive to incur unnecessary costs if such costs generated no additional revenue. If such costs generated some revenue and demand were inelastic at the allowable price under the dollar-for-dollar pass-through rule, sufficient incentive may exist to incur these costs.[25] The incentives to incur unnecessary costs are less, however, when cost increases are passed through on a dollar-for-dollar basis than when passed through with a markup for the profit margin.

24. See proposition 7 in the appendix to this chapter.
25. For exact conditions, see proposition 8 in the appendix to this chapter.

*Fractional Cost Pass-Through*

Another proposal was to place a percentage limit on cost increases that the firm could pass through in a price increase.[26] One idea was not to permit increases in overhead costs to be part of a justification for price increases. The logic of the proposal was that it would encourage firms to cut costs where they had some control, thus improving the enforceability of the regulation that unnecessary cost increases were not allowable. The commission never seriously considered not allowing a particular cost increase as long as the increase was not large. As noted, however, it did place the limit on increases in labor cost at 6.2 percent (that is, 5.5 percent plus 0.7 percent for fringe benefits).

In a few cases, the Price Commission permitted only a dollar-for-dollar pass-through of specific cost increases. For example, when the price of hides doubled, the commission permitted shoe and leather manufacturers to pass these costs along only on a dollar-for-dollar basis.[27] Similar actions were taken in other problem areas, including meat and lumber.[28]

Alternative types of allowable-cost rules are virtually infinite in number. Whether such rules affect a particular firm either more or less adversely than do other rules depends upon which costs are increasing. One aspect seems clear: that not allowing a pass-through of a cost increase (unless it is a completely discretionary or unnecessary cost increase or one offset by some other means) will affect some firms inequitably and adversely when applied across the board.

26. In general, any allowable-cost strategy, including the ones discussed above, can be stated by the following formula, in which there are $n$ different kinds of costs:

(1)      $dP/P = k_1 f_1 dC_1/C_1 + k_2 f_2 dC_2/C_2 + \ldots + k_n f_n dC_n/C_n - mMdC/C,$

where $dC_i/C_i$ = the percentage increase of the $i$th cost element; $f_i$ = the proportion the $i$th cost element is to total costs; $k_i$ = the fraction of the $i$th cost increase permitted; and $m$ = the amount of the margin, $M$, taken off the percentage increase in total cost, $dC/C$. Alternatively, (1) can be written as:

(2)      $dP/P = k_1(1 - m_1M)f_1 dC_1/C_1 + \ldots + k_n(1 - m_nM)f_n dC_n/C_n,$

where $m_i$ is the amount of the margin taken off the $i$th cost increase. Under the Price Commission's general rule, all $k_i$s equal 1 and $m$ equals 0. Under the dollar-for-dollar pass-through, all $k_i$s would equal 1 and $m$ would equal 1 in equation (1). Under the general rule of the Price Commission, if $C_1$ were a discretionary cost, then in (2), $k_1$ and $m_1$ both would be 0.

27. An empirical analysis of this regulation is presented in Chapter 10.

28. Details on several actions are presented in Chapter 6.

## Conclusion

It should be stressed that the foregoing analysis of the effects of the regulations and the proposed alternatives represents a strictly partial equilibrium (firm by firm) analysis. A full theoretical assessment of the aggregate effects is beyond the scope of this book, because (a) an adequate general economywide model would be made up of several equations, and the conclusions would depend upon the relative sizes of various parameters; and (b) the proper theoretical analysis for the limited span of Phase II is probably a disequilibrium analysis rather than an equilibrium assessment. An econometric assessment of the aggregate effects of the program is presented in the following chapter.

## APPENDIX

This appendix rigorously defines and proves some propositions used in the chapter.

The first proposition shows that for the single-product firm, the Price Commission's allowable-cost strategy implies a constant profit margin.

*Proposition 1: If the percentage increase in price is equal to the percentage increase in unit cost of production (factor cost increases less productivity gains), the profit margin is constant.*

*Proof:* Since $PY = \Sigma v_i x_i + \pi$, where $P$ is the price of output, $Y$ is output, $v_i$ is the price of the $i$th factor, $x_i$ is the quantity of the $i$th factor, and $\pi$ is profit; the profit margin is

$$M = \frac{\pi}{PY} = 1 - \frac{\Sigma v_i x_i}{PY}.$$

Therefore, $dM = 0$ implies

$$\frac{dP}{P} = \Sigma f_i \left[ \frac{dv_i}{v_i} + \frac{dx_i}{x_i} \right] - \frac{dY}{Y} = \frac{dAC}{AC},$$

where

$$f_i = \frac{v_i x_i}{\Sigma v_i x_i},$$

the proportion of total cost expended on the $i$th factor, and

$$AC = \frac{\Sigma v_i x_i}{Y},$$

the average cost of production.

The allowable price after all costs have increased is illustrated in
Figure 7-1 for a profit-maximizing firm that would be constrained by
the regulations. Because the profit margin is, by definition, $1 - AC/$
$P = M$, where $AC$ is average cost, then $P/AC = 1/(1 - M) = k$,
where $k$ is a constant. Thus, the allowable-price curve, $L$, is parabolic

Figure 7-1. *Price-Output Combinations for Profit-Controlled
and Profit-Uncontrolled Firms*[a]

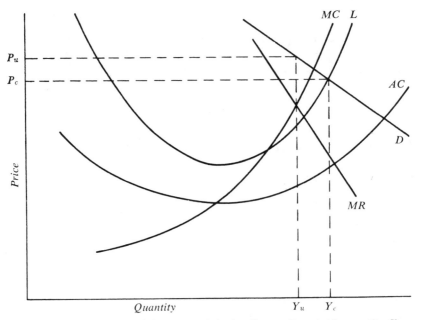

a. $P_u$ = profit-maximizing price; $P_c$ = controlled price; $Y_u$ = profit-maximizing quantity; $Y_c$ =
quantity produced under controls; $AC$ = average cost after cost increases have been incurred;
$MC$ = marginal cost; $D$ = demand curve; $MR$ = curve marginal to $D$; $L$ = allowable price curve.

to the average-cost curve, reaching a minimum and being closest, in
absolute terms, to the average-cost curve where it is a minimum.

The figure illustrates the differences in the price-quantity relation for
a firm constrained by the allowable-cost regulation or, equivalently, by
the profit-margin limitation. The controlled price, $P_c$, is less than the
profit-maximizing price, $P_u$, and the quantity produced under controls,
$Y_c$, is greater than the profit-maximizing quantity, $Y_u$.

It is also true that the profit-maximizing firm will be unaffected by controls or price at the limit given by curve $L$, which is proven in Proposition
1-A.

*Proposition 1-A: For the profit-maximizing firm, either the profit-margin constraint holds with equality or marginal cost equals marginal revenue.*

*Proof:* To maximize $PY - C(Y)$ subject to $[PY - C(Y)]/PY \leq M$, a constant, requires:

(a) $\quad \dfrac{\partial L}{\partial Y} = \dfrac{\partial(PY)}{\partial Y} - \dfrac{\partial C}{\partial Y} + \lambda(M-1)\dfrac{\partial(PY)}{\partial Y} + \lambda\dfrac{\partial C}{\partial Y} \leq 0$ and

(b) $\quad \dfrac{\partial L}{\partial \lambda} = (M-1)PY + C(Y) \geq 0.$

Thus, if $\lambda > 0$,

$$\frac{PY - C(Y)}{PY} = M.$$

If $Y > 0$, $\lambda = 0$, and

$$\frac{\partial(PY)}{\partial Y} = \frac{\partial C}{\partial Y}.$$

*Proposition 2: Purely wasteful expenditures will be incurred by the profit-maximizing firm if demand is inelastic at the allowable price.* Formally, if $\pi = PY - C(Y, \alpha)$, where $\alpha \geq 0$, $\partial C/\partial \alpha \equiv 1$, and $\partial(PY)/\partial \alpha = 0$, then if $\alpha > 0$, $\partial(PY)/\partial Y = 0$ and $(PY - C)/PY = M$. If $\alpha = 0$ and $(PY - C)/PY = M$, then $\partial C/\partial Y \geq \partial(PY)/\partial Y$, where $\alpha$ = totally wasteful expenditures.

*Proof:* To maximize $\pi = PY - C(Y, \alpha)$ subject to $[PY - C(Y, \alpha)]/PY \leq M > 0$, requires:

(a) $\quad \dfrac{\partial L}{\partial Y} = \dfrac{\partial(PY)}{\partial Y} - \dfrac{\partial C}{\partial Y} + \lambda(M-1)\dfrac{\partial(PY)}{\partial Y} + \lambda\dfrac{\partial C}{\partial Y} \leq 0;$

(b) $\quad \dfrac{\partial L}{\partial \alpha} = -\dfrac{\partial C}{\partial \alpha} + \lambda\dfrac{\partial C}{\partial \alpha} \leq 0;$ and

(c) $\quad \dfrac{\partial L}{\partial \lambda} = (M-1)PY + C(Y, \alpha) \geq 0.$

Therefore, if $Y > 0$ and $\lambda = 0$, then $\alpha = 0$, and

$$\frac{\partial(PY)}{\partial Y} = \frac{\partial C}{\partial Y}.$$

If $Y > 0$ and $\alpha > 0$, then $\lambda = 1$ or

$$\frac{PY - C}{PY} = M \quad \text{and} \quad M\frac{\partial(PY)}{\partial Y} = 0 \quad \text{or} \quad \frac{\partial(PY)}{\partial Y} = 0.$$

*Proposition 3: If unnecessary expenditures are not purely wasteful, there will be a greater incentive to incur such costs.* Formally, if $\pi = PY + R(\alpha) - C(Y, \alpha)$, $\partial C/\partial \alpha \equiv 1$ and $1 > \partial R/\partial \alpha > 0$, then $\alpha > 0$ implies $\partial C/\partial Y > \partial(PY)/\partial Y > 0$, where $R$ is revenue from expenditure level $\alpha$. Here, $\alpha$ is unproductive in the sense that a dollar's expenditure yields less than a dollar in revenue.

*Proof:* To maximize $PY + R(\alpha) - C(Y, \alpha)$ subject to $(PY - C)/PY \leq M$, requires:

(a)   $$\frac{\partial L}{\partial Y} = \frac{\partial(PY)}{\partial Y} - \frac{\partial C}{\partial Y} + \lambda(M - 1)\frac{\partial(PY)}{\partial Y} + \lambda\frac{\partial C}{\partial Y} \leq 0;$$

(b)   $$\frac{\partial L}{\partial \alpha} = \frac{\partial R}{\partial \alpha} - \frac{\partial C}{\partial \alpha} + \lambda\frac{\partial C}{\partial \alpha} \leq 0; \text{ and}$$

(c)   $$\frac{\partial L}{\partial \lambda} = MPY - PY + C \geq 0.$$

Therefore, if $Y > 0$ and $\lambda = 0$, then $\partial(PY)/\partial Y = \partial C/\partial Y$ and $\alpha = 0$. If $Y > 0$ and $\alpha > 0$, then $1 > \lambda = (1 - \partial R)/\partial \alpha > 0$, and $(PY - C)/PY = M$. It follows from (a) that

$$\lambda = \frac{\dfrac{\partial C}{\partial Y} - \dfrac{\partial(PY)}{\partial Y}}{(M - 1)\dfrac{\partial(PY)}{\partial Y} + \dfrac{\partial C}{\partial Y}} = \frac{\dfrac{\partial C}{\partial Y} - \dfrac{\partial(PY)}{\partial Y}}{\dfrac{\partial C}{\partial Y} - \dfrac{C}{PY}\dfrac{\partial(PY)}{\partial Y}} > 0.$$

Because $\partial C/\partial Y - \partial(PY)/\partial Y < 0$ implies $\lambda > 1$, $\partial C/\partial Y > \partial(PY)/\partial Y > 0$.

*Proposition 4: At normal output, target-rate-of-return pricing implies a constant unit profit, and price increases are equivalent to a dollar-for-dollar pass-through.*

*Proof:* $P = \Sigma v_i x_i/Y + \pi/Y$, where $v_i$ = price of $i$th factor and $x_i$ = $i$th factor. If $d(\pi/Y) = 0$, then

$$\frac{dP}{P} = \frac{\Sigma v_i x_i(dv_i/v_i + dx_i/x_i)}{PY} - \frac{\Sigma v_i x_i}{PY^2}dY; \text{ and}$$

$$\frac{dP}{P} = \Sigma h_i\left(\frac{dv_i}{v_i} + \frac{dx_i}{x_i}\right) - \frac{\Sigma v_i x_i}{PY}\frac{dY}{Y}, \quad h_i = \frac{v_i x_i}{PY} = \frac{\Sigma v_i x_i}{PY}f_i, \quad f_i = \frac{v_i x_i}{\Sigma v_i x_i}$$

$$= \Sigma h_i\left(\frac{dv_i}{v_i} + \frac{dx_i}{x_i} - \frac{dY}{Y}\right)$$

$$= \Sigma(1 - M)f_i\left(\frac{dv_i}{v_i} + \frac{dx_i}{x_i} - \frac{dY}{Y}\right).$$

*Proposition 5: If P is the allowable price under constant profit margin regulation and P\* is the desired price under target-rate-of-return pricing, then*

$$\frac{dP}{P} \gtrless \frac{dP^*}{P^*} \text{ as } \Sigma f_i \left( \frac{dv_i}{v_i} + \frac{dx_i}{x_i} - \frac{dY}{Y} \right) \gtrless \frac{f_f}{M^*} \frac{dY}{Y},$$

*where $f_f$ is the fraction of fixed costs to total costs and $M^*$ is the profit margin at normal output.*

*Proof:* At $Y^*$, normal output, $P^* Y^* = \Sigma v_i x_i^* + \pi^*$, $r^* = \pi^*/K$; $dr^* = 0$ implies $d\pi^* = 0$, where $r^*$ is the target rate of return; and

$$\frac{dP^*}{P^*} = \frac{\Sigma f_i(dv_i/v_i + dx_i^*/x_i - dY^*/Y)}{\Sigma v_i x_i^*/Y^*}(1 - M^*), \quad M^* = \frac{\pi^*}{P^* Y^*}.$$

By definition,

$$\frac{dP}{P} = \Sigma f_i \left( \frac{dv_i}{v_i} + \frac{dx_i}{x_i} - \frac{dY}{Y} \right) - f_f \frac{dY}{Y}.$$

Thus,

$$\frac{dP}{P} \gtrless \frac{dP^*}{P^*}$$

implies

$$\Sigma f_i \left( \frac{dv_i}{v_i} + \frac{dx_i}{x_i} - \frac{dY}{Y} \right) - f_f \frac{dY}{Y} \gtrless (1 - M^*) \Sigma f_i^* \left( \frac{dv_i}{v_i} + \frac{dx_i^*}{x_i^*} - \frac{dY^*}{Y^*} \right).$$

Because $dY^* \equiv 0$, if

$$f_i \left( \frac{dx_i}{x_i} - \frac{dY}{Y} \right) = f_i^* \frac{dx_i^*}{x_i^*} \bigg|_{dY^* = 0},$$

then

$$\sum_{var} f_i \left( \frac{dv_i}{v_i} + \frac{dx_i}{x_i} - \frac{dY}{Y} \right) (M^*) \gtrless f_f \frac{dY}{Y},$$

or

$$\sum_{var} f_i \left( \frac{dv_i}{v_i} + \frac{dx_i}{x_i} - \frac{dY}{Y} \right) \gtrless \frac{f_f}{M^*} \frac{dY}{Y}.$$

*Proposition 6: The effect on the total margin of the multiproduct firm depends upon relative price-quantity movements. Formally, if by definition*

$$M = \frac{\sum_j P_j Y_j - \sum_j \sum_i v_{ij} x_{ij}}{\sum_j P_j Y_j}, \quad M_j = \frac{P_j Y_j - \sum_i v_{ij} x_{ij}}{\sum_i v_{ij} x_{ij}},$$

and

$$\frac{dP_j}{P_j} = \sum_i f_{ij}\left(\frac{dv_{ij}}{v_{ij}} + \frac{dx_{ij}}{x_{ij}} - \frac{dY_j}{Y_j}\right), f_{ij} = \frac{x_{ij}v_{ij}}{\sum_i x_{ij}v_{ij}},$$

then

$$dM = \Sigma(M_j - M)g_j\left(\frac{dP_j}{P_j} + \frac{dY_j}{Y_j}\right), \text{ where } g_j = \frac{P_jY_j}{\Sigma P_jY_j}.$$

*Proof:*

$$dM = -\frac{\Sigma\Sigma(dv_{ij}x_{ij} + v_{ij}dx_{ij})}{\Sigma P_jY_j} + \frac{\Sigma\Sigma v_{ij}x_{ij}}{(\Sigma P_jY_j)^2}\Sigma(dP_jY_j + P_jdY_j);$$

therefore,

$$\frac{1}{1-M}dM = \Sigma g_j\left(\frac{dP_j}{P_j} + \frac{dY_j}{Y_j}\right) - \sum_j\sum_i f_jf_{ij}\left(\frac{dv_{ij}}{v_{ij}} + \frac{dx_{ij}}{x_{ij}}\right),$$

where

$$f_j = \frac{\sum_i x_{ij}v_{ij}}{\sum_j\sum_i x_{ij}v_{ij}},$$

or

$$\frac{1}{1-M}dM = \sum_j(g_j - f_j)\left(\frac{dP_j}{P_j} + \frac{dY_j}{Y_j}\right) = \sum_j\left(\frac{M_j - M}{1 - M}\right)g_j\left(\frac{dP_j}{P_j} + \frac{dY_j}{Y_j}\right).$$

Thus,

$$dM = \sum_j(M_j - M)g_j\left(\frac{dP_j}{P_j} + \frac{dY_j}{Y_j}\right).$$

*Proposition 7: There are conditions in which a dollar-for-dollar pass-through is more profitable for the firm.* Formally, if $\pi^*$ equals profits when price increases are based on a dollar-for-dollar pass-through, $d(\pi/Y) = 0$, and $\pi$ equals profits under a constant profit margin price increase; and if $dY > 0$ and $dAC/dY < 0$, then $d\pi^* > d\pi$.

*Proof:* Because

$$d\pi^* = PY\left(\frac{dP}{P} + \frac{dY}{Y}\right) - C\frac{dC}{C} \quad \text{and} \quad \frac{dP^*}{P} = (1 - M)\frac{d(C/Y)}{C/Y},$$

then

$$d\pi^* = PY\left[(1 - M)\left(\frac{dC}{C} - \frac{dY}{Y}\right) + \frac{dY}{Y}\right] - dC = \pi\frac{dY}{Y}.$$

For a constant profit margin,

$$\frac{dP}{P} = \frac{d(C/Y)}{C/Y} \quad \text{and}$$

$$d\pi = PY\left(\frac{dC}{C} - \frac{dY}{Y} + \frac{dY}{Y}\right) - C\frac{dC}{C} = \pi\frac{dC}{C}.$$

Therefore, if

$$\frac{dY}{Y} > \frac{dC}{C} \quad \text{or} \quad \frac{dC}{C} - \frac{dY}{Y} < 0,$$

then

$$\frac{d\pi^*}{\pi} > \frac{d\pi}{\pi}.$$

*Proposition 8: Under a dollar-for-dollar pass-through of cost increases, the incentive to incur unnecessary costs is less, as is evident by comparing what follows with Proposition 3.* Formally, if $\pi = PY + R(\alpha) - C(Y, \alpha)$ and $d(\pi/Y) = 0$, where $\partial C/\partial\alpha \equiv 1$ and $1 > \partial R/\partial\alpha > 0$, then $\alpha > 0$, implies

$$\frac{\pi}{Y}\frac{(1 - \partial R/\partial\alpha)}{\partial R/\partial\alpha} = \frac{\partial C}{\partial Y} - \frac{\partial(PY)}{\partial Y} > 0.$$

*Proof:* To maximize $PY + R(\alpha) - C(Y, \alpha)$, subject to $\pi/Y \leq k$, a constant, requires

$$\frac{\partial L}{\partial Y} = \frac{\partial(PY)}{\partial Y} - \frac{\partial C}{\partial Y} + \lambda k - \lambda\left(\frac{\partial(PY)}{\partial Y} - \frac{\partial C}{\partial Y}\right) \leq 0;$$

$$\frac{\partial L}{\partial\alpha} = \frac{\partial R}{\partial\alpha} - \frac{\partial C}{\partial\alpha} + \lambda\frac{\partial C}{\partial\alpha} \leq 0; \text{ and}$$

$$\frac{\partial L}{\partial\lambda} = kY - PY + C \geq 0.$$

Therefore, if $\lambda = 0$, $\alpha = 0$, and if $Y > 0$, $\partial(PY)/\partial Y = \partial C/\partial Y$. If $\lambda > 0$, $\alpha > 0$, then $\lambda = (1 - \partial R/\partial\alpha)$. If $Y > 0$, then

$$\frac{\partial(PY)}{\partial Y} - \frac{\partial C}{\partial Y} + \left(1 - \frac{\partial R}{\partial\alpha}\right)\left(k - \frac{\partial(PY)}{\partial Y} + \frac{\partial C}{\partial Y}\right) = 0$$

or

$$\left(1 - \frac{\partial R}{\partial\alpha}\right)k + \frac{\partial R}{\partial\alpha}\left(\frac{\partial(PY)}{\partial Y} - \frac{\partial C}{\partial Y}\right) = 0.$$

Thus,

$$\frac{\pi}{Y}\frac{(1 - \partial R/\partial\alpha)}{\partial R/\partial\alpha} = \frac{\partial C}{\partial Y} - \frac{\partial(PY)}{\partial Y} > 0.$$

# VIII

# Effect on Prices at the Aggregate Level

The most commonly referenced indicator of inflation, the consumer price index, exhibited a rather favorable response during Phase II. It increased an average of 3.7 percent annually from 1965 to 1968, more than double its average gain in 1962–65 (Table 8-1). From 1968 to 1970, the average rise climbed to nearly 6 percent. The rate of increase in total CPI appeared to slow to less than 4 percent in the eight months before the freeze in August 1971, but this was somewhat illusory because mortgage interest costs fell at an annual rate of more than 16 percent over this same period. The remainder of the CPI was rising at a rate of close to 5 percent, an increase dominated largely by services and food. For the controls period as a whole, including the freeze, all major components showed a moderation in their rates of increase, the least being food prices and the most dramatic, services (excluding mortgage-interest rates) and medical-care costs.

The first four months of Phase II were characterized by a bulge in consumer prices; the CPI, less used cars and mortgage-interest costs, advanced at an annual rate of 4.5 percent. During the latter part of Phase II, food price increases were moderately less than their bulge rates, as were almost all other major components shown in Table 8-1. The exceptions were nondurable commodities (excluding food), which increased at the target rate of about 2.5 percent during both the early bulge and the later months of Phase II, and medical care, which doubled its rate of increase.

The wholesale price index (WPI) shows a somewhat different picture: during the controls period it rose by about the same amount as during the eight months prior to the freeze, a rate substantially above its recent historical average performance (Table 8-1). The problem areas in the WPI were food, lumber, hides, leather, and textile products. The major components that experienced the most moderate price increases over the control period were durables (0.9 percent increase during controls, compared with 3.0 percent average annual rate of increase immediately before controls) and producer finished goods (1.5 percent during controls, compared with 3.7 percent before).

The major implicit price deflators for the national income accounts behaved more like the CPI than the WPI (see Table 8-2). The implicit price deflator for gross national product rose at an annual rate of 2.7 percent over the controls period, compared with a rate of 4.9 percent prior to controls. For the private nonfarm deflator, the rate of increase during the entire controls period averaged 1.8 percent, compared with 4.2 percent in the first three quarters of 1971 and an average of 5.0 percent for the two years prior to that.[1]

The three indexes of unit labor costs listed in Table 8-2 showed substantial moderation in the first three quarters of 1971 as the recovery built up steam; unit labor costs in the manufacturing sector fell by an annual rate of 2.6 percent. For the private economy and the private nonfarm sector, unit labor costs increased over the controls period at an annual rate only slightly less than during the first nine months of 1971.

These observations raise a number of possible and potentially conflicting assessments. If certain uncontrolled items such as raw food price increases (the only alternative to which was rationing) are excluded from the CPI, the reduction in the rate of consumer price increases is significant. But wholesale prices, an area in which the major constrictures of the program should have been concentrated, continued to increase at a high rate. Likewise, if competitive sectors in which shortages occurred (especially lumber, food, and hides) are excluded from the WPI, a substantial moderation appears in the remainder of the index.

The major price deflators and wage indicators show some moderation—more so for price increases than for wage increases—over the high rates that prevailed immediately prior to controls. This picture is clouded, however, by the significant moderation of unit labor costs that had occurred prior to controls and was not changed substantially during the controls program. The central issue raised by the indexes remains whether the rate of inflation was higher or lower than it would have been if past structural relations had persisted through the controls period.

Comparison between the actual rate of inflation and what would have occurred requires turning back the clock and estimating what would have occurred without controls. Thus, assessment of the effectiveness of controls, as measured by price indexes for a short-lived controls experiment such as Phase II, will be circumscribed by qualifications and

1. A detailed discussion of wage performance during Phase II is given in a companion study, Arnold R. Weber and Daniel J. B. Mitchell, manuscript in preparation.

Table 8-1. *Rate of Change in Selected Consumer and Wholesale Price Indexes, Various Periods, 1962–72*
Seasonally adjusted annual rates in percent

| Product category | 1962–65[a] | 1965–68[a] | 1968–70[a] | December 1970– August 1971 | Phase I[b] | Bulge period[c] | Controls period after bulge[d] | Phases I and II[e] |
|---|---|---|---|---|---|---|---|---|
| *Consumer price index* | | | | | | | | |
| All items | 1.6 | 3.7 | 5.8 | 3.8 | 2.0 | 3.7 | 3.3 | 3.2 |
| Food | 2.2 | 3.1 | 4.7 | 5.0 | 1.7 | 7.2 | 4.0 | 4.4 |
| Nonfood commodities[f] | 0.8 | 3.0 | 4.7 | 2.6 | 1.0 | 3.0 | 2.2 | 2.2 |
| Durables[f] | 0.5 | 2.3 | 5.1 | 2.5 | 0.3 | 4.6 | 1.5 | 2.0 |
| Nondurables | 1.2 | 3.6 | 4.3 | 3.0 | 1.4 | 2.6 | 2.5 | 2.3 |
| Services[g] | 2.9 | 4.9 | 7.6 | 7.2 | 3.2 | 4.7 | 3.7 | 3.8 |
| Rent | 1.0 | 2.1 | 4.2 | 4.3 | 2.8 | 3.6 | 3.4 | 3.3 |
| Medical care | 2.4 | 6.4 | 6.7 | 6.2 | 1.6 | 2.1 | 4.2 | 3.2 |
| CPI less used cars and mortgage-interest costs | 1.4 | 4.0 | 5.7 | 4.9 | 1.5 | 4.5 | 3.2 | 3.3 |

Wholesale price index

| | | | | | | | | |
|---|---|---|---|---|---|---|---|---|
| All items | 1.2 | 1.8 | 3.5 | 5.3 | −0.3 | 5.6 | 7.0 | 5.2 |
| Consumer finished goods | 1.3 | 2.0 | 3.1 | 4.1 | −1.1 | 4.8 | 5.0 | 3.8 |
| Food | 2.6 | 1.9 | 2.7 | 6.8 | 0.3 | 7.4 | 9.4 | 7.1 |
| Nonfood | 0.4 | 2.0 | 3.4 | 2.2 | −0.4 | 3.3 | 2.0 | 1.9 |
| Durables | −0.1 | 1.7 | 3.2 | 3.0 | −3.9 | 6.1 | 0.4 | 0.9 |
| Nondurables | 0.6 | 2.2 | 3.5 | 1.8 | 0.4 | 1.9 | 3.2 | 2.3 |
| Producer finished goods | 1.0 | 3.4 | 4.7 | 3.7 | −2.0 | 5.0 | 1.1 | 1.5 |
| Intermediate materials[h] | 0.9 | 2.1 | 3.5 | 6.5 | −0.7 | 3.4 | 4.2 | 3.1 |
| Crude materials[h] | 2.7 | 0.4 | 7.4 | 3.3 | 2.3 | 12.1 | 9.6 | 8.8 |

Sources: Derived from official consumer and wholesale price indexes of the U.S. Bureau of Labor Statistics. For short periods of time, the seasonally adjusted annual rate may differ significantly depending upon the seasonal adjustment factors that are used. In this table, the seasonal adjustment factors released early each year by the BLS, which are based primarily on data for the preceding year, were used for adjusting indexes for that year.

a. Calculated from seasonally unadjusted December-over-December figures.
b. August 1971–November 1971.
c. November 1971–March 1972.
d. March 1972–December 1972.
e. August 1971–December 1972.
f. Excludes used cars.
g. Not seasonally adjusted; data contain almost no seasonal movement. Excludes mortgage-interest costs and includes other items not shown separately.
h. Excludes food and feed for further processing; crude materials also excludes plant and animal fibers, oilseeds, and leaf tobacco.

Table 8-2. *Rate of Change in Selected Price, Unit Labor Costs, and Productivity Series, Various Periods, 1962–72*
Seasonally adjusted annual rates in percent

| Series | 1962–65 | 1965–68 | 1968–70 | December 1970– August 1971 | Phase I[a] | Bulge period[b] | Controls period after bulge[c] | Phases I and II[d] |
|---|---|---|---|---|---|---|---|---|
| *Price* | | | | | | | | |
| Private nonfarm deflator | 1.2 | 3.3 | 5.0 | 4.2 | −0.3 | 4.5 | 1.8 | 1.8 |
| Personal consumption deflator | 1.3 | 3.2 | 4.7 | 4.1 | 1.2 | 3.0 | 2.5 | 2.2 |
| GNP deflator | 1.6 | 3.7 | 5.3 | 4.9 | 1.1 | 6.0 | 2.5 | 2.7 |
| *Unit labor cost*[e] | | | | | | | | |
| Private economy | 1.0[f] | 4.4 | 6.5 | 2.4 | 1.6 | 11.1 | 1.1 | 2.3 |
| Private nonfarm economy | 1.1[f] | 4.3 | 6.6 | 2.2 | 1.3 | 9.4 | 0.7 | 1.9 |
| Manufacturing[g] | −0.6 | 3.8 | 5.0 | −2.6 | 3.9 | 1.8 | 0.3 | 1.1 |
| *Productivity* | | | | | | | | |
| Private economy | 3.5 | 2.6 | 0.3 | 6.0 | 3.0 | 5.2 | 5.0 | 4.3 |
| Private nonfarm economy | 3.1 | 2.3 | 0.2 | 5.8 | 3.8 | 3.0 | 5.4 | 4.3 |
| Manufacturing | 4.1 | 2.2 | 1.7 | 10.5 | 0.0 | 10.3 | 4.9 | 4.7 |

Sources: U.S. Department of Commerce, *Survey of Current Business*, various issues; and Department of Commerce, *Business Conditions Digest*, various issues.
a. August 1971–November 1971.
b. November 1971–March 1972.
c. March 1972–December 1972.
d. August 1971–December 1972.
e. Adjusted for interindustry shifts and for overtime in manufacturing.
f. Includes data for 1964–65 only.
g. Not seasonally adjusted.

interlaced with judgment. Several obvious questions arise concerning which variables should be held constant or adjusted in order to portray the picture as it would have been. Because a hypothetical set of conditions for the period of controls can be constructed in a myriad of ways, the results produced may give contradictory indications of what the results would have been without controls.

This chapter reviews the results of various economic studies that have appeared and compares them with the results of other econometric models. As such, this material represents only a first step toward determining the total impact of price controls. Despite the importance of aggregate figures to policymakers, the basic evaluation of the success or failure of the controls experiment (properly defined and qualified) requires a longer-run context. Therefore, Chapters 9 and 10 contain an industry-by-industry assessment of the effects of the controls program before the aggregate question is reexamined in Chapter 11.

## Aggregate Wage-Price Models Developed by the Price Commission

Two basic types of models for estimating the impact of the controls programs were developed within the Price Commission during Phase II: (a) quarterly wage-price models for the private nonfarm sector of the economy and (b) monthly wage-price models using average hourly earnings in manufacturing, the WPI, and the CPI.

### Quarterly Models for the Private Nonfarm Sector

Three quarterly wage-price models were estimated; though basically similar, each has a slightly different approach. Each model consists of two primary, estimated relations, one for wages and one for prices, which then are linked by a series of identities and estimated lagged relations among variables. Each model was estimated first over the sample period 1955:1–1971:2 (the first and second quarters of the respective years) and then reestimated through 1972:4, with a dummy variable for Phases I and II, covering the period 1971:3–1972:4. Each model predicts the quarterly rate of change in the private nonfarm price deflator and the quarterly rate of change in average hourly earnings of production workers, adjusted to exclude industry shifts and overtime and to include fringe benefits.

The first model, model EB, is constructed along the lines suggested by Otto Eckstein and Roger Brinner.[2] The most distinguishing feature of the Eckstein-Brinner approach is the use of an inflationary expectations variable that becomes positive when the rate of inflation, as measured by the private consumption deflator, exceeds a 2.5 percent annual rate, on average, for a period of two years. Virtually all econometric models estimated prior to the late 1960s underpredict price changes. The Eckstein-Brinner technique uses the inflationary expectations variable—which is 0 for the 1960s and becomes positive in the third quarter of 1967—to track the increase in the rate of wage increase that occurred in 1968. The expectations variable is used in conjunction with the aggregate rate of civilian unemployment.

George Perry has argued that the aggregate measure of unemployment does not adequately measure labor-market tightness when the composition of the labor force changes, especially when the proportion of women and teenagers increases as it did during the late 1960s.[3] Using Perry's measures of the dispersion of unemployment and adding two proxies for excess demand, disguised unemployment and the unemployment of hours, Robert J. Gordon estimated a wage-price model using involved lagged relations.[4] Perry's model estimates a significant guidepost dummy variable, as does the Eckstein-Brinner model. Gordon's use of additional unemployment variables rejects the guidepost dummy. The second model, model G, follows the Gordon approach by using similar lagged relations with no guidepost dummy variable, but it was found that the aggregate unemployment rate performed as well as the Perry-Gordon measures of unemployment.

The third model, Model SZ, follows the work of Calvin Siebert and Mahmood Zaidi.[5] The principal distinguishing feature of Model SZ is the inclusion in the wage equation of profits, the rate of change in the ag-

2. Otto Eckstein and Roger Brinner, *The Inflation Process in the United States*, Study for the Joint Economic Committee, 92 Cong. 2 sess. (1972). The detailed equations and statistics for all models are presented in the technical appendix to this chapter.

3. George L. Perry, "Changing Labor Markets and Inflation," *Brookings Papers on Economic Activity* (3:1970), pp. 411–41. (*Hereafter BPEA.*)

4. Robert J. Gordon, "Inflation in Recession and Recovery," *BPEA* (1:1971), pp. 105–58; and "Wage-Price Controls and the Shifting Phillips Curve," *BPEA* (2:1972), pp. 385–421.

5. Calvin Siebert and Mahmood A. Zaidi, "The Short-Run Wage-Price Mechanism in U.S. Manufacturing," *Western Economic Journal*, vol. 9 (September 1971), pp. 278–88.

gregate civilian unemployment rate, and productivity, all of which are omitted in the other two models. The independent variables in the model SZ price equation are the current change in average hourly earnings, the current change in output per man-hour, and two demand-related variables, the rate of change in capacity utilization, and the rate of change in the ratio of unfilled orders to sales.

Both models EB and G estimate quarterly changes in the private nonfarm deflator to be a function of standard unit labor costs, deviations from this trend, and a demand related variable. These two models also include the effects of changes in employee taxes in the wage equation; model SZ does not. Model G contains a variable for the effects of employer contributions to social security; the other two do not.

PROJECTIONS OF THE MODELS. First, the models, labeled "historical models," are estimated over the period 1955:1–1971:2.[6] With the estimated wage and price equations linked by a series of identities and estimated lagged relations among some of the variables, the controls period (1971:3–1972:4) was simulated using the actual values of the exogenous variables. The average value of actual change in the private nonfarm deflator was 1.7 percent (quarterly changes at annualized rate). Comparable values predicted by the historical models are: EB, 3.6 percent; G, 5.3; and SZ, 1.9.

For model SZ, several wage and price equations were estimated that differed from the approach employed in models EB and G. The results (tracking ability and the like) were, for the most part, less than satisfactory. Because the statistical qualities of models EB and G are superior to model SZ, the conclusions of the first two models will be examined more closely.

The models were used in two ways to assess the effects of the freeze and Phase II on wage and price inflation. Model EB indicates that price changes would have averaged 1.9 percentage points higher per quarter if conditions prior to the freeze were unchanged, whereas model G estimates that the average price change would have been 3.6 percentage points higher. (All models, when simulated from 1971:3, overpredict prices.)

The period from 1968 on was characterized by actual price movements in excess of those values being predicted by various econometric models. If the historical models (estimated through 1971:2) are simu-

6. See section A in the appendix to this chapter.

lated from 1955, with prices and wages endogenous to the models, they also underpredict changes in prices after 1968. If the simulations are begun in 1955, for the controls period the simulated values are: EB, 2.7; G, 4.0; and SZ, 1.9.

DUMMY VARIABLES FOR THE CONTROLS PERIOD. The next step was to estimate the above models over the full period 1955:1–1972:4 and include a dummy variable in each price and wage equation to pick up any structural shift that occurred over the Phase I–Phase II period.[7] The annualized values of the coefficients (with the corresponding $t$-statistics in parentheses), indicating the marginal impact of quarterly rate of change in prices, are: EB, −1.56 (−3.38); G, −1.97 (−2.95); and SZ, −1.29 (−2.93).

The dummy variable in the price equation is significantly negative for all three models. In the wage equation, the dummy variable is significantly positive in models EB and SZ and negative but insignificant in model G.

The dummy variables, having a value of 1 over the six quarters of controls, pick up any structural shift that occurred.[8] Although there are many potential sources for such changes, a logical candidate is the change induced by Phases I and II. Even so, these coefficients show marginal impacts: that is, the price equation is estimated using actual values of wage change, productivity, demand, and so forth. Thus, the proper interpretation of the coefficient for the dummy variable in the price equation is: given the rate of change in wages and other exogenous variables, the rate of change in wages (prices) would have been X percentage points higher each quarter, on the average. Therefore, the impact shown in these models on the quarterly rate of change in the private nonfarm deflator, given the actual rate of change in wages, ranges from −1.3 to −2.0 percentage points.

RELIABILITY OF THE MODELS. The reliability of the estimates shown above depends in part upon how well the models track the actual price and wage changes over the period of controls. The results of simulations of the three controls models (estimated over the period 1955:1–

7. See section A in the appendix to this chapter. The dummy-variable approach is limited because it assumes that only the constant was affected by controls. No significant changes occurred, however, in the estimated coefficients of the independent variables.

8. Two dummy variables also were tried, one for the freeze and one for Phase II; the estimated coefficients were not significantly different.

1972:4) for average (annualized) quarterly percentage change, with the actual change 1.7 percent, are: EB, 1.3 percent; G, 1.5 percent; and SZ, 0.6 percent.

In terms of the average quarterly change over the period of controls, model G comes the closest to predicting price change, missing the actual values by 0.2 percentage point. The more usual criterion, however, is the mean square error—the variance of the predicted values plus the square of the difference between the means of the actual and predicted. On this score, model G clearly is superior, having a lower mean square error. Both models G and EB actually have mean square errors that are less than the variances of the actual data, whereas model SZ is relatively poor at following actual changes in the data. All control models underpredict actual changes.

ALTERING EXOGENOUS VARIABLES. The determination of the total impact of prices requires some assumption as to the interaction among prices and the exogenous variables. That is, if prices were held down by controls, as is indicated by the dummy variables in the models, what adjustments should be made in the values of the exogenous variables to simulate hypothetical conditions? Alternatively, what is the price-control elasticity of real output? This is, of course, a moot task, but what the models say would have occurred under a specific set of alternative assumptions can be compared with actual data.

One alternative is to assume that any reduction in the rate of inflation had no effect on real production—that is, a price-control elasticity of 0. This would be equivalent to postulating that real production was somehow fixed prior to the controls period and remained unchanged.

The second clear alternative is to assume that the actions of the monetary authorities and fiscal policy were unaffected by controls—that is, that monetary and fiscal policy fixed the nominal level of gross national product before the freeze of August 1971. Thus, the price-control elasticity of real output would be equal to 1, and each percentage reduction in the rate of inflation would be transformed into an equal percentage increase in real output. This conclusion may be deduced as well by another line of reasoning: if consumption, investment, and government dollar expenditures are determined on the basis of last year's money income, and this aggregate demand is unitarily elastic with respect to price, then any reduction in the rate of price inflation will result in an equal increase in the rate of real production, in percentage terms.

To the extent (a) that inflation wastes resources through hedging and other efforts on the part of individuals to come out ahead in what is collectively a negative-sum game, and (b) that monetary and fiscal policy were more expansionary than they would have been without controls, nominal GNP would have been lower without a system of controls. If the price elasticity of aggregate demand is approximately 1, then the price-control elasticity of real output would be greater than 1. On the other hand, to the extent that the controls program induced real inefficiencies into the system so that real costs of production were increased, it would tend to reduce the price-control elasticity of real output. In any event, a price-control elasticity of real output equal to 1 is assumed, and this is incorporated into the models for purposes of comparison.

Given an assumption as to the relation between the effect on price and the effect on output, the effects on other exogenous variables can be deduced. The percentage change in output is approximately equal to the sum of the percentage changes in output per man-hour, the number of persons employed, and hours worked.[9] It seems reasonable to assume that the impact on these variables is proportionally equivalent to the relation among these variables over the controls period. From 1971:3 to 1972:4, real output increased 8.6 percent; number employed, by 3.2 percent; average hours, 0.3 percent; and output per man-hour, 5.1 percent, all annual rates. Therefore, a proportional impact would imply that the effect on the number employed would be 0.372 times the effect on real output, and the change in productivity would be 0.593 times the effect on real output.[10]

The impact on the rate of unemployment would depend further upon the effects of increased output on the size of the labor force. That a weak labor market reduces the size of the labor force is well known.[11] Over the controls period, however, the labor force participation rate was

9. Because by definition $Y = L \cdot H \cdot Y/LH$, where $Y$ is output, $L$ is number employed, and $H$ is hours worked: $dY/Y = dL/L + dH/H + d(Y/LH)/(Y/LH)$.

10. That is, $3.2 \div 8.6 = 0.372$ and $5.1 \div 8.6 = 0.593$. These data conform quite closely to Okun's law, which says that a 3 percent increase in output will lower the rate of unemployment by approximately 1 percentage point. See Arthur M. Okun, "Upward Mobility in a High-pressure Economy," *BPEA* (1:1973), pp. 207–52, for additional discussion of short-run versus long-run relations between output and number employed, originally stated in Okun, "Potential GNP: Its Measurement and Significance," in American Statistical Association, *Proceedings of the Business and Economic Statistics Section* (1962), pp. 98–104. The source of the data in the text above is U.S. Department of Commerce, *Survey of Current Business,* various issues.

11. See, for example, Alfred Tella, "The Relation of Labor Force to Employment," *Industrial and Labor Relations Review,* vol. 17 (April 1964), pp. 454–69; and N. J. Simler and Alfred Tella, "Labor Reserves and the Phillips Curve," *Review of Economics and Statistics,* vol. 50 (February 1968), pp. 32–49.

fairly constant. Furthermore, the interaction between labor force and the level of economic activity is a complicated and lagged process. Therefore, the size of the labor force is assumed to have been unaffected by controls.

With these assumptions incorporated into each model, and by using the predicted rate of inflation with controls and the rate of change in adjusted hourly earnings, each model can be solved simultaneously for the implied rate of inflation without controls.[12] These results, with the actual rate 1.7 percent, are: EB, 3.0 percent; G, 3.8; and SZ, 2.9. Both historical models EB and SZ underpredict when simulated from 1955 through 1972. Thus, a better comparison exists between the rates predicted with controls (the average predicted by the control models with the dummy variable having a value of 1 for the controls period) and the above rates predicted without controls (predicted assuming a price elasticity of output equal to 1, dummy variables having a value of 0, and a proportional impact on productivity, employment, and hours worked).

The reduction in the rate of inflation by the controls program can be assessed relative to any of the above results. The impact of the controls program, during the period 1971:3–1972:4, on the private nonfarm sector in terms of annualized quarterly percentage change, can be seen in the figures for models EB, G, and SZ, respectively, in various measures: the marginal coefficients of dummy variables, −1.6, −2.0, and −1.3; the difference between actual (1.7) and predicted change with historical models when simulated for the period 1971:3–1972:4, −1.9, −3.6, and −0.2; the difference between actual and predicted change with historical models when simulated from 1955 through 1972, −1.0, −2.3, and 0; and the difference between predicted with controls when simulated from 1955 and predicted without controls incorporating adjusted exogenous variables, −1.8, −2.3, and −1.8. These figures suggest a significant reduction in the rate of increase in the private nonfarm deflator.[13]

12. Details of these changes are given in section B of the appendix to this chapter. Except for the variables above and the various transformations and profits for model SZ that are discussed in the appendix, the other exogenous variables such as taxes are assumed to be unchanged by controls. The models were estimated through 1972:4 and revised to incorporate a price-control elasticity equal to 1, as shown in section B of the appendix.

13. The assumed unitary price-control elasticity of 1 may be unreasonable, but it has little effect on the estimated retardation of the rate of price increase over the controls period.

*Monthly Models of the CPI and WPI*

The Price Commission staff also began work on a monthly forecasting model that had been developed and used to assess the effect of the program on the CPI and WPI. Two such models were estimated, one that contains the price of farm products endogenously, model A, and one for which farm prices are exogenous, model B.

Model A is a stage-of-processing model that contains nine separate estimated relations. The dependent variables are (1) the rates of change of six components of the WPI, (2) rate of change in the price of raw industrial materials, (3) the rate of change in adjusted average hourly earnings in manufacturing, and (4) the rate of change in the CPI.[14] The exogenous variables for model A are (5) the Federal Reserve Board index of industrial production in manufacturing, (6) an index of man-hours in manufacturing, (7) the aggregate civilian unemployment rate, (8) the level of unfilled orders in manufacturing, and (9) personal income.

In model B, the estimated relation for the price of farm products is deleted. The price of farm products is added as an exogenous variable, and personal income is deleted.[15]

Both models were estimated over the period 1960–72, with a dummy variable in each estimated equation that was retained where significant. The dummy variable was significant in the CPI equation and in the equation for the price of intermediate goods excluding foods and feeds. These marginal impacts on the CPI and WPI components and on adjusted average hourly earnings in manufacturing (annualized) can be seen in the values for the structural shifts in the CPI equation, −1.95 percent, and in the equation for price of intermediate goods excluding food, −1.63 percent. Because intermediate goods excluding food have a weight of about 0.4 in the WPI, the implied shift in the WPI equation is −0.65 percent. (In arriving at these figures, the dummy variable also was significant, but positive, in the wage equation, the structural shift being +2.82 percent.)

The models were then simulated for the period 1971:3–1972:4, once with the dummy variables set equal to 1 for the controls period and once with the dummy variables set equal to 0 for the controls period.

14. See section C of the appendix to this chapter.
15. See section C of the appendix to this chapter.

The latter simulation is equivalent to assuming that the price control elasticity of real output is equal to 0. Because the quarterly models indicated a relatively small change in the results when the price control elasticity of real output was assumed to be equal to 1, this more conservative assumption was adopted here.

The predictions for the average monthly percentage change (annualized) in the CPI and WPI, respectively, for the period August 1971 through December 1972, were: model A without controls, 5.1 and 3.6; and model B without controls, 5.6 and 5.5. Actual change was—for the CPI and WPI, respectively—3.2 and 5.1 percent.

In determining the difference that controls made on the rate of inflation, the changes predicted with controls can be compared with those predicted without controls, or the actual changes with those predicted without controls, as shown below:

|  | First comparison | | Second comparison | |
| --- | --- | --- | --- | --- |
|  | Model A | Model B | Model A | Model B |
| CPI | −2.4 | −2.5 | −1.9 | −2.4 |
| WPI | −0.5 | −0.5 | +1.5 | −0.4 |

For the CPI, these differences conform roughly to the effect on the private nonfarm deflator as determined by the quarterly models. But although the change in CPI appears to have been reduced by about 2 percentage points, the WPI is much less. In Chapters 9 and 10, the data are examined by industry in some detail.

## Other Studies Assessing Phases I and II

Through 1973 only a few articles had been published that attempted to evaluate the effects of Phase I, Phase II, or both. With the exception of the study by Feige and Pearce,[16] these assessments conform roughly to the general impressions that can be drawn from the analysis in the preceding section.

One of the earlier analyses of Phase II was developed by Gordon using quarterly wage-price models of the private nonfarm sector that

16. Edgar L. Feige and Douglas K. Pearce, "The Wage-Price Control Experiment—Did It Work?" *Challenge,* vol. 16 (July/August 1973), pp. 40–44.

give results quite similar to those presented above.[17] On the basis of data through the second quarter of 1972, Gordon used his historical model to simulate price changes to compare with actual changes. His results (in annual percentage rates of change) for two alternative simulations, one with wage change exogenous and one with both wages and prices endogenous, are not significantly different from those in the preceding section, as shown below:

| Variable | Actual | Predicted by model | Difference |
|---|---|---|---|
| Prices, with wages exogenous | 2.14 | 3.61 | −1.47 |
| Prices, with wages and prices interacting | 2.14 | 3.99 | −1.85 |

Using the CPI, the WPI, and various wage indexes, Bosworth evaluated the performance of wages and prices under controls.[18] Like Gordon, Bosworth had recourse to data only through mid-1972. He concluded that, essentially, there had been a significant slowdown in consumer prices that was particularly dramatic in the area of medical-care services, but that the effect on wholesale prices was much less impressive. In terms of cause and effect, Bosworth comments: "What these statistics do not prove, however, is that the controls are responsible for the improvement. . . . The major impact on prices and wages does not appear to come from specific decisions of the Pay Board or the Price Commission. . . . The restraint appears to come instead from the changed environment in which price and wage decisions are made—particularly the published 5.5 percent (or 6.2 percent) general wage standard."[19]

Popkin analyzes price trends in the CPI and WPI during Phase II.[20] Without drawing major conclusions or implications, he notes that most major groups of commodities and services in the CPI and WPI rose at

17. Gordon, "Wage-Price Controls."

18. Barry Bosworth, "Phase II: The U.S. Experiment with an Incomes Policy," *BPEA* (2:1972), pp. 343–83.

19. Ibid, p. 375. See Bosworth, "The Current Inflation: Malign Neglect?" *BPEA* (1:1973), pp. 263–83, for a continuation of this analysis through 1972 and into 1973; and Robert J. Gordon, "The Response of Wages and Prices to the First Two Years of Controls," *BPEA* (3:1973), pp. 765–78, for an analysis through the third quarter of 1973.

20. Joel Popkin, "Prices in 1972: An Analysis of Changes During Phase 2," *Monthly Labor Review*, vol. 96 (February 1973), pp. 16–23.

a slower rate during Phase II than during the eight months preceding the freeze in 1971. In addition, he emphasizes the exceptions to typical relations that occurred under Phase II: retail prices of nonfood commodities rose less rapidly than their wholesale counterparts (particularly nondurables); and the price of services (excluding mortgage-interest costs) increased. Although prices for services rose more than those for nonfood commodities, the increase was closer to that for nonfood commodities in the CPI than any year since 1964, with the exception of 1967. The slowdowns were most marked in areas having a prevalence of small, exempt service firms.

Feige and Pearce[21] argue that the annual rate of inflation as measured by the CPI slowed by about 1.3 percentage points during Phases I and II relative to the rate for the sixteen months prior to the freeze. As measured by the WPI, however, the annual rate of inflation increased by 1.9 percentage points compared with the sixteen months prior to the control program. Both of these observations are simple comparisons of the actual data. To establish hypothetical data for what would have occurred without controls, Feige and Pearce estimated a time-series model through August 1971, based solely upon the past history of a given price series.[22] The actual results for the prefreeze period May 1970–August 1971 and the freeze and postfreeze period September 1971 through December 1972 for the CPI and WPI are compared below with predictions of the model:[23]

|  | Actual prefreeze | Actual postfreeze | Predicted |
|---|---|---|---|
| CPI | 4.5 | 3.2 | 3.2 |
| WPI | 3.5 | 5.4 | 4.0 |

Feige and Pearce conclude that on the basis of past variations, the rate of change in the CPI would have slowed down by exactly the

21. Feige and Pearce, "The Wage-Price Control Experiment," p. 41.

22. Each series (that is, the CPI and WPI) is represented as a stochastic process of autoregressive integrated moving average form, an ARIMA model. The predictive ability of ARIMA models relative to large-scale econometric models has been assessed favorably by Charles R. Nelson in "The Prediction Performance of the FRB-MIT-PENN Model of the U.S. Economy," *American Economic Review*, vol. 62 (December 1972), pp. 902–17.

23. From Feige and Pearce, "The Wage-Price Control Experiment," Tables 1 and 2, pp. 41, 43.

amount it did, giving a zero impact to the controls program. The average change in the WPI, on this basis, was 1.4 percentage points higher. If the December figures for the WPI are omitted, the actual average change for the 15 months from September 1971 to November 1972 is 4.2 percent, whereas the model predicts 4.0 for the same period, thus changing the impact on the WPI to +0.2 percentage point. Thus, on the basis of how each series moved independently in the past, Feige and Pearce conclude the slowdown in prices would have occurred anyway.[24]

Because this contrasts sharply with the results in the monthly model, a further test was undertaken. The monthly model indicated that most of the reduction occurred in the CPI equation. Therefore, a simple two-equation model was constructed, one for the CPI and one for adjusted average hourly earnings in manufacturing, estimated from 1960 to just before the freeze in August 1971.[25] The model then was simulated from August 1971 forward, taking the actual WPI as an exogenous variable. The results—the average monthly rate of change (annualized) in the CPI, actual, 3.2 percent, and predicted, 5.4 percent—conform fairly well to the impact shown by the monthly forecasting model, showing an impact of −2.2 percentage points.

Thus, looking at the inflation problem from a structural point of view, the Feige-Pearce results must be rejected. The rate of inflation, under historical structural conditions, would not have slowed as it did.

## Conclusions

Comparisons of actual changes in prices at the aggregate level, and estimates of what would have occurred under historical conditions without price and wage controls, indicates, first, a significant reduction in the rate of inflation for consumer prices (around 2.0 percentage points) and, second, a much smaller impact on wholesale prices (no more than 0.5 percentage point). These conclusions seem to follow from a variety of different approaches using aggregate, private nonfarm data.

24. Alternatively, the ARIMA model may be predicting the institution of controls on prices to bring the rates of change during the sixteen-month period of controls into line with historical experience. If this is indeed the case, price controls succeeded.

25. See section D of the appendix to this chapter for details. Cost considerations prohibited the estimation and simulation of the full monthly forecasting model for the period 1960 to August 1971.

# APPENDIX

The first section of this appendix presents the detailed equations for three quarterly models of wage and price change for the private nonfarm sector. Following the details of the estimated models, the alterations in the models for a price-control elasticity of output equal to unity are set forth in section B. (Assuming the price-control elasticity of output were equal to zero would only require setting the values of the dummy variable, Phase II, equal to zero in the controls models.) Section C presents the monthly forecasting models developed by the Price Commission staff to assess the effects of the stabilization program on the consumer and wholesale price indexes. The final section discusses a simple two-equation historical model used to simulate forward from July 1971 over the controls period.

## A. Details of Three Quarterly Models

Each model was first estimated over the sample period 1955:1–1971:2 (historical models) and then over the period 1955:1–1972:4 (price-control models).

### The Eckstein-Brinner Model: Model EB

EXOGENOUS VARIABLES

$QL$ = the quarterly rate of change in output per man-hour

$CMH$ = the quarterly rate of change in compensation per man-hour

$TW$ = the quarterly rate of change in the ratio of personal income to personal income less personal tax payments and personal contributions to social security

$OR$ = index of real orders in manufacturing

$CAP$ = index of industrial capacity in manufacturing

$U$ = aggregate civilian unemployment rate

$GP$ = guidepost dummy variable (values are 1962:1, 0.25; 1962:2, 0.50; 1962:3, 0.75; 1962:4–1966:4, 1.0; 1967:1, 0.75; 1967:2, 0.50; 1967:3, 0.25; and 0 for all other quarters)

$PHASE2$ = an economic stabilization program price-control dummy (values are 1971:3–1972:4, 1; and 0 for all other quarters)

ENDOGENOUS VARIABLES

$PNFD$ = the quarterly rate of change in the private nonfarm deflator

$W2$ = the quarterly rate of change in average hourly earnings of production workers adjusted to exclude industry shifts and overtime and to include fringe benefits

The variables are estimated by the following two equations:

(EB1)
$$PNFD = a_0 + a_1[\overline{W2}(-1) - 0.0065] + a_2[W2 - \overline{W2}(-1)]$$
$$+ a_3[\overline{QL}(-1) - 0.0065] + a_4[QL - \overline{QL}(-1)]$$
$$+ a_5(\overline{W2} - \overline{CMH}) + a_6 DEMAND + a_7 PHASE2$$

(EB2)
$$W2 = b_0 + b_1\overline{PCD} + b_2 PCDEXP + b_3/U$$
$$+ b_4 GP + b_5\overline{TW} + b_6 PHASE2,$$

where the identities below define the variables.

ESTIMATED LAGGED RELATION

(EB3)
$$PCD = c_0 + \sum_{i=1}^{8} c_i PNFD(1 - i)$$

where $PCD$ = quarterly rate of change in the private consumption deflator.

IDENTITIES

(EB4)
$$\overline{W2} = 0.4W2 + 0.3W2(-1) + 0.2W2(-2)$$
$$+ 0.1W2(-3)$$

(EB5)
$$\overline{QL} = 0.4QL + 0.3QL(-1) + 0.2QL(-2)$$
$$+ 0.1QL(-3)$$

(EB6)
$$\overline{CMH} = 0.4CMH + 0.3CMH(-1) + 0.2CMH(-2)$$
$$+ 0.1CMH(-3)$$

(EB7)
$$\overline{PCD} = 0.4PCD + 0.3PCD(-1) + 0.2PCD(-2)$$
$$+ 0.1PCD(-3)$$

(EB8)
$$PCDEXP = \left[\sum_{i=0}^{7} PCD(-i) - 5.0\right], \text{ if positive}; = 0, \text{ otherwise}$$

(EB9)
$$\overline{TW} = 10TW - 4.5TW(-1) - 3TW(-2) - 1.5TW(-3)$$

(EB10)   $DEMAND = (OR/CAP) - [OR(-1)/CAP(-1)]$

SUMMARY

The quarterly rate of change in the private nonfarm deflator for model EB is a function of the following (in which the notation corresponds with that in Table 8-3):

$a_1$, the deviation of a four-quarter weighted average of quarterly rates of change in wages from the trend quarterly rate of change in output per man-hour in the private nonfarm sector (0.0065)

$a_2$, the deviation of current rates of change in wages from the past four-quarter average

$a_3$, the deviation of a four-quarter weighted-average change in productivity from its long-term average quarterly change

$a_4$, the difference between the current rate of change in output per man-hour and the average over the past year

$a_5$, the difference in wage changes and compensation per man-hour

$a_6$, demand pressures as expressed by the positive value of the change in the ratio of real orders to capacity in manufacturing

$a_7$, a dummy variable for controls in Phases I and II

Changes in adjusted average hourly earnings for production workers in the private nonfarm sector are a function of the following:

$b_1$, a four-quarter weighted average of changes in the private consumption deflator, which, in turn, is estimated to be an eight-quarter weighted average of changes in the private nonfarm deflator

$b_2$, an expectations variable that is the actual value of the private consumption deflator if greater than 5.0 percent over the prior eight quarters, 0 elsewhere

$b_3$, the inverse of the unemployment rate

$b_4$, a guidepost dummy variable

$b_5$, a weighted average of the past four-quarter changes in the ratio of gross personal income to net personal income, with the weights summing to 1.0

$b_6$, a dummy variable for controls in Phases I and II

The best distributed lag relations between the personal consumption deflator and the private nonfarm deflator over the past eight quarters is as shown by the coefficients $c_1$ through $c_8$ in equation (EB3).

The statistics for the three estimated equations are presented in Table 8-3 for the periods 1955:1–1971:2 and 1955:1–1972:4.

Table 8-3. Regression Coefficients for Wage and Price Equations, Model EB, Two Periods, 1955–72[a]

First quarter 1955–second quarter 1971

| Equation | Variable[b] and coefficient | | | | | | | | | $\bar{R}^2$ | Durbin-Watson statistic | Standard error |
|---|---|---|---|---|---|---|---|---|---|---|---|---|
| (EB1) | $a_0$ 0.001 (0.90) | $a_1$ 0.91 (10.22) | $a_2$ 0.37 (3.90) | $a_3$ −0.22 (−3.11) | $a_4$ −0.12 (3.41) | $a_5$ −0.42 (−3.12) | $a_6$ 0.055 (1.82) | | | 0.73 | 2.29 | 0.0021 |
| (EB2) | $b_0$ 0.003 (2.24) | $b_1$ 0.13 (0.65) | $b_2$ 0.17 (3.77) | $b_3$ 0.034 (3.84) | $b_4$ −0.002 (−2.61) | $b_5$ 0.022 (2.99) | $b_6$ ... ... | | | 0.68 | 2.22 | 0.0024 |
| (EB3) | $c_0$ 0.001 (1.08) | $c_1$ 0.865 (12.68) | $c_2$ 0.112 (2.46) | $c_3$ −0.088 (−2.26) | $c_4$ −0.043 (−1.67) | $c_5$ 0.038 (1.11) | $c_6$ 0.046 (1.58) | $c_7$ −0.032 (−1.17) | $c_8$ −0.109 (−2.62) | 0.74 | 1.76 | 0.0030 |

First quarter 1955–fourth quarter 1972[c]

| Equation | Variable[b] and coefficient | | | | | | | | $\bar{R}^2$ | Durbin-Watson statistic | Standard error |
|---|---|---|---|---|---|---|---|---|---|---|---|
| (EB1) | $a_0$ 0.001 (1.19) | $a_1$ 0.873 (9.93) | $a_2$ 0.455 (5.39) | $a_3$ −0.233 (−3.33) | $a_4$ −0.138 (−4.04) | $a_5$ −0.431 (−3.19) | $a_6$ 0.046 (1.51) | $a_7$ −0.004 (−3.38) | 0.73 | 2.35 | 0.0021 |
| (EB2) | $b_0$ 0.003 (2.13) | $b_1$ 0.238 (1.11) | $b_2$ 0.137 (2.91) | $b_3$ 0.032 (3.44) | $b_4$ −0.002 (−2.60) | $b_5$ 0.021 (3.01) | $b_6$ 0.003 (2.32) | | 0.64 | 2.14 | 0.0026 |

Source: Model EB, described in the text.
a. The numbers in parentheses are $t$-statistics.
b. $a_0$, $b_0$, and $c_0$ are constant terms. The definitions of the other variables are given in the text of section A. (Although not significantly different from zero, $b_1$ was retained to conform to the Eckstein-Brinner approach.)
c. Data for equation (EB3) are identical to those in the first part of the table.

## The Gordon Model: Model G

### EXOGENOUS VARIABLES

$WTCR$ = ratio of the index of average hourly earnings for production workers in the private nonfarm sector (adjusted for overtime [manufacturing only], interindustry shifts, and fringe benefits) to the index of compensation per man-hour in the private nonfarm sector

$UOKR$ = the ratio of unfilled orders to capacity in manufacturing

$JQ$ = index of output per man-hour in the private nonfarm sector

$T$ = time dummy variable where in 1947:1, $T = 1$ and in 1972:4, $T = 104$

$U$ = aggregate civilian unemployment rate[26]

$TW$ = the quarterly rate of change in the ratio of personal income to personal income less personal tax payments and personal contributions to social security

$TF$ = the quarterly rate of change in the ratio of personal income to personal income less the firms' contributions to social insurance

### ENDOGENOUS VARIABLES

$PNFD$ = the quarterly rate of change in the private nonfarm deflator

$W3$ = the quarterly rate of change in standard unit labor costs (that is, the change in the ratio of average hourly earnings divided by an index of standard productivity: $W3 = W2 - [J - J(-1)]/J(-1)$; $J = \exp(f_0 + f_1 T)$; $T$ is time, where in 1947:1, $T = 1$ and in 1972:4, $T = 104$

The variables are estimated by the following equations:

(G1)  $$PNFD = a_0 + a_1 OC + a_2 DUFK + a_3 PHASE2 + a_4 QLR_L + a_5 W3_L$$

(G2)  $$W3 = b_0 + b_1/U + b_2 TW + b_3 TFG + b_4 PHASE2 + b_5 PCD_L + b_6 PDIFF_L,$$

where $PHASE2$ is an economic stabilization price-control dummy variable, and the other variables are described in the identities below.

---

26. In the original formulation, Gordon used three indications of labor-market tightness. The inverse unemployment rate performed equally as well and was substituted for his original variables. Robert J. Gordon, "Inflation in Recession and Recovery," *BPEA* (1:1971), pp. 105–58.

Table 8-4. Regression Coefficients for Wage and Price Equations, Model G, Two Periods, 1955–72[a]

### First quarter 1955–second quarter 1971

| Equation | Variable[b] and coefficient | $\bar{R}^2$ | Durbin-Watson statistic | Standard error |
|---|---|---|---|---|
| (G1) | $a_0$ 0.001 (1.06); $a_1$ −0.44 (−2.39); $a_2$ 0.023 (2.36); $a_3$ …; $a_4$ −0.28 (−2.00); $a_5$ 0.98 (7.00) | 0.73 | 2.42 | 0.0021 |
| (G2) | $b_0$ −0.009 (−4.61); $b_1$ 0.029 (3.28); $b_2$ 0.071 (0.97); $b_3$ 1.15 (4.61); $b_4$ …; $b_5$ 1.64 (9.11); $b_6$ 0.435 (1.41) | 0.79 | 2.42 | 0.0019 |
| (G3) | $c_0$ 0.001 (1.08); $c_1$ 0.865 (12.68); $c_2$ 0.112 (2.46); $c_3$ −0.088 (−2.26); $c_4$ −0.043 (−1.67); $c_5$ 0.384 (1.11); $c_6$ 0.046 (1.58); $c_7$ −0.032 (−1.17); $c_8$ −0.109 (−2.62) | 0.74 | 1.76 | 0.0030 |
| (G4)[c] | $d_0$ 0.114 (1.82); $d_1$ −0.008 (−6.95) | 0.36 | 0.06 | 0.254 |
| (G5)[c] | $f_0$ −0.56 (−133.26); $f_1$ 0.007 (88.20) | 0.99 | 0.31 | 0.0168 |

### First quarter 1955–fourth quarter 1972[d]

| Equation | Variable[b] and coefficient | $\bar{R}^2$ | Durbin-Watson statistic | Standard error |
|---|---|---|---|---|
| (G1) | $a_0$ 0.001 (1.27); $a_1$ −0.420 (−2.29); $a_2$ 0.021 (2.14); $a_3$ −0.005 (−2.95); $a_4$ −0.27 (−1.83); $a_5$ 0.95 (6.69) | 0.72 | 2.51 | 0.0021 |
| (G2) | $b_0$ −0.009 (−4.43); $b_1$ 0.029 (3.16); $b_2$ 0.067 (0.93); $b_3$ 1.249 (4.92); $b_4$ −0.001 (−0.79); $b_5$ 1.67 (8.47); $b_6$ 0.306 (0.95) | 0.75 | 2.4 | 0.0021 |

Source: Model G, described in the text.

a. The numbers in parentheses are $t$-statistics.

b. $a_0$, $b_0$, $c_0$, $d_0$, and $f_0$ are constant terms. The definitions of the other variables are given in the text of section A.

c. Equations (G4) and (G5) were estimated over the period 1948:4–1969:4 in order to establish a long-term trend.

d. Data for equations (G3), (G4), and (G5) are identical with those in the first part of the table.

ESTIMATED RELATIONS

(G3) (= EB3)

$$PCD = c_0 + \sum_{i=1}^{8} c_i PNFD(1 - i)$$

(G4) $\quad UOKT = \exp(d_0 + d_1 T)$

(G5) $\quad J = \exp(e_0 + f_1 T) = \text{trend rate in productivity}$

IDENTITIES

(G6) $\quad a_5 W3_L = \sum_{i=1}^{10} g_i W3(1 - i)$

(G7) $\quad b_5 PCD_L = \sum_{i=1}^{24} h_i PCD(1 - i)$

(G8) $\quad b_6 PDIFF_L = \sum_{i=1}^{8} k_i PDIFF(-i)$

(G9) $\quad QLR_L = \sum_{i=1}^{8} j_i QLR(1 - i)$

(G10) $\quad DUFK = \dfrac{DUOK - DUOK(-1)}{DUOK(-1)}$

(G11) $\quad DUOK = UOKR/UOKT$

(G12) $\quad QLR = [JQ/J - JQ(-1)/J(-1)]/[JQ(-1)/J(-1)]$

(G13) $\quad OC = 0.25\left(\dfrac{WTCR}{WTCR(-4)}\right) - 1.00$

(G14) $\quad TFG = TF - 0.5TF(-1) - 0.33TF(-2) - 0.17TF(-3)$

(G15) $\quad PDIFF = PNFD - PCD$

SUMMARY

In model G the quarterly rate of change in the private nonfarm deflator is estimated to be a function of the following (the notation corresponds with that in Table 8-4):

$a_1$, one-fourth of the annual rate of change in the ratio of adjusted average hourly earnings to compensation per man-hour

$a_2$, the quarterly rate of change in the actual ratio of unfilled orders to capacity to the trend of that ratio as estimated by equation (G10)

$a_3$, economic stabilization program price-control dummy variable

$a_4$, a weighted average over the last eight quarters of the quarterly rate of change in the ratio of output per man-hour to the trend in productivity ($\sum_{i=1}^{8} j_i$), the trend being estimated by equation (G12)

$a_5$, a weighted average, over the past ten quarters, of the quarterly rate of change in standard unit labor costs ($\sum_{i=1}^{10} g_i$) (average hourly earnings divided by standard productivity [equation (G12)])

The quarterly rate of change in standard unit labor costs is a function of:

$b_1$, the inverse of the unemployment rate

$b_2$, the quarterly rate of change in the ratio of gross personal income to net personal income

$b_3$, weighted average (with weights summing to 0 over the past four quarters) of personal income to personal income net of firms' contributions for social security

$b_4$, an economic stabilization program price-control dummy

$b_5$, a weighted average over the past twenty-four quarters of changes in the private consumption deflator ($\sum_{i=1}^{24} h_i$)

$b_6$, a weighted average over the last eight quarters of the quarterly rate of change in the difference between the private nonfarm deflator and the private consumption deflator ($\sum_{i=1}^{8} k_i$)

Model G contains five estimated lagged relations: four simply create new variables and the other relates changes in the private nonfarm deflator to changes in the private consumption deflator—the same linking equation used in model EB.

The statistics for model G are given in Table 8-4 for the periods 1955:1–1971:2 and 1955:1–1972:4.

### The Siebert-Zaidi Model: Model SZ

As noted in the text, several different equations that differed from models EB and G were estimated for model SZ. The best results are as follows.

EXOGENOUS VARIABLES

$QL$ = the quarterly rate of change in output per man-hour in the private nonfarm sector

$UFS$ = the ratio of the quarterly rate of change in unfilled orders for manufacturing to sales for manufacturing and trade

$PHASE2$ = an economic stabilization program price-control dummy variable

$U$ = aggregate civilian unemployment rate

$PROF$ = the quarterly rate of change in corporate profits

$CUR$ = the quarterly rate of change in the Federal Reserve Board index of capacity utilization for manufacturing

ENDOGENOUS VARIABLES

(SZ1) $PNFD = a_0 + a_1W2 + a_2RMP + a_3CUR + a_4QL$
$+ a_5UFS + a_6PHASE2$

(SZ2) $W2 = b_0 + b_1/U + b_2[U - U(-1)/U(-1)] + b_3PCD$
$+ b_4PNFD + b_5QL + b_6PROF + b_7W2(-1)$
$+ b_8PHASE2$

ESTIMATED LAGGED RELATIONS

(SZ3) $PCD = c_0 + \sum_{i=1}^{8} c_iPNFD(1 - i)$

(SZ4) $RMP = d_0 + \sum_{i=1}^{8} d_iPNFD(1 - i)$

SUMMARY

Model SZ estimates the quarterly rate of change in the private nonfarm deflator to be a function of the following (the notation corresponds to that in Table 8-5):

$a_1$, the rate of change in adjusted average hourly earnings

$a_2$, the quarterly rate of change in raw materials price index in the wholesale price index

$a_3$, the rate of change in capacity utilization

$a_4$, the rate of change in productivity

$a_5$, demand as given by the rate of change in the ratio of unfilled orders to sales

$a_6$, an economic stabilization program price-control dummy

The rate of change in average hourly earnings in the private nonfarm sector is given by:

$b_1$, the inverse of the unemployment rate

$b_2$, quarterly rate of change in the unemployment rate

Table 8-5. Regression Coefficients for Wage and Price Equations, Model SZ, Two Periods, 1955–72[a]

Variable[b] and coefficient

First quarter 1955–second quarter 1971

| Equation | | | | | | | | | | $\bar{R}^2$ | Durbin-Watson statistic | Standard error |
|---|---|---|---|---|---|---|---|---|---|---|---|---|
| (SZ1) | $a_0$ -0.001 (-1.16) | $a_1$ 0.662 (9.27) | $a_2$ -0.002 (-0.22) | $a_3$ -0.025 (-1.32) | $a_4$ -0.153 (-3.28) | $a_5$ 0.069 (2.08) | | | | 0.64 | 1.93 | 0.0024 |
| (SZ2) | $b_0$ 0.002 (1.09) | $b_1$ 0.007 (0.74) | $b_2$ -0.002 (-0.34) | $b_3$ 0.499 (3.10) | $b_4$ 0.320 (2.28) | $b_5$ 0.107 (1.98) | $b_6$ -0.014 (-1.54) | $b_7$ 0.227 (2.21) | | 0.66 | 2.13 | 0.0025 |
| (SZ3) | $c_0$ 0.001 (1.08) | $c_1$ 0.865 (12.68) | $c_2$ 0.112 (2.46) | $c_3$ -0.088 (-2.26) | $c_4$ -0.043 (-1.67) | $c_5$ 0.038 (1.11) | $c_6$ 0.046 (1.58) | $c_7$ -0.032 (-1.17) | $c_8$ -0.109 (-2.62) | 0.74 | 1.76 | 0.0030 |
| (SZ4) | $d_0$ 0.022 (2.02) | $d_1$ 5.898 (5.98) | $d_2$ -0.713 (-1.08) | $d_3$ -2.858 (-5.98) | $d_4$ -2.652 (-7.10) | $d_5$ -1.634 (-3.23) | $d_6$ -0.763 (-1.81) | $d_7$ -0.425 (-1.07) | $d_8$ -0.427 (-0.71) | 0.52 | 1.66 | 0.0429 |

First quarter 1955–fourth quarter 1972[c]

| Equation | | | | | | | | | | $\bar{R}^2$ | Durbin-Watson statistic | Standard error |
|---|---|---|---|---|---|---|---|---|---|---|---|---|
| (SZ1) | $a_0$ -0.001 (-1.32) | $a_1$ 0.669 (9.94) | $a_2$ -0.002 (-0.24) | $a_3$ -0.025 (-1.40) | $a_4$ -0.152 (-3.38) | $a_5$ 0.070 (2.19) | $a_6$ -0.003 (-2.93) | | | 0.65 | 1.96 | 0.0024 |
| (SZ2) | $b_0$ 0.003 (1.16) | $b_1$ 0.001 (0.14) | $b_2$ -0.008 (-1.48) | $b_3$ 0.429 (2.69) | $b_4$ 0.481 (3.70) | $b_5$ 0.167 (3.79) | $b_6$ -0.002 (-0.60) | $b_7$ 0.186 (1.91) | $b_8$ 0.002 (1.80) | 0.66 | 2.12 | 0.0025 |

Source: Model SZ, described in the text.

a. The numbers in parentheses are $t$-statistics.

b. $a_0$, $b_0$, $c_0$, and $d_0$ are constant terms. The definitions of the other variables are given in the text of section A.

c. Data for equations (SZ3) and (SZ4) are identical to those in the first part of the table.

$b_3$, the quarterly rate of change in the private consumption deflator
$b_4$, the rate of change in the private nonfarm deflator
$b_5$, the rate of change in productivity
$b_6$, the rate of change in corporate profits
$b_7$, average hourly earnings lagged one quarter
$b_8$, an economic stabilization program price-control dummy

The estimated lagged relations are the relation between *PNFD* and *PCD*, as used in models EB and G (coefficients $c_1$ through $c_8$), and an estimated relation between *PNFD* and the change in the raw materials component of the WPI, *RMP* (coefficients $d_1$ through $d_8$). The coefficients for model SZ are given in Table 8-5. The rate of change in profits has the wrong sign for both periods, although it is not significant for the historical period 1955:1–1971:2.

## B. Changes in the Quarterly Models to Incorporate the Assumption That the Price Control Elasticity of Real Output Is Equal to Unity

### Model EB

The changes in model EB involve the productivity rate, *QL*, compensation per man-hour, *CMH*, the unemployment rate, *U*, and the dummy variable, *PHASE2*. The ratio of real orders to capacity and the ratio of gross to net personal income are assumed to be unchanged by controls.

The model is first solved for the simulated rate of inflation and rate of change in wages with controls, *PNFDW* and *W2W*. The additional endogenous variables added to the model are *QLWO*, productivity without controls; *UWO*, unemployment without controls; *CMHWO*, compensation per man-hour without controls; *PNFDWO*, quarterly rate of change in the private nonfarm deflator without controls; and *W2WO*, wage change without controls. In all places, these variables replace their like counterparts used for simulation.

Then, the following identities are added to the model:

(EB11)     $QLWO = QL + 0.593(PNFDW - PNFDWO)$

(EB12)     $UWO = \dfrac{U - 0.4884(PNFDW - PNFDWO)}{1 - 0.372(PNFDW - PNFDWO)}$

(EB13)   $CMHWO = CMH\left(\dfrac{W2W}{W2WO}\right)$

The additional exogenous variables are then *PNFDW*, the simulated rate of inflation with controls; and *W2W*, the simulated rate of wage change with controls. Also, the value of the dummy variable, *PHASE2*, is set equal to 0 for the period 1971:3–1972:4.

### Model G

In model G, the new endogenous variables are *PNFDWO*, the quarterly rate of change in the private nonfarm deflator without controls; and *W3WO*, the quarterly rate of change in standard unit labor costs without controls. Using the simulated values for what actually took place as additional exogenous variables, *PNFDW* and *W3W*, the added identities to model G are:

$$(G16) \quad \frac{JQWO}{JQWO(-1)} = \frac{JQ}{JQ(-1)} + 0.593(PNFDW - PNFDWO)$$

$$(G17) \quad UWO = \frac{U - 0.4884(PNFDW - PNFDWO)}{1 - 0.372(PNFDW - PNFDWO)},$$

where $JQWO$ = the index of output per man-hour without controls, and $UWO$ = the rate of aggregate civilian unemployment without controls. $UWO$ then replaces $U$ and $JQWO$ replaces $JQ$ everywhere in the model. The effect on average hourly earnings is assumed to be equal to the effect on compensation per man-hour so that their ratio, *WTCR*, is unchanged. Also, unfilled orders to capacity and employee and employer taxes are assumed to be unaffected by controls.

### Model SZ

Model SZ is modified in a similar manner. The new endogenous variables become *PNFDWO* and *W2WO* and replace *PNFD* and *W2* in equations (SZ1) through (SZ4). The added equations to the model are:

$$(SZ5) \quad UWO = \frac{U - 0.4884(PNFDW - PNFDWO)}{1 - 0.372(PNFDW - PNFDWO)}$$

$$(SZ6) \quad QLWO = QL + 0.593(PNFDW - PNFDWO)$$

$$(SZ7) \quad PROFWO = PROF + 4.94[W2W - W2WO - 0.402(PNFDW - PNFDWO)]$$

$$(SZ8) \quad CURWO = -0.0114 + 0.979(JFRB + PNFDW - PNFDWO),$$

where *UWO* replaces *U*, *QLWO* replaces *QL*, *PROFWO* replaces *PROF*, and *CURWO* replaces *CUR* everywhere in (SZ1) through (SZ4). Equation (SZ7) is derived in the following way. Income originating in corporate business comprises profits, net interest, and compensation to employees. Assuming that the effect on value added per unit of output is equal to the effect on prices and that the impact on net interest was 0, it follows that

$$\%\Delta\pi = -\frac{wL}{\pi}(\%\Delta w + \%\Delta L),$$

where

$\%\Delta\pi$ = impact on the percentage change in profits

$wL$ = compensation to employees

$\%\Delta w$ = impact on wage change

$\%\Delta L$ = impact on employment (number employed plus hours)

Thus, in equation (SZ7), 4.94 is the ratio of compensation to profits, and the value 0.402 follows from the prior assumptions about the impact on employment.

Equation (SZ8) was derived by first regressing *CUR* on the quarterly rate of change in the FRB index of industrial production, *JFRB*, which gave the following relation:

$$CUR = -0.0114 + 0.979 JFRB$$

$\bar{R}^2 = 0.993$; Durbin-Watson statistic = 2.66; standard error = 0.0019; $\rho = 0.776$.

Then, because the impact on the percentage change in prices equals the impact on output, equation (SZ8) follows.

The added exogenous variables to model SZ are the simulated values *PNFDW* and *W2W* and the quarterly rate of change in the index of industrial production, *JFRB*. *PHASE2* is set at 0 when solving for the rate of inflation without controls.

## C. Monthly Forecasting Models

One of the models developed by the Price Commission staff, A, treats the price of farm products endogenously; the other, B, exogenously.

*Technique of Estimation*

To overcome some of the difficulties of capturing monthly changes in prices, several general strategies were undertaken. First, the variables usually were estimated in a weighted-ratio form, previously suggested by Eckstein and Wyss.[27] The symbol $R$ denotes the following ratio form for a variable, $X$:

$$XR = \frac{X}{0.4X(-1) + 0.3X(-2) + 0.2X(-3) + 0.1X(-4)}.$$

The algebraic properties of $XR$ incorporate smooth and positive serial correlation, because $XR$ is more responsive to deviations from a trend rate of growth in $X$.

Because the models use monthly data, there is no a priori reason why a four-period weighted-average ratio would be appropriate. Other periods were tried, but overall the foregoing form generated the best results. Thus, it was utilized uniformly in the models. In several equations, lagged values of the dependent variable proved significant as explanatory variables. A polynomial distributed lag for one of the independent variables also was used. Both of these techniques add to the ability of the regression equations to capture adjustment processes greater than four months.

No seasonally adjusted data were used. Therefore, each estimated equation included seasonal dummy variables that were retained in the equation where significant.

Food prices in monthly models of the CPI and WPI usually generate the greatest month-to-month variation. Therefore, to estimate consistent relations among the various components, the WPI first was decomposed into categories excluding food. Furthermore, because lags vary by stage of process, both the food and nonfood components were separated into stage-of-processing categories. The resulting six categories that, when weighted, approximately add up to the WPI (see equation [12], below) are:

*PCM[*, the price of crude materials excluding food
*PIG[*, the price of intermediate goods excluding food
*PPFG*, the price of producer-finished goods
*PCFG[*, the price of consumer finished goods excluding food

27. Otto Eckstein and David Wyss, "Industry Price Equations," in Otto Eckstein (ed.), *The Econometrics of Price Determination: Conference* (Board of Governors of the Federal Reserve System, 1972), pp. 133–65.

*PFP*, the price of farm products
*PPFF*, the price of processed foods and feeds

The latter two are equivalent to the WPI codes 01 and 02 with the same names, respectively. The first four are not regularly published by the Bureau of Labor Statistics and were constructed. Because of data limitations, however, the actual six series contain some overlap of commodities. Consequently, the weights had to be adjusted for this overlap, and the result is equation (I2)—an approximation to the WPI, labeled *WPIX*.

Even this process proved troublesome, because it is quite difficult to forecast weather and the machinations of the corn-hog cycle by using national income accounts data. Therefore, two models were constructed: one that predicts farm prices endogenously and one that has farm prices exogenous to the model.

### General Form

The principal endogenous variables in both models are the WPI and the CPI, neither seasonally adjusted. Model A, which contains farm prices endogenously, consists of eighteen identities, nine estimated relations, five exogenous variables, and three dummy variables. Model B, with farm prices exogenous, consists of seventeen identities, eight estimated relations, five exogenous variables (*PFP* becomes an exogenous variable and personal income is dropped from model B), and the same three dummy variables.

The dependent variables for the nine estimated relations are the prices, in ratio form, of raw materials, crude materials for further processing, intermediate goods, producer-finished goods, consumer-finished goods, farm products, processed foods and feeds, average hourly earnings in manufacturing adjusted for overtime and interindustry shifts, *W*, and consumer goods (the CPI).

### Model A

EXOGENOUS VARIABLES

$JFRB$ = FRB index of industrial production in manufacturing
$JMHM$ = index of man-hours in manufacturing
$U$ = aggregate civilian unemployment rate
$OUM$ = unfilled orders in manufacturing
$YP$ = personal income

DUMMY VARIABLES

$T$, time trend: January 1960, $T = 1$; December 1973, $T = 168$

$Si$, monthly dummy: January 1960, $S1 = 1$; February 1960, $S2 = 1$; ...
November 1973, $S11 = 11$

$ESP$, controls period dummy: January 1960 to July 1971, $ESP = 0$; August
1971 to December 1972, $ESP = 1$; January 1973, $ESP = 0$

$GPD$, guidepost dummy: January 1962 to March 1962 and July 1967 to
September 1967, $GPD = 0.25$; April 1962 to June 1962 and April 1967
to June 1967, $GPD = 0.50$; July 1962 to September 1962 and January
1967 to March 1967, $GPD = 0.75$; October 1962 to December 1966,
$GPD = 1.0$; otherwise, $GPD = 0$

ESTIMATED RELATIONS

(E1) $$CPIR = a_0 + a_1 CPIR(-1) + a_2 WPIR + a_3 JFRB + a_4 ESP$$
$$+ \sum_{i=1}^{11} s_{ai} Si$$

(E2) $$PRMR = b_0 + b_1 PRMR(-1) + b_2 PRMR(-2) + b_3 U\%FRBR$$
$$+ b_4 ESP + \sum_{i=1}^{11} s_{bi} Si$$

(E3) $$PCM[R = c_0 + c_1 PCM[R(-1) + c_2 PRMR + c_3 PRMR(-1)$$
$$+ c_4 JFRB + \sum_{i=1}^{11} s_{ci} Si$$

(E4) $$PIG[R = d_0 + d_1 PIG[R(-1) + d_2 PCM[R + d_3 ULCMR$$
$$+ d_4 T + d_5 ESP + \Sigma s_{di} Si$$

(E5) $$PPFGR = f_0 + f_1 PPFGR(-1) + f_2 ULCMR + \Sigma s_{fi} Si$$

(E6) $$PCFG[R = g_0 + g_1 PCFG[R(-1) + \sum_{i=0}^{13} w_{gi} ULCMR(-i) + \Sigma s_{gi} Si$$

(E7) $$PFPR = h_0 + h_1 PFPR(-1) + h_2 PFPR(-2) + h_3 JFRBR(-2)$$
$$+ h_4 YPR + \Sigma s_{hi} Si$$

(E8) $$PPFFR = j_0 + j_1 PPFFR(-1) + j_2 PPFFR(-2) + j_3 PFPR$$
$$+ j_4 PFPR(-3) + \Sigma s_{ji} Si$$

(E9) $$WR = k_0 + k_1 JQR + k_2/U(-2) + k_3 CPIR(-2)$$
$$+ k_4 GPD + k_5 ESP + \Sigma s_{ki} Si$$

The identities in the models define all the variables when coupled with
the definition of the exogenous and dummy variables.

IDENTITIES FROM ESTIMATED RELATIONS

(I1) $$CPI = CPIR\{0.4CPI(-1) + 0.3CPI(-2) + 0.2CPI(-3) + 0.1CPI(-4)\}$$

(I2) $$WPIX = 0.028PCM[ + 0.398PIG[ + 0.097PPFG + 0.207PCFG[ + 0.106PFP + 0.165PPFF$$

(I3) $$PCM[ = PCM[R\{0.4PCM[(-1) + 0.3PCM[(-2) + 0.2PCM[(-3) + 0.1XPCM[(-4)\}$$

(I4) $$PIG[ = PIG[R\{0.4PIG[(-1) + 0.3PIG[(-2) + 0.2PIG[(-3) + 0.1PIG[(-4)\}$$

(I5) $$PPFG = PPFGR\{0.4PPFG(-1) + 0.3PPFG(-2) + 0.2PPFG(-3) + 0.1PPFG(-4)\}$$

(I6) $$PCFG[ = PCFG[R\{0.4PCFG[(-1) + 0.3PCFG[(-2) + 0.2PCFG[(-3) + 0.1PCFG[(-4)\}$$

(I7) $$PFP = PFPR\{0.4PFP(-1) + 0.3PFP(-2) + 0.2PFP(-3) + 0.1PFP(-4)\}$$

(I8) $$PPFF = PPFFR\{0.4PPFF(-1) + 0.3PPFF(-2) + 0.2PPFF(-3) + 0.1PPFF(-4)\}$$

(I9) $$W = WR\{0.4W(-1) + 0.3W(-2) + 0.2W(-3) + 0.1W(-4)\}$$

IDENTITIES FOR ESTIMATED RELATIONS

(I10) $$WPIR = WPI/\{0.4WPI(-1) + 0.3WPI(-2) + 0.2WPI(-3) + 0.1WPI(-4)\}$$

(I11) $$ULCMR = JULCM/\{0.4JULCM(-1) + 0.3JULCM(-2) + 0.2JULCM(-3) + 0.1JULCM(-4)\}$$

(I12) $$JFRBR = JFRB/\{0.4JFRB(-1) + 0.3JFRB(-2) + 0.2JFRB(-3) + 0.1JFRB(-4)\}$$

(I13) $$JQR = JQ/\{0.4JQ(-1) + 0.3JQ(-2) + 0.2JQ(-3) + 0.1JQ(-4)\}$$

(I14)    $JULCM = W/JQ$

(I15)         $JQ = JFRB/JMHM$

(I16)    $U\%FRB = OUM/JFRBM$

(I17)        $YPR = YP/\{0.4\,YP(-1) + 0.3\,YP(-2) + 0.2\,YP(-3)$
$+ 0.1\,YP(-4)\}$

(I18)  $U\%FRBR = U\%FRB/\{0.4\,U\%FRB(-1) + 0.3\,U\%FRB(-2)$
$+ 0.2\,U\%FRB(-3) + 0.1\,U\%FRB(-4)\}$

SUMMARY

Equation (E1) is a function of the following[28] (the notation corresponds with that in Table 8-6):

$a_1$, the consumer price index lagged one quarter

$a_2$, the wholesale price index

$a_3$, the quarterly rate of change in the Federal Reserve Board index of industrial production

$a_4$, a dummy for the controls period, *ESP*

Following the model by stage of process, equation (E2), estimates the change in the price of raw materials, *PRMR*, as a function of the following:

$b_1$ and $b_2$, *PRMR* lagged one and two months

$b_3$, the ratio of unfilled orders in manufacturing to the FRB index of production, $U\%FRBR$

$b_4$, a dummy for the controls period (which was significant)

Equation (E3) determines the change in the price of crude materials, *PCM[*, on the following basis:

$c_1$, crude-materials price changes last month

$c_2$ and $c_3$, current and past month's changes in raw-materials prices

$c_4$, the level of the FRB index of production in manufacturing, *JFRB*

In equation (E4), changes in both consumer and producer finished goods were expected to depend upon intermediate-goods prices, crude-materials

---

28. All equations contain seasonals (this will not be repeated for each equation). All equations were tested for significant intercept changes for both the guidepost period and the controls period. Only significant changes are shown.

prices, or both, but the only variable that proved significant, in addition to their own lagged values, was the change in unit labor costs. The price change of intermediate goods, $PIG[$, is a function of:

$d_1$, $PIG[$ lagged one month
$d_2$, change in crude-materials prices
$d_3$, change in unit labor costs
$d_4$, a time-trend dummy
$d_5$, a controls-period dummy

Equation (E5) estimates the change in producer finished goods, $PPFG$, on the basis of:

$f_1$, $PPFG$ lagged one month
$f_2$, the change in unit labor costs

Equation (E6) estimates the change in consumer finished goods, $PCFG[$, from:

$g_1$, $PCFG[$ lagged one month

$g_2$, the change in unit labor costs, $\sum_{i=0}^{13} w_{g_i} ULCMR(-i)$

Equation (E7) estimates the change in farm prices, $PFP$, on the basis of:

$h_1$ and $h_2$, $PFP$ lagged one month and two months
$h_3$, the change in industrial production lagged two months
$h_4$, the current change in personal income

In equation (E8), the change of processed foods and feeds prices, $PPFFR$, is a function of:

$j_1$ and $j_2$, $PPFFR$ lagged one month and two months
$j_3$ and $j_4$, the current and three-month–lagged changes in farm prices

Equation (E9) estimates wage change on the following basis:

$k_1$, change in output per man-hour, $JQR$
$k_2$, the inverse of the aggregate civilian unemployment rate lagged two months
$k_3$, a two-month lag in the change in the consumer price index
$k_4$ and $k_5$, dummy variables for both the guideposts and the controls periods

Table 8-6. *Regression Coefficients for Monthly Price Equations, Model A, 1960–72*[a]

| Equation | Variable[b] and coefficient | | | | | | $\bar{R}^2$ | Durbin-Watson statistic | Standard error |
|---|---|---|---|---|---|---|---|---|---|
| (E1) | $a_0$ | $a_1$ | $a_2$ | $a_3$ | $a_4$ | | 0.81 | 1.93 | 0.0014 |
| | 0.266 | 0.576 | 0.156 | 0.005 | −0.002 | | | | |
| | (4.32) | (10.00) | (5.33) | (3.74) | (−3.61) | | | | |
| (E2) | $b_0$ | $b_1$ | $b_2$ | $b_3$ | $b_4$ | | 0.66 | 1.97 | 0.0147 |
| | 0.243 | 0.932 | −0.260 | 0.086 | 0.009 | | | | |
| | (2.98) | (12.22) | (−3.44) | (1.30) | (2.28) | | | | |
| (E3) | $c_0$ | $c_1$ | $c_2$ | $c_3$ | $c_4$ | | 0.72 | 1.88 | 0.0066 |
| | 0.319 | 0.497 | 0.296 | −0.119 | 0.011 | | | | |
| | (6.35) | (7.02) | (8.76) | (−2.91) | (2.99) | | | | |
| (E4) | $d_0$ | $d_1$ | $d_2$ | $d_3$ | $d_4$ | $d_5$ | 0.79 | 1.51 | 0.0018 |
| | 0.211 | 0.722 | 0.038 | 0.028 | 0.00002 | −0.00135 | | | |
| | (3.62) | (14.04) | (2.85) | (1.29) | (2.77) | (−2.31) | | | |

| | 0 | 1 | 2 | 3 | 4 | 5 | | | |
|---|---|---|---|---|---|---|---|---|---|
| (E5) | $f_0$ 0.177 (3.82) | $f_1$ 0.786 (15.80) | $f_2$ 0.038 (1.60) | | | | 0.70 | 2.01 | 0.0020 |
| (E6) | $g_0$ 0.270 (3.82) | $g_1$ 0.520 (15.80) | $g_2$ 0.211 (4.10) | | | | 0.56 | ... | 0.0020 |
| (E7) | $h_0$ −0.083 (−0.33) | $h_1$ 0.611 (7.88) | $h_2$ −0.205 (−2.63) | $h_3$ 0.198 (2.22) | $h_4$ 0.478 (1.91) | | 0.39 | 2.06 | 0.0165 |
| (E8) | $j_0$ 0.344 (6.65) | $j_1$ 0.400 (6.23) | $j_2$ −0.143 (−2.15) | $j_3$ 0.343 (13.64) | $j_4$ 0.057 (2.05) | | 0.76 | 1.94 | 0.0056 |
| (E9) | $k_0$ 0.233 (1.98) | $k_1$ 0.287 (7.95) | $k_2$ 0.017 (2.41) | $k_3$ 0.487 (4.33) | $k_4$ −0.002 (−2.63) | $k_5$ 0.002 (2.58) | 0.78 | 1.61 | 0.0031 |

Source: Monthly forecasting Model A, described in the text.
a. Seasonals were included where significant but are not reported here. Numbers in parentheses are $t$-statistics.
b. $a_0, b_0, \ldots, k_0$ are constant terms. The definition of the other variables is given in the text of section C.

*Model B*

Identity (I7NF) replaces (I7) of model A:

(I7NF)   $PFPR = PFP/\{0.4PFP(-1) + 0.3PFP(-2) + 0.2PFP(-3)$
$+ 0.1PFP(-4)\}$

The estimated equation for farm prices, (E7), also is deleted from model A to form model B. Consequently, *PFP* becomes an exogenous variable and *YP* is deleted. Otherwise, model B is equivalent to model A.

*Statistical Results*

All equations were estimated over the period 1960:1–1972:12. The results are given in Table 8-6. As expected, the raw crude materials and farm price equations, (E2) and (E7), present the greatest difficulties with their high standard errors. The Durbin-Watson statistic, although presented, is not indicative of significance because of lagged dependent variables. Table 8-7 indicates the tracking ability of the monthly rate of change in the CPI, WPI, and W (the average hourly earnings in industry) over the sample period 1961–72 and the Phases I and II subperiods.

# D. A Simple Two-Equation Historical Model

Equations (E1) and (E9)[29] were estimated over the sample period 1960–1971:7. The results (excluding seasonals) are:

$$CPIR = 0.244 + 0.585CPIR(-1) + 0.169WPIR + 0.0043JFRB$$
$$\quad (3.78) \quad (9.76) \qquad\qquad (5.02) \qquad\qquad (3.40)$$

$\bar{R}^2 = 0.82$; Durbin-Watson statistic $= 1.95$; standard error $= 0.0014$.

$$WR = 0.248 + 0.206JQR + 0.0111/U(-2) + 0.554CPIR(-2)$$
$$\quad (2.25) \quad (7.69) \qquad (1.71) \qquad\qquad (4.99)$$

$$- 0.0019GPD$$
$$(-3.06)$$

$\bar{R}^2 = 0.77$; Durbin-Watson statistic $= 1.71$; standard error $= 0.0029$.
The numbers in parentheses are *t*-statistics.

---

29. Equations (E1) and (E9) are presented in section C, where detailed definitions of all the variables are given.

Table 8-7. *Actual and Predicted Average Monthly Rates of Change in the Consumer and Wholesale Price Indexes and in Average Hourly Earnings, 1961–72 and Phases I and II*[a]

Percent

| | Rate of change | | |
|---|---|---|---|
| *Item* | *Actual* | *Predicted by Model A* | *Predicted by Model B* |
| *1961–72*[b] | | | |
| Consumer price index | 0.248 | 0.256 | 0.252 |
| | (0.0400) | (0.0157) | (0.0186) |
| Wholesale price index | 0.179 | 0.184 | 0.175 |
| | (0.1346) | (0.0288) | (0.1055) |
| Average hourly earnings in manufacturing | 0.371 | 0.370 | 0.368 |
| | (0.3256) | (0.2050) | (0.2047) |
| *August 1971–December 1972* | | | |
| Consumer price index[c] | 0.260 | 0.225 | 0.252 |
| | (0.0133) | (0.0110) | (0.1020) |
| Wholesale price index[c] | 0.413 | 0.252 | 0.404 |
| | (0.2498) | (0.0528) | (0.1732) |

Sources: Models A and B, described in the text.

a. The numbers in parentheses are the mean squared errors.

b. Although the sample period began with 1960, insufficient computer space precluded solving the models from 1960.

c. Not seasonally adjusted data.

The model then was simulated from 1971:7 forward with the actual changes in the WPI, output per man-hour, the unemployment rate, and the FRB index of industrial production exogenous. The results, discussed at the end of Chapter 8, conform fairly well to the results from the monthly forecasting model described in section C.

# IX

# Price Behavior in Sixteen Selected Manufacturing Industries

Analysis of price behavior in specific industries during Phase II is presented in two parts: sixteen manufacturing industries amenable to econometric modeling are examined in this chapter, and the remaining sectors of the economy are studied in the following chapter.

To analyze price movements on an industry-by-industry basis, indexes of both input and output prices were constructed. The approach was similar to that of Eckstein and Wyss.[1] For output prices, first the correspondence between the elements of the wholesale price index and the standard industrial classification was established at the four-digit SIC level. These four-digit SIC codes then were aggregated to the input-output classifications of the 1958 input-output table.[2] With constructed price series for each input-output code, the two-digit index was constructed by a weighting, based upon 1958 value of shipments, of the input-output codes. Input prices were based primarily on the input-output coefficients as weights and the output price indexes. These price series were constructed on a nonseasonally adjusted monthly basis and then converted to a quarterly basis by simple averaging.

## Price and Profit-Margin Movements

The inflation problem is illustrated on an industry-by-industry basis without exception in the first two columns of Table 9-1. During the five-year period 1961–65, the average annual percentage change for the sixteen manufacturing industries ranged from −1.6 percent to +1.5 percent, with the average being near 0. The period 1968–70 was characterized by a uniform upward movement in prices in all of these

1. See Otto Eckstein and David Wyss, "Industry Price Equations," in Eckstein (ed.), *The Econometrics of Price Determination: Conference* (Board of Governors of the Federal Reserve System, 1972).
2. *Survey of Current Business*, vol. 44 (November 1964).

Table 9-1. *Change in Wholesale Price Indexes, Selected Manufacturing Industries, Various Periods, 1961–72*[a]

Percent

| | Average annual change | | | Actual change | | |
|---|---|---|---|---|---|---|
| Industry[b] | 1961–65[c] | 1968–70[c] | December ber 1970– August 1971 | Phase I[d] | Phase II[e] | Phases I and II |
| Food processing | 1.0 | 4.0 | 7.7 | −0.5 | 10.8 | 10.3 |
| Tobacco | 0.8 | 4.3 | −6.4 | 0.0 | 0.5 | 0.5 |
| Textiles | −0.4 | 1.3 | 3.5 | 0.1 | 11.6 | 11.7 |
| Apparel | 0.4 | 2.8 | −2.9 | 0.2 | 2.4 | 2.6 |
| Lumber | 0.2 | 4.9 | 18.8 | −2.8 | 15.5 | 12.3 |
| Furniture | 0.7 | 4.0 | −4.4 | −0.1 | 3.1 | 3.0 |
| Paper | −0.7 | 2.2 | −11.2 | 0.0 | 3.8 | 3.9 |
| Chemicals | −0.7 | 0.1 | 0.9 | −0.3 | 0.3 | 0.0 |
| Rubber | −0.8 | 3.5 | −5.6 | −0.3 | 0.5 | 0.2 |
| Stone, clay, and glass | −0.1 | 4.2 | 11.2 | −0.2 | 3.8 | 3.7 |
| Ferrous metals | 0.0 | 4.5 | 0.8 | 0.1 | 1.7 | 1.7 |
| Nonferrous metals | 1.5 | 7.7 | −7.0 | −0.7 | 1.2 | 0.5 |
| Fabricated metals and instruments | 0.7 | 3.6 | −7.6 | 0.2 | 2.7 | 2.9 |
| Nonelectrical machinery | 0.8 | 4.0 | −5.2 | −0.1 | 2.6 | 2.5 |
| Electrical machinery | −1.6 | 2.7 | 4.8 | −0.4 | −0.6 | −0.9 |
| Motor vehicles | −0.1 | 2.8 | −4.5 | 0.3 | 2.7 | 3.0 |

Sources: The wholesale price index for each industry is based on fixed weights derived from the 1958 input-output table published in *Survey of Current Business*, vol. 44 (November 1964); and detailed data tapes of wholesale price indexes provided by the U.S. Bureau of Labor Statistics.

a. The price series were constructed from monthly nonseasonally adjusted data, after which they were converted to a quarterly basis by simple averaging.

b. The industries correspond to those in the standard industrial classification. See the discussion in the text.

c. Computed from yearly averages.

d. August 1971–November 1971.

e. November 1971–December 1972.

industries. The average annual change ranged from 0.1 percent in the chemical industry, which had been characterized by falling prices, to 7.7 percent in nonferrous metals, an industry with relatively volatile prices.

In the months preceding the freeze in August 1971, there were many indications the rate of inflation was falling, but the picture was not clear. Lumber prices were rising rapidly in the face of a boom in housing construction. Wholesale prices for processed foods were rising at an annual rate of nearly 8 percent. With the economy barely out of the trough of the recession, several industries were characterized by falling prices: prices of paper were falling at an annual rate of 11 percent;

fabricated metals and instrument prices were down by more than 7 percent; and those of nonferrous metals were off by 7 percent. In general, prices were either rising or falling at a rather significant rate for these industries; few prices were stable.

Although the freeze lasted only three months, price behavior during it differed markedly from that of the previous eight months of 1971. No industry evidenced price changes of any substantial amount; the greatest increase during the three-month freeze was 0.3 percent for motor vehicles.

During the more than thirteen months of Phase II, from November 1971 to December 1972, prices in three of the sixteen industries rose rapidly: food processing by nearly 11 percent, textile mill products by nearly 12 percent, and lumber prices by more than 15 percent. Two industries—paper and stone, clay, and glass—had moderately high price increases of 3.8 percent, furniture increased by 3.1 percent, and nine other industries experienced price increases of less than 3 percent over Phase II. In contrast, prices of electrical machinery fell as they did during the stable years of 1961–65.

The influence of Price Commission regulations on these data is far from clear. In fact, Table 9-2 suggests little impact from Price Commission price authorizations to firms in these industries. The wholesale price index for lumber increased nearly five times the weighted-average price increase granted by the commission. On the other hand, from November 1971 to December 1972, the WPI for electrical machinery actually fell by 0.6 percent, although the commission granted average price increases in excess of 2 percent (Table 9-2).

The difference between authorizations and actual price changes may be caused by lack of directly comparable data. The most serious difference in the two averages is the result of the weights used in their calculation. The constructed WPI for each industry is based upon fixed weights derived from the 1958 input-output table, whereas the average price increase granted by the commission is weighted by the applicable sales for each increase granted other than to firms with TLP agreements. Thus, to the extent that applicable sales for price-increase requests differ from the weights in the constructed index, the two averages could differ without being indicative of violations or of regulations that were far too loose. In general, on the basis of the weighting differences, the Price Commission average would be expected to be greater than the wholesale index.

Table 9-2. *Changes in Constructed Wholesale Price Indexes Compared with Weighted-Average Increases Granted by the Price Commission, Selected Manufacturing Industries, November 1971–December 1972*
Percent

| Industry | Change in constructed price index | Weighted-average increase granted by Price Commission[a] | | |
|---|---|---|---|---|
| | | Total | Firms without term limit pricing agreements | Firms with term limit pricing agreements |
| Food processing | 10.8 | 2.3 | 2.6 | 1.9 |
| Tobacco | 0.5 | 2.3 | 2.6 | 2.0 |
| Textiles | 11.6 | 2.9 | 3.0 | 2.0 |
| Apparel | 2.4 | 4.0 | 4.1 | 3.4 |
| Lumber | 15.5 | 3.3 | 5.2 | 2.0 |
| Furniture | 3.1 | 2.9 | 3.6 | 2.0 |
| Paper | 3.8 | 3.3 | 3.8 | 2.0 |
| Chemicals | 0.3 | 2.2 | 3.6 | 1.9 |
| Rubber | 0.5 | 2.3 | 2.9 | 2.0 |
| Stone, clay, and glass | 3.8 | 3.7 | 5.0 | 2.0 |
| Ferrous metals | 1.7 | 4.2 | 4.7 | 2.0 |
| Nonferrous metals | 1.2 | 2.9 | 5.2 | 1.8 |
| Fabricated metals and instruments | 2.7 | 3.3 | 4.0 | 1.9 |
| Nonelectrical machinery | 2.6 | 3.1 | 4.2 | 1.7 |
| Electrical machinery | −0.6 | 2.2 | 3.1 | 1.9 |
| Motor vehicles | 2.7 | 3.5 | 3.6 | 1.9 |

Sources: Column 1, Table 9-1; other columns, calculated from Price Commission data.
a. Weighted on the basis of applicable sales, from Price Commission data.

Another reason the Price Commission authorizations figure would be expected to be biased upward is that price increases granted were not always fully implemented by the firms. On the other hand, the definition of base price would tend to lower the commission average. Because the base price was defined as the highest price charged to 10 percent of a given class of customers, prices less than the defined base price could be increased without approval from the commission. If a firm received permission to increase prices under the volatility rule—passing volatile raw-materials cost increases along on a dollar-for-dollar basis and lowering prices when such costs declined—these price increases would not be reported to the commission. Volatility was interpreted quite literally, however, and such treatments were limited primarily to raw agricultural products in the food-processing industry.

Table 9-3. *Implied Increase in Revenue to Tier I Firms from Price Commission Grants Compared with Revenue Implied by Changes in Industry Wholesale Price Indexes, November 1971–December 1972*
Amounts in billions of dollars

| Industry | Increase in revenue to tier I firms from commission-approved price increases (1) | Tier I sales as a percent of total corporate sales (2) | If all price increases were equal to grants to tier I firms (3) | Implied by WPI (4) | Ratio of revenue implied by WPI to increases granted[a] (5) |
|---|---|---|---|---|---|
| | | | *Industry revenue* | | |
| Food processing | 0.793 | 32 | 2.478 | 11.443 | 4.6 |
| Tobacco | 0.116 | 48 | 0.242 | 0.057 | 0.2 |
| Textiles | 0.328 | 49 | 0.669 | 2.661 | 4.0 |
| Apparel | 0.094 | 10 | 0.940 | 0.564 | 0.6 |
| Lumber | 0.113 | 25 | 0.452 | 2.117 | 4.7 |
| Furniture | 0.063 | 30 | 0.210 | 0.225 | 1.1 |
| Paper | 0.422 | 58 | 0.728 | 0.844 | 1.2 |
| Chemicals | 0.729 | 54 | 1.350 | 0.186 | 0.1 |
| Rubber | 0.118 | 28 | 0.421 | 0.102 | 0.2 |
| Stone, clay, and glass | 0.245 | 35 | 0.700 | 0.735 | 1.1 |
| Ferrous metals | 0.614 | 50 | 1.228 | 0.483 | 0.4 |
| Nonferrous metals | 0.026 | 5 | 0.520 | 0.225 | 0.4 |
| Fabricated metals and instruments | 0.539 | 29 | 1.859 | 1.492 | 0.8 |
| Nonelectrical machinery | 0.599 | 33 | 1.815 | 1.550 | 0.9 |
| Electrical machinery | 0.248 | 16 | 1.550 | −0.413 | −0.3 |
| Motor vehicles | 1.635 | 70 | 2.336 | 1.796 | 0.8 |
| Total | 6.682 | 37 | 17.498 | 24.067 | 1.38 |
| Total, excluding food and lumber | 5.776 | 39 | 14.568 | 10.507 | 0.72 |

Source: Price Commission data.
a. Ratio of column (4) to column (3).

It was assumed in constructing Table 9-2 that all prices of firms granted TLP agreements were increased by the amount of the TLP. One of the major attributes of the TLP, the flexibility to raise individual prices in excess of their cost justification,[3] would contribute to a discrepancy among the figures on an industry-by-industry basis. Price increases were granted directly only to tier I firms. Thus, to the extent that tiers II and III raised prices differently from tier I, the two series could differ. (This possibility belies theories both of competition, which suggest equal prices, and of administered prices, which assert prices are set by the larger firms in each industry.) Finally, firms could raise their list prices, which in many cases are the prices reported to the Bureau of Labor Statistics, without requesting a price increase as long as they did not raise the actual transaction prices.

Even with all these qualifications taken into consideration, it would seem that an effective price-control program would have produced a closer concordance with the WPIs constructed for these manufacturing industries, because these indexes avoid many of the problem areas such as exempt items and raw agricultural products. Further adjustments are shown in Table 9-3 to generate comparability and indicate areas of differences. Column (1) gives the implied increase in revenue from applicable sales as shown on the standard PC-1 increase-request forms and by TLP agreements. Column (2) is the estimated percentage that these applicable sales are of total industry sales (applicable sales divided by 1971 corporate sales). The relative implied revenues are shown in column (5).

For the sixteen industries, the rate of increase in the index of wholesale prices was 38 percent more than the sales-weighted increase granted by the commission. If food is deleted (on the ground that some food products were under the volatility rule), as well as lumber (because multiple wholesaling reportedly occurred to circumvent the regulations, and transaction prices thus may have been incorporated in the WPI even though not granted to lumber manufacturers), the ratio of the WPI increases to the total granted price increases for the remaining fourteen manufacturing industries drops to 0.72 (see the last two rows of Table 9-3, column (5)).[4]

---

3. At first, no limits were placed on individual price increases. In one case, the TLP plan submitted to the Price Commission called for a price increase of 300 percent on a minor item that had been mispriced in 1971 (that is, priced far below what the actual costs of production turned out to be). Later, the commission placed a maximum of 8 percent on individual price increases.

4. Wholesale prices for textile mill products increased rapidly during Phase II because of increases in cotton and wool prices. Many of the tier I textile firms are vertically integrated, so their price increase requests may have occurred only during Phase II. Thus, textile increases were not excluded.

The data in Table 9-3 suggest that apparent violations occurred in some industries, and that the allowed price adjustments were too generous in others. With the ratio between 0.7 and 1.3 as an arbitrary range for "effective control," six industries fall into the "controlled" category; in three industries, actual price increases were in substantial excess of Price Commission authorizations; and for seven industries, the price-increase authorizations substantially exceeded actual price movements. The sixteen industries as thus categorized are as follows:

| Controlled industries | Noncompliant industries | Industries receiving overgenerous authorizations |
|---|---|---|
| Furniture | Food processing | Tobacco |
| Paper | Textiles | Apparel |
| Stone, clay, and glass | Lumber | Chemicals |
| Fabricated metals | | Rubber |
| Nonelectrical machinery | | Ferrous metals |
| Motor vehicles | | Nonferrous metals |
| | | Electrical machinery |

The second line of defense, the profit-margin limitation, generally exercised much less constraint than the cost-justification rule for price increases. For these sixteen industries, only five (tobacco; chemicals; stone, clay, and glass; ferrous metals; and motor vehicles) had base-period profit margins below the average of 1960–72 (see Table 9-4). On the basis of these industry data, only four industries (food processing, apparel, lumber, and furniture) were restrained by the profit-margin limitation (see Table 9-5).

Industry data are not equivalent to data for a firm; firms are classified in the Securities and Exchange Commission–Federal Trade Commission data reports on the basis of sales and profits of the firms' major activities. These data are indicative, however, of the relative insignificance of the profit-margin limitation across firms in these industries—an observation confirmed by the total of only $3.5 million in rollbacks and refunds ordered by the Price Commission for profit-margin violations, compared with the $4.6 billion in price increases granted by the commission to tier I firms in the manufacturing and service sectors. Furthermore, the largest proportion of the rollbacks occurred in the retail and wholesale sectors.

Table 9-4. *Phase II Base-Period and 1960–72 Pretax Profit Margins, Selected Manufacturing Industries*

Percent

| Industry | Base-period profit margin[a] | Long-run average profit margin[b] | Range of profit margin, 1960–72[c] |
|---|---|---|---|
| Food processing | 4.9 | 4.8 | 4.6– 5.0 |
| Tobacco | 11.3 | 11.4 | 10.6–12.1 |
| Textiles | 5.9 | 5.3 | 4.1– 7.0 |
| Apparel | 4.3 | 3.7 | 3.0– 4.5 |
| Lumber | 8.1 | 5.6 | 3.3– 8.4 |
| Furniture | 6.5 | 5.6 | 3.8– 6.8 |
| Paper | 8.2 | 8.0 | 4.3– 9.7 |
| Chemicals | 12.3 | 12.9 | 10.7–14.1 |
| Rubber | 7.6 | 7.0 | 5.1– 8.3 |
| Stone, clay, and glass | 8.8 | 9.2 | 6.4–14.4 |
| Ferrous metals | 7.2 | 7.7 | 3.6– 9.8 |
| Nonferrous metals | 10.0 | 9.2 | 4.5–13.7 |
| Fabricated metals and instruments | 9.8 | 9.4 | 6.8–11.2 |
| Nonelectrical machinery | 10.7 | 9.9 | 7.9–11.7 |
| Electrical machinery | 7.9 | 7.6 | 6.1– 9.8 |
| Motor vehicles | 9.8 | 10.5 | 3.5–13.7 |

Source: Data Resources, Inc., data bank.

a. Average of highest two years, 1968, 1969, or 1970.

b. 1960–72.

c. Lowest and highest annual profit margin.

The exceptions to the general ineffectiveness of the profit-margin constraint occurred in those industries in which profit margins show little cyclical variation (notably food processing), and on a firm-by-firm basis, wherein a firm may have experienced low profits in the base years, for a variety of reasons, but was unable to obtain an exception from the Price Commission. A firm that was constrained from raising prices because of an abnormal base period or other reasons could thereby make it difficult for other firms to do so—depending, of course, upon the degree of competition.

Whether the rates of change in prices, wages, and profit margins differed from past structural relations can be better answered by means of econometric equations that explain price and profit-margin variation over time.

Table 9-5. *Profit Margins for Phase II Base Period and Controls Period, Selected Manufacturing Industries*

Percent

| Industry | Base-period profit margin[a] | Four-quarter moving average of pretax profit margins during controls | | | | |
|---|---|---|---|---|---|---|
| | | 1971:4 | 1972:1 | 1972:2 | 1972:3 | 1972:4 |
| Food processing | 4.9 | 4.9[b] | 4.8 | 4.7 | 4.6 | 4.6 |
| Tobacco | 11.3 | 10.8 | 11.0 | 10.9 | 11.0 | 11.2 |
| Textiles | 5.9 | 4.6 | 4.8 | 4.8 | 4.8 | 4.7 |
| Apparel | 4.3 | 4.3[b] | 4.6[b] | 4.5[b] | 4.4[b] | 4.3[b] |
| Lumber | 8.1 | 6.8 | 7.2 | 7.8 | 8.1[b] | 8.0 |
| Furniture | 6.5 | 5.9 | 6.3 | 6.7[b] | 6.8[b] | 7.0[b] |
| Paper | 8.2 | 4.3 | 4.5 | 5.2 | 5.7 | 6.8 |
| Chemicals | 12.3 | 10.8 | 11.0 | 10.9 | 11.0 | 11.2 |
| Rubber | 7.6 | 6.6 | 7.0 | 7.2 | 7.3 | 7.4 |
| Stone, clay, and glass | 8.8 | 7.7 | 8.0 | 8.0 | 8.1 | 8.0 |
| Ferrous metals | 7.2 | 4.1 | 3.9 | 3.5 | 4.3 | 5.0 |
| Nonferrous metals | 10.0 | 4.7 | 4.5 | 4.4 | 5.2 | 5.6 |
| Fabricated metals and instruments | 9.8 | 8.0 | 8.3 | 8.5 | 8.7 | 9.0 |
| Nonelectrical machinery | 10.7 | 8.3 | 8.5 | 8.8 | 9.2 | 9.2 |
| Electrical machinery | 7.9 | 6.4 | 6.6 | 6.7 | 6.8 | 7.2 |
| Motor vehicles | 9.8 | 8.7 | 8.9 | 9.4 | 9.1 | 9.1 |

Source: Data Resources, Inc., data bank.
a. Average of highest two years, 1968, 1969, or 1970.
b. Four-quarter average is over or same as the base-period average.

## Price and Profit-Margin Equations

Price and profit-margin equations were estimated for the sixteen industries, first over the period 1959:3–1971:2 and then over the period 1959:3–1972:4, with a dummy variable included in each equation for the freeze and Phase II period of controls. These results are summarized here; some details are presented in the technical appendix to this chapter.

### Definitions

Price adjustment, particularly in the short run, is conceptually a function of many variables. In dealing with rather broad market aggregates, the most notable of the variables is change in unit cost: that is, factor price increases less factor productivity gains. Other influential market characteristics at a given point in time include: (a) the degree of excess demand and its perceived permanence; (b) the elasticity of demand as seen by the individual firms; (c) the current productive capacity and the marginal costs associated with greater or lesser output; (d) the costs of price changes (for example, the cost of changing a price list, advertising plans, and the like); (e) the reliability and speed of information flows; (f) the motivations of buyers and sellers (for example, whether they are profit-maximizing, sales-maximizing, or nonprofit institutions; and whether they are buying for final consumption or as inputs into other productive processes); (g) the ease of entry and exit; and (h) other "institutional" factors such as support prices, international markets and foreign policy, national defense subsidies, and regulation by various governmental bodies.

These factors depend, in turn, upon other facets of the exchange process. The degree of excess demand depends upon changing preferences, income, other price changes, the state of technology, and any combination of these. The elasticity of demand as seen by the firm depends upon a complex interaction of market demand and market structure (from pure competition to monopoly) coupled with any institutional ethic that has developed about various forms of price discrimination (from multiple prices to perfect price discrimination) or other marketing practices. Technology and past investment in an industry will partially determine current capacity and marginal costs of altered production. Given these and a number of other factors, substantial differences would be expected among regressions for two-digit SIC manufacturing industries.

Profit margins are, by definition, a function of output price, level of output, and unit or average costs of production. Essentially, they are a residual of what happens to other variables. As such, equations that explain changes in profit margins do not suffer from the same theoretical morass as optimal price adjustment, but they do suffer from inadequate profit data. Therefore, the values of the parameters reveal something about the industry. Furthermore, in cases of sufficiently small standard error, such equations should also be useful in assessing the potential impact of any system of price controls that relies in part upon a profit-margin limitation.

Table 9-6. Coefficients for Price Equations, Selected Manufacturing Industries, 1959:3–1971:2[a]

| Industry | Constant | Output[b] | Demand[e] | Wages[d] | Materials[e] | Interest rate[e] | Bond rate | $\rho_1$ | $\rho_2$ | $R^2$ | Durbin-Watson statistic | Standard error |
|---|---|---|---|---|---|---|---|---|---|---|---|---|
| Food processing | 0.0165 (2.32) | ... | −0.0979 (−1.68) | ... | 0.4800 (8.63) | ... | ... | 0.80 | ... | 0.91 | 1.82 | 0.0097 |
| Tobacco | 0.0036 (0.35) | ... | ... | 0.2900 (2.01) | ... | −0.0373 (−1.58) | 0.1070 (2.78) | 0.95 | −0.20 | 0.79 | 1.94 | 0.0099 |
| Textiles | −0.0419 (−2.86) | 0.0862 (1.97) | ... | 1.007 (3.26) | 0.2078 (1.89) | ... | ... | 1.50 | −0.80 | 0.89 | 1.89 | 0.0099 |
| Apparel | 0.0112 (2.00) | ... | ... | ... | 0.0659 (2.03) | ... | ... | 1.40 | −0.50 | 0.94 | 2.07 | 0.0029 |
| Lumber | −0.0574 (−1.54) | 0.5360 (3.04) | ... | 1.499 (2.05) | ... | ... | ... | 1.20 | −0.50 | 0.70 | 2.23 | 0.0396 |
| Furniture | −0.0077 (−2.54) | ... | ... | 0.7428 (10.27) | 0.0233 (1.88) | ... | ... | 1.10 | −0.50 | 0.95 | 2.31 | 0.0037 |
| Paper | −0.0087 (−0.55) | ... | ... | 0.3344 (1.52) | 0.0590 (2.10) | ... | ... | 1.10 | −0.45 | 0.78 | 2.03 | 0.0079 |
| Chemicals | −0.0060 (−0.71) | ... | 0.0508 (3.69) | 0.1821 (1.25) | ... | ... | ... | 0.90 | ... | 0.86 | 2.01 | 0.0036 |
| Rubber | −0.0077 (−0.55) | ... | ... | 0.7148 (2.07) | 1.363 (4.11) | ... | ... | 0.90 | −0.20 | 0.79 | 1.83 | 0.0154 |
| Stone, clay, and glass | −0.0205 (−5.31) | ... | ... | 1.1129 (9.86) | ... | ... | ... | 1.17 | −0.48 | 0.95 | 2.08 | 0.0044 |
| Ferrous metals | ... | ... | ... | ... | 0.2306 (2.70) | ... | ... | 1.20 | −0.20 | 0.96 | 1.77 | 0.0046 |
| Nonferrous metals | 0.0017 (0.08) | ... | −0.0830 (−1.59) | 0.9153 (1.86) | ... | ... | ... | 1.40 | −0.70 | 0.86 | 1.97 | 0.0225 |
| Fabricated metals and instruments | −0.0023 (−1.05) | ... | 0.0215 (1.74) | 0.3873 (5.44) | 0.4533 (8.17) | ... | ... | 0.80 | −0.40 | 0.97 | 1.72 | 0.0028 |
| Nonelectrical machinery | 0.0055 (0.75) | ... | ... | 0.2525 (1.62) | 0.4389 (4.26) | ... | ... | 0.90 | ... | 0.97 | 1.79 | 0.0027 |
| Electrical machinery | 0.0023 (0.41) | −0.1329 (−2.97) | ... | ... | ... | ... | ... | 1.40 | −0.60 | 0.90 | 2.09 | 0.0076 |
| Motor vehicles | −0.0054 (−1.29) | ... | ... | ... | 0.9347 (5.59) | ... | ... | 0.85 | −0.25 | 0.83 | 1.95 | 0.0083 |

Sources: Alternate equations (1) through (31) in the appendix to Chapter 9, where the variables are defined.

a. Numbers in parentheses are t-statistics.
b. Capacity utilization for electrical machinery; production for other industries.
c. Ratio of inventories to shipments for chemicals; ratio of inventories to sales for other industries.
d. Variations of average hourly earnings, $AHE/F$, which are defined in the respective equations in the appendix to Chapter 9.
e. Variations of input prices, which are defined in the respective equations in the appendix to Chapter 9.

*Summary of Industry Price and Profit-Margin Equations*

A summary of the estimated price and profit-margin equations is presented in Tables 9-6 and 9-7.[5] In two industries, textiles and lumber, increased output is associated with increased prices; in one industry, electrical machinery, reduced output is associated with increased prices; but output has no significant effect on price changes in the remaining thirteen industries. Excess demand, however, raises prices in food processing and nonferrous metals, whereas in fabricated metals and chemicals, an increase in the inventory-to-sales ratio is associated significantly with rising prices. Thus, a total of seven industries show prices responsive either to excess demand or to changes in production.

In no case is there a negative relation between wage change and price change. The wage variable has a significantly positive impact on price adjustments in eleven of the sixteen industries. Similarly, input prices have significantly positive coefficients for only ten of the industries. A decline in the four-quarter rate of change in the profits-to-equity ratio in tobacco is associated with price increases. In addition, the four-quarter rate of change in Moody's Aaa corporate bond rate is related positively to price movements for tobacco. Otherwise, such variables exhibit no significant relation to price changes among all the other industries. For all industries except electrical machinery, at least one cost variable is significant, and both wages and input prices are significant in six of the sixteen industries.

Increases in production raise profit margins in every industry except food processing, in which this variable is not significant. And in fourteen of the industries, the estimated elasticity of profit margins with respect to output is greater than 1 (see Table 9-7). At a profit margin of 0.07, however, a 1 percent output increase in, say, textiles, would increase margins by 2.5 percent, to 0.0718.

A significantly positive relation exists between price changes and profit-margin changes in only five industries: tobacco, textiles, lumber, paper, and nonferrous metals. In three industries—food processing, apparel, and chemicals—price increases are associated with falling margins, indicating that price increases do not compensate fully for rising average costs. As was expected, the coefficient on the wage variable is positive (and significant) in apparel and chemicals to make up for the negative

5. The exact equations are presented in the appendix to this chapter.

## Table 9-7. Coefficients for Profit-Margin Equations, Selected Manufacturing Industries, 1959:3–1971:2[a]

| Industry | Constant | Output | Demand | Price[b] | Wages[c] | Input prices[d] | Other costs[e] | $\rho_1$ | $\rho_2$ | $R^2$ | Durbin-Watson statistic | Standard error |
|---|---|---|---|---|---|---|---|---|---|---|---|---|
| Food processing | 0.0087 (0.66) | ... | ... | −0.4297 (−1.62) | ... | ... | ... | 0.60 | ... | 0.45 | 1.71 | 0.0349 |
| Tobacco | −0.0359 (−1.84) | 0.4349 (2.59) | ... | 1.572 (3.13) | ... | ... | ... | 0.60 | ... | 0.42 | 2.00 | 0.0441 |
| Textiles | −0.0558 (−2.32) | 2.524 (7.89) | ... | 2.265 (3.36) | ... | ... | −0.5889 (−2.66) | 0.23 | ... | 0.82 | 1.91 | 0.0962 |
| Apparel | −0.2156 (−3.07) | 3.165 (3.41) | 1.549 (1.51) | −10.33 (−3.01) | 6.040 (4.01) | ... | ... | ... | ... | 0.43 | 1.62 | 0.1922 |
| Lumber | −0.2362 (−1.59) | 5.982 (4.65) | ... | 1.274 (1.49) | f | ... | ... | 0.45 | ... | 0.68 | 1.76 | 0.2988 |
| Furniture | −0.0782 (−2.19) | 3.994 (6.87) | ... | ... | ... | −0.7323 (−1.74) | ... | ... | −0.31 | 0.50 | 1.73 | 0.2197 |
| Paper | 0.0540 (0.78) | 1.674 (4.19) | ... | 1.596 (1.71) | −4.660 (−3.43) | ... | ... | 0.94 | ... | 0.86 | 2.10 | 0.0512 |
| Chemicals | −0.1562 (−4.01) | 1.333 (5.94) | ... | −2.762 (−2.40) | 1.265 (1.46) | ... | ... | 0.60 | ... | 0.76 | 1.92 | 0.0352 |
| Rubber | −0.2502 (−4.96) | 1.715 (6.77) | ... | ... | 2.142 (1.94) | −5.623 (−3.83) | ... | 0.25 | ... | 0.66 | 1.42 | 0.1086 |
| Stone, clay, and glass | −0.1025 (−3.18) | 2.285 (4.74) | ... | ... | ... | ... | ... | 0.30 | ... | 0.44 | 1.99 | 0.1442 |
| Ferrous metals | 0.0740 (0.75) | 1.500 (4.67) | ... | ... | −4.460 (−1.94) | ... | ... | 0.39 | ... | 0.59 | 1.49 | 0.2300 |
| Nonferrous metals | −0.0670 (−1.60) | 1.578 (7.99) | ... | 1.369 (4.10) | −1.809 (−1.50) | ... | ... | 0.30 | ... | 0.73 | 1.95 | 0.1059 |
| Fabricated metals and instruments | −0.0775 (−2.52) | 2.240 (7.68) | ... | ... | ... | ... | ... | 0.65 | ... | 0.79 | 1.78 | 0.0703 |
| Nonelectrical machinery | −0.0573 (−1.97) | 1.007 (3.13) | ... | ... | ... | ... | ... | 0.85 | −0.29 | 0.72 | 2.05 | 0.0745 |
| Electrical machinery | −0.0605 (−1.19) | 1.542 (4.61) | ... | ... | ... | ... | −0.3955 (−1.89) | 0.70 | ... | 0.64 | 2.02 | 0.0849 |
| Motor vehicles | −0.0681 (−1.15) | 1.948 (7.68) | ... | ... | ... | ... | −0.8485 (−1.47) | 0.33 | ... | 0.64 | 2.06 | 0.2217 |

Sources: Alternate equations (2) through (32) in the appendix to Chapter 9, where the variables are defined.

a. Numbers in parentheses are $t$-statistics.

b. Lagged for food, tobacco, and apparel.

c. Variations of average hourly earnings, $AHE[F$, which are defined in the respective equations in the appendix to Chapter 9.

d. Lagged for furniture.

e. Moody's Aaa corporate bond rate for textiles and motor vehicles; depreciation costs for electrical machinery.

f. Two wage variables were used in this equation: the four-quarter rate of increase in average hourly earnings in SIC 24 in the current quarter and one quarter lagged. The coefficients and $t$-statistics are 7.876 (2.29) and −5.348 (−1.54), respectively.

sign on the price variable. In four industries the coefficient on wage increases is positive, but it is negative for three industries; wages are insignificant for the other nine industries.

Input-price changes have a negative impact on profit margins only in the furniture and rubber industries; otherwise, input prices are not significant in their relation to profit margins. In no industry are the three variables—price change, wage change, and input price change—all significant, suggesting that price adjustments occur with average cost changes, as is confirmed by the price equations.

Changes in interest rates have a significantly negative impact on margins in textiles and motor vehicles. Depreciation has a significantly negative coefficient in electrical machinery and is not a significant explanatory variable for the other fifteen industries.

## Structural Shifts in Price and Profit-Margin Equations

The impact of the Economic Stabilization Program can be examined by estimating the structural shift that occurred in price and profit-margin equations for these sixteen manufacturing industries. The technique is a simple one: extending the period of estimation from 1971:2 to 1972:4 for the previously estimated equations and adding to each equation a dummy variable, whose value is 0, for 1959:3–1971:2 and 1 for 1971:3–1972:4.

Using the estimated coefficient for a dummy variable in a price, wage, or profit-margin equation leaves a great deal unanswered about the effect of the program. First, assuming that the program was totally responsible for any structural change that occurred, the impact of the program among the independent and dependent variables was marginal. Second, to determine the actual impact, a model should be constructed that would compare simulated values without controls to simulated values with controls or with actual data. This exercise was far too complicated and required too many questionable assumptions to be undertaken here. Nonetheless, the results from the aggregate studies discussed in Chapter 8 may be used in conjunction with the industry results to generate some idea of where, on an industry-by-industry basis, any aggregate impact occurred.

The results of the reestimation of each equation through 1972:4 are shown in Tables 9-8 and 9-9. In general, little change occurs in the value

Table 9-8. Coefficients of Price Equations, Selected Manufacturing Industries, 1959:3–1972:4[a]

| Industry | Constant | Output | Demand | Wages | Materials | Interest rate | Bond rate | Economic stabilization program dummy | $p_1$ | $p_2$ | $R^2$ | Durbin-Watson statistic | Standard error |
|---|---|---|---|---|---|---|---|---|---|---|---|---|---|
| Food processing | 0.0142 (1.85) | ... | -0.1257 (-2.13) | ... | 0.3923 (7.41) | ... | ... | -0.0059 (-0.57) | 0.80 | ... | 0.89 | 1.72 | 0.0106 |
| Tobacco | 0.0050 (0.51) | ... | ... | 0.2727 (2.08) | ... | 0.0967 (2.71) | -0.0204 (-2.00) | -0.0204 (-2.00) | 0.94 | -0.18 | 0.80 | 2.02 | 0.0099 |
| Textiles | -0.0492 (-3.07) | 0.0764 (1.60) | ... | 1.277 (3.84) | 0.1501 (1.80) | ... | ... | 0.0059 (0.62) | 1.50 | -0.80 | 0.91 | 1.89 | 0.0112 |
| Apparel | 0.0109 (2.68) | ... | ... | ... | 0.0570 (1.86) | ... | ... | 0.0079 (2.85) | 1.40 | -0.50 | 0.93 | 2.05 | 0.0030 |
| Lumber | -0.0537 (-1.48) | 0.5243 (3.20) | ... | 1.466 (2.08) | ... | ... | ... | 0.0758 (2.24) | 1.20 | -0.50 | 0.83 | 2.23 | 0.0084 |
| Furniture | -0.0079 (-2.68) | ... | ... | 0.7406 (10.62) | 0.0189 (1.62) | ... | ... | -0.0036 (-1.17) | 1.10 | -0.50 | 0.94 | 2.25 | 0.0036 |
| Paper | -0.0103 (-1.31) | ... | ... | 0.3674 (2.29) | 0.0531 (2.20) | ... | ... | 0.0091 (1.38) | 1.10 | -0.45 | 0.81 | 2.00 | 0.0075 |
| Chemicals | -0.0083 (-1.08) | ... | 0.0505 (3.70) | 0.2105 (1.62) | ... | ... | ... | 0.0011 (0.31) | 0.90 | ... | 0.85 | 1.97 | 0.0036 |
| Rubber | -0.0103 (-0.75) | ... | ... | 0.7428 (2.18) | 1.204 (3.80) | ... | ... | -0.0148 (-1.04) | 0.90 | -0.20 | 0.77 | 1.87 | 0.0153 |
| Stone, clay, and glass | -0.0257 (-4.49) | ... | ... | 1.070 (8.33) | ... | ... | ... | 0.0065 (1.17) | 1.00 | -0.38 | 0.94 | 2.16 | 0.0059 |
| Ferrous metals | ... | ... | ... | ... | 0.2277 (1.59) | ... | ... | 0.0319 (4.42) | 1.46 | -0.54 | 0.93 | 1.81 | 0.0078 |
| Nonferrous metals | 0.0125 (0.66) | ... | -0.0596 (1.41) | 0.3887 (0.91) | ... | ... | ... | -0.0001 (0.00) | 1.40 | -0.70 | 0.85 | 1.79 | 0.0230 |
| Fabricated metals and instruments | -0.0025 (-1.20) | ... | 0.0203 (1.81) | 0.3951 (5.98) | 0.4430 (8.66) | ... | ... | -0.0001 (-0.04) | 0.80 | -0.40 | 0.97 | 1.89 | 0.0028 |
| Nonelectrical machinery | 0.0019 (0.21) | ... | ... | 0.3143 (1.68) | 0.3610 (3.03) | ... | ... | 0.0001 (0.03) | 0.90 | ... | 0.95 | 1.93 | 0.0034 |
| Electrical machinery | 0.0042 (0.80) | -0.0667 (-2.26) | ... | ... | ... | ... | ... | 0.0006 (0.09) | 1.40 | -0.60 | 0.89 | 1.85 | 0.0076 |
| Motor vehicles | -0.0052 (-1.12) | ... | ... | ... | 0.8363 (4.65) | ... | ... | 0.0037 (0.45) | 0.85 | -0.25 | 0.80 | 2.16 | 0.0094 |

Sources: Same as Table 9-6.
a. See notes to Table 9-6.

Table 9-9. Coefficients for Profit-Margin Equations, Selected Manufacturing Industries, 1959:3–1972:4[a]

| Industry | Constant | Independent variables | | | | | | | $\rho_1$ | $\rho_2$ | $R^2$ | Durbin-Watson statistic | Standard error |
|---|---|---|---|---|---|---|---|---|---|---|---|---|---|
| | | Output | Demand | Price | Wages | Input prices | Other costs | Economic stabilization program dummy | | | | | |
| Food processing | 0.0059 (0.43) | ... | ... | -0.3524 | ... | ... | ... | -0.0224 (-0.76) | 0.60 | ... | 0.42 | 1.86 | 0.0367 |
| Tobacco | -0.0338 (1.80) | 0.3679 (2.44) | ... | 1.453 (3.02) | ... | ... | ... | -0.0316 (0.91) | 0.60 | ... | 0.41 | 1.97 | 0.0434 |
| Textiles | -0.0618 (2.12) | 2.687 (7.52) | ... | 1.599 (2.25) | ... | ... | -0.5754 (-1.71) | -0.1420 (-1.71) | 0.23 | ... | 0.75 | 1.77 | 0.1100 |
| Apparel | -0.2042 (2.67) | 3.260 (3.32) | 1.300 (1.19) | -10.00 (-2.79) | 5.863 (3.67) | ... | ... | -0.0282 (-0.25) | ... | ... | 0.34 | 1.71 | 0.2106 |
| Lumber | -0.2457 (1.70) | 6.184 (4.97) | ... | 1.203 (1.44) | 6.573 (2.00) | ... | ... | -0.1290 (-0.59) | 0.45 | ... | 0.68 | 1.74 | 0.2735 |
| Furniture | -0.0748 (2.08) | 3.796 (6.58) | ... | ... | ... | -0.5895 (1.41) | ... | 0.0441 (0.39) | ... | ... | 0.47 | 1.59 | 0.2214 |
| Paper | -0.0519 (0.63) | 2.346 (5.08) | ... | 1.844 (1.56) | -2.634 (-1.60) | ... | ... | 0.1225 (1.94) | 0.95 | -0.30 | 0.85 | 2.07 | 0.0651 |
| Chemicals | -0.1777 (3.91) | 1.281 (5.59) | ... | -2.554 (-2.21) | 1.134 (1.36) | ... | ... | 0.0383 (1.24) | 0.60 | ... | 0.74 | 1.85 | 0.0368 |
| Rubber | -0.2767 (4.34) | 1.823 (5.63) | ... | ... | 2.671 (1.91) | -6.266 (-3.46) | ... | 0.2213 (2.30) | 0.25 | ... | 0.58 | 2.01 | 0.1396 |
| Stone, clay, and glass | -0.1033 (3.21) | 2.296 (4.82) | ... | ... | ... | ... | ... | 0.0647 (0.77) | 0.30 | ... | 0.45 | 1.96 | 0.1443 |
| Ferrous metals | -0.0152 (0.24) | 1.728 (7.02) | ... | ... | -2.401 (-1.60) | ... | ... | 0.3906 (3.04) | 0.39 | ... | 0.57 | 2.02 | 0.2651 |
| Nonferrous metals | -0.1384 (1.75) | 2.146 (6.33) | ... | 1.501 (2.47) | -0.4316 (-0.20) | ... | ... | 0.0413 (0.27) | 0.30 | ... | 0.58 | 1.76 | 0.1931 |
| Fabricated metals and instruments | -0.0790 (2.32) | 2.173 (7.14) | ... | ... | ... | ... | ... | 0.0313 (0.51) | 0.65 | ... | 0.76 | 1.90 | 0.0706 |
| Nonelectrical machinery | -0.0478 (1.74) | 0.9239 (3.59) | ... | ... | ... | ... | ... | 0.0001 (0.00) | 0.85 | -0.30 | 0.71 | 2.00 | 0.0748 |
| Electrical machinery | -0.0679 (1.38) | 1.474 (4.67) | ... | ... | ... | ... | -0.3497 (-1.76) | 0.0744 (1.00) | 0.70 | ... | 0.64 | 2.01 | 0.0831 |
| Motor vehicles | -0.0586 (0.98) | 1.567 (6.45) | ... | ... | ... | ... | -0.7404 (-1.30) | -0.1922 (-1.34) | 0.30 | ... | 0.54 | 2.17 | 0.2367 |

Sources: Same as Table 9-7.
a. See notes to Table 9-7.

Table 9-10. *Impact of the Economic Stabilization Controls Program on Equations for Manufacturing Industries, 1971:3–1972:4*[a]

| Impact on price equations | | Impact on profit-margin equations | |
|---|---|---|---|
| Positive | Negative | Positive | Negative |
| Apparel[b] | Tobacco[b] | Paper[c] | Textiles[d] |
| Lumber[d] | | Chemicals[b] | Motor vehicles[c] |
| Paper[c] | | Rubber[b] | |
| Ferrous metals[b] | | Ferrous metals[b] | |

Sources: Tables 9-8 and 9-9.
a. Industry equations in which the economic stabilization program dummy is significant at the 10 percent level.
b. Indicates price increases granted were too generous.
c. Indicates a controlled industry in terms of price increases granted versus increases in the wholesale price index.
d. Indicates a noncompliant industry.

of the coefficients for the independent variables or the general statistical properties of the equations.

Table 9-10 summarizes the cases in which the controls period dummy is significant at the 10 percent level and compares these results with those obtained from examining price approvals versus movements in the industry price equations. In general, there appears to be little impact of the controls program, at least in the downward direction. In only one industry, tobacco, is the dummy variable significantly negative, and only in textiles and motor vehicles is it significant for the profit-margin equations. On the other hand, the dummy variable is significantly positive for four industries in the price equation, as well as for four industries in the profit-margin equation.

The negative impact implied by the price equation in the tobacco industry can be largely discounted, since most of the approved price increases were not put into effect (compare Table 9-2). Thus, either market forces or other structures must have been operating in tobacco. The aggregate data show the tobacco industry to be close to, but not over, its profit margin, which may have been a restraining influence on price increases.

The implied negative impact on profit margins from the textile-industry equation is rather surprising in view of the fact that prices increased 11.7 percent during Phases I and II, four times the rate granted by the Price Commission during Phase II. This can imply only that textile price increases would have been higher than 11.7 percent, an implication that is not supported by the textile price equation.

The impact shown by the equations on profit margins in motor vehicles, although not supported by the aggregate industry data (see Table 9-5), is supported by company announcements made during Phase II.

## Summary

The impact of Price Commission regulations on these manufacturing industries appears to be minimal. The aggregate performance for these sixteen industries during the controls program can be compared with previous experience. The price indexes for each industry were aggregated to a quarterly, fixed-weight index, the weights being the relative value of shipments for each industry in 1958 to conform to the original construction of each industry index. The first five years of the 1960s were marked by virtual price stability for these industries. In 1961–65 the average annual rate of increase was 0.2 percent; in 1968–70, 3.3 percent. The rate of increase moderated slightly to 2.9 percent from the first quarter of 1971 to the second, only to increase over the period of controls—1971:3–1972:4—by an average of 3.8 percent. (The averages 2.9 and 3.8 are for overlapping four-quarter rates of change to overcome seasonal factors.) Thus, relative to prices before controls, prices increased 0.9 percentage point.

Thus, the available data suggest that little of the aggregate effects of the controls experiment, as determined in the preceding chapter, can be detected in these parts of the manufacturing sector.

# APPENDIX

This appendix details the price and profit-margin equations estimated over the sample period 1959:3–1971:2. For the industries for which the price and profit-margin equations were either positive or negative, these equations were reestimated with an added dummy variable for the controls period. The results are contained in Tables 9-6 through 9-10 and in the main body of the chapter.

## Techniques and Data[6]

The form of the variables, for those expressing rates of change, is a four-quarter rate of change, denoted by an $F$ postcript:

$$XF = \frac{X - X(-4)}{X(-4)}.$$

To capture lags in adjustment, a weighted average, with weights summing to 1, proved useful at times. This formulation is denoted by a $WA$ postscript:

$$XFWA = 0.4XF + 0.3XF(-1) + 0.2XF(-2) + 0.1XF(-3).$$

Four-quarter percentage rates of change (current, lagged, or weighted-lagged values) are preferable to the levels of the variables that have a high degree of multicollinearity, because they actually are determined simultaneously. For example, wages are not exogenous to price determination. A feedback process actually occurs between these variables—and others—in response to common forces at work within the economic system, such as changes in the level of aggregate demand or changes in the rate of unemployment.

The use of four-quarter rates of change reduces the multicollinearity between variables in a statistical sense, although it does not eliminate the problem. At first it was assumed, in using four-quarter rates of change, that $(x_t - x_{t-4})/x_{t-4} = a + b(y_t - y_{t-4})/y_{t-4} + \mu_t$, where $\mu_t \sim NID(0, \sigma^2)$, where $NID$ stands for normally and independently distributed. If the Durbin-Watson statistic indicates the presence of autocorrelation, it is assumed that $\mu_t = p\mu_{t-1} + \delta$ or $\mu_t = p_1\mu_{t-1} + p_2\mu_{t-2} + \delta$, where $\delta \sim NID(0, \sigma^2)$.[7]

6. Precise definitions are presented below.

7. It was not assumed that a constant fraction of the dependent variable changes every quarter with the same parametric response to the same independent variables (or the equivalent), as postulated, for example, by George L. Perry, *Unemployment, Money Wage Rates, and Inflation* (M.I.T. Press, 1966).

Eckstein and Wyss, in "Industry Price Equations," suggest the use of the ratio of current level of variables to a four-quarter weighted average as a means of reducing artificial autocorrelation introduced by the assumption that the true mechanism works quarterly with a random error. Experimentation with both one-quarter rates and the Eckstein-Wyss construction indicated that many other factors were at work within the period of a year. Four-quarter rates were used because it is postulated that one-quarter rates of change would be of the form $(x_t - x_{t-1})/x_{t-1} = f[(y_t - y_{t-1})/y_{t-1}, (z_t - z_{t-1})/z_{t-1}, \mu_t]$, where $z_t$ are unobservable variables with the property that $z_t - z_{t-4} = 0$. Seasonal adjustment would not be adequate if the $z_t$ are not solely determined

The data used to estimate the price equations generally are of the two-digit standard industrial classification (SIC) level of compilation. The variables are largely self-explanatory except for the indexes of output and input prices, which were described in the first section of this chapter.

The computation and meaning of the other variables used is straightforward. Data were not seasonally adjusted except for the profit and sales series for ferrous metals; these data required adjustment to correct for a change in classification.

## The Estimating Equations

The equations are estimated over the period 1959:3–1961:2, depending upon the lags involved, to 1971:2, because some of the data are available only from 1958, and because 1971:2 is the last quarter before the price and wage freeze occurred. All equations are corrected for first- and second-order autocorrelation, if present, by a combination of the Hildreth-Lu technique and nonlinear least-squares estimation. The Hildreth-Lu technique was used to search over a grid of values to ensure that the nonlinear estimates were a global minimum, not just a local minimum for the residual sum of squares.

All variables are fixed-weight indexes except for the profit-margin variable. That is, because the profit-margin variable is total before tax profits divided by total industry sales, it will fluctuate for a variety of reasons. Consequently, the profit-margin equations were not expected to have particularly high $\bar{R}^2$s or low standard errors.

In the equations, the dependent variables for each industry are the four-quarter rate of change in output prices and the four-quarter rate of change in profit margins of the form $PQ\_F$ and $PM\_F$, respectively (for example, $PQ20F$ = four-quarter rate of change in output prices for SIC 20).

by the quarter or if the function $f$ is not linear. Thus, no artificial autocorrelation is introduced by these assumptions. Consequently, ordinary least squares or the nonlinear regression for when $p \neq 0$ or when $p_1$ and $p_2 \neq 0$ produces unbiased efficient estimators of the coefficients. For a discussion of the problems generated by the Perry type of assumption, see S. W. Black and H. H. Kelejian, "The Formulation of the Dependent Variable in the Wage Equation," *Review of Economic Studies*, vol. 39 (January 1972), pp. 55–59; or J. C. R. Rowley and D. A. Wilton, "Quarterly Models of Wage Determination: Some New Efficient Estimates," *American Economic Review*, vol. 63 (June 1973), pp. 380–89.

The variable $AHE[\_F$ used in several equations is the four-quarter rate of change in adjusted average hourly earnings. For all equations, the numbers in parentheses are $t$-statistics.

*Food Processing (SIC 20)*

(1)     $PQ20F = 0.01645 - 0.0979INV\%SC20F + 0.480PIN20F$
             (2.32)        (−1.68)                    (8.63)

$\bar{R}^2 = 0.91$; standard error $= 0.00967$; Durbin-Watson statistic $= 1.82$; $\rho = 0.80$.

(2)     $PM20F = 0.009 - 0.430PQ20F(-1)$
             (0.66)    (−1.62)

$\bar{R}^2 = 0.45$; standard error $= 0.03486$; Durbin-Watson statistic $= 1.71$; $\rho = 0.60$.

where

$INV\%SC20F =$ four-quarter rate of change in the inventory to sales ratio; and

$PIN20F =$ four-quarter rate of change in input prices for the food-processing industry.

*Tobacco (SIC 21)*

(3)     $PQ21F = 0.004 + 0.2900AHE[21FWA(-2)$
                       (2.01)

                       $- 0.037ZADP\%EQF(-2) + 0.107RMAAAF$
                       (−1.58)                            (2.78)

$\bar{R}^2 = 0.79$; standard error $= 0.010$; Durbin-Watson statistic $= 1.94$;
                       $\rho_1 = 0.95$; $\rho_2 = -0.20$.

(4)     $PM21F = -0.036 + 0.435JFRB21F + 1.57PQ21F(-1)$
             (−1.84)    (2.59)              (3.13)

$\bar{R}^2 = 0.42$; standard error $= 0.04405$; Durbin-Watson statistic $= 2.00$; $\rho = 0.59$.

where

$AHE[21FWA(-2) = 0.4AHE[21F(-2) + 0.3AHE[21F(-3)$
                              $+ 0.2AHE[21F(-4) + 0.1AHE[21F(-5)$;

$ZADP\%EQF(-2) =$ the ratio of the four-quarter rate of change in profits after tax, plus depreciation, to equity, lagged two quarters;

$RMAAAF$ = four-quarter rate of change in Moody's corporate Aaa bond rate; and

$JFRB2IF$ = four-quarter rate of change in the Federal Reserve Board (FRB) index of industrial production for tobacco.

*Textiles* (*SIC 22*)

(5)    $PQ22F = -0.042 + 0.086JFRB22F + 1.01AHE[22FWA$
$\qquad\quad (-2.86)\quad (1.97)\qquad\qquad\quad (3.26)$

$\qquad\qquad + 0.208PIN22F$
$\qquad\qquad\quad (1.89)$

$\bar{R}^2 = 0.89$; standard error $= 0.00988$; Durbin-Watson statistic $= 1.89$;
$\rho_1 = 1.5; \rho_2 = -0.8.$

(6)    $PM22F = -0.056 + 2.27PQ22F + 2.52JFRB22F$
$\qquad\quad (-2.32)\quad (3.36)\qquad\quad (7.89)$

$\qquad\qquad - 0.589RMAAAF$
$\qquad\qquad\quad (-2.66)$

$\bar{R}^2 = 0.82$; standard error $= 0.096$; Durbin-Watson statistic $= 1.91$; $\rho = 0.23$.

where

$JFRB22F$ = four-quarter rate of change in the FRB index of textile production;

$AHE[22FWA = 0.4AHE[22F + 0.3AHE[22F(-1) + 0.2AHE[22F(-2) + 0.1AHE[22F(-3)$; and

$PIN22F$ = four-quarter rate of change in input prices for the textile industry.

*Apparel* (*SIC 23*)

(7)    $PQ23F = 0.011 + 0.066PQ22F(-1)$
$\qquad\quad (2.00)\quad (2.03)$

$\bar{R}^2 = 0.94$; standard error $= 0.00286$; Durbin-Watson statistic $= 2.07$;
$\rho_1 = 1.40; \rho_2 = -0.5.$

(8)    $PM23F = -0.216 + 3.16JFRB23F + 6.04AHE[23F(-1)$
         $(-3.07)$   $(3.41)$                $(4.01)$

              $- 10.33PQ23F + 1.55CNCS58F$
              $(-3.0)$            $(1.51)$

$\bar{R}^2 = 0.43$; standard error $= 0.1922$; Durbin-Watson statistic $= 1.62$.

where

$JFRB23F =$ four-quarter rate of change in the FRB index of production
           for apparel; and
$CNCS58F =$ four-quarter rate of change in real consumption expenditures
           (1958 dollars) on apparel.


*Lumber (SIC 24)*

(9)    $PQ24F = -0.057 + 1.50AHE[24FWA(-1) + 0.536JFRB24F$
         $(-1.54)$   $(2.05)$                       $(3.04)$

$\bar{R}^2 = 0.70$; standard error $= 0.0396$; Durbin-Watson statistic $= 2.23$;
                    $\rho_1 = 1.20; \rho_2 = -0.50$.

(10)   $PM24F = -0.236 + 5.98JFRB24F + 1.27PQ24F$
         $(-1.59)$   $(4.65)$              $(1.49)$

              $+ 7.88AHE[24F - 5.35AHE[24F(-1)$
              $(2.29)$              $(-1.54)$

$\bar{R}^2 = 0.68$; standard error $= 0.2988$; Durbin-Watson statistic $= 1.76$; $\rho = 0.45$.

where

$AHE[24FWA = 0.4AHE[24F + 0.3AHE[24F(-1) + 0.2AHE[24F(-2)$
            $+ 0.1AHE[24F(-3)$; and
$JFRB24F =$ four-quarter rate of change in the FRB index of industrial
           production for lumber.


*Furniture (SIC 25)*

(11)   $PQ25F = -0.008 + 0.743AHE[25FWA + 0.023PQ24F(-2)$
         $(-2.54)$   $(10.29)$              $(1.88)$

$\bar{R}^2 = 0.95$; standard error $= 0.0037$; Durbin-Watson statistic $= 2.31$;
                    $\rho_1 = 1.10; \rho_2 = -0.50$.

(12)   $PM25F = -0.078 + 3.99JFRB25F - 0.732PQ24F(-1)$
              $(-2.19)$   $(6.87)$          $(-1.74)$

$\bar{R}^2 = 0.50$; standard error $= 0.2197$; Durbin-Watson statistic $= 1.73$.

where

$AHE[25FWA = 0.4AHE[25F + 0.3AHE[25F(-1) + 0.2AHE[25F(-2)$
           $+ 0.1AHE[25F(-3)$; and
   $JFRB25F =$ four-quarter rate of change in the FRB index of production for furniture.

*Paper (SIC 26)*

(13)   $PQ26F = -0.009 + 0.334AHE[26F + 0.059PQ24F(-1)$
           $(-0.85)$   $(1.52)$        $(2.10)$

$\bar{R}^2 = 0.78$; standard error $= 0.0079$; Durbin-Watson statistic $= 2.03$;
                 $\rho_1 = 1.12$; $\rho_2 = -0.45$.

(14)   $PM26F = 0.054 + 1.67JFRB26F - 4.66AHE[26F(-1)$
          $(0.78)$   $(4.19)$        $(-3.43)$

        $+ 1.5955PQ26F$
          $(1.71)$

$\bar{R}^2 = 0.86$; standard error $= 0.05118$; Durbin-Watson statistic $= 2.10$;
                 $\rho_1 = 0.94$; $\rho_2 = -0.31$.

where

$JFRB26F =$ four-quarter rate of change in the FRB index of production for paper.

*Chemicals (SIC 28)*

(15)   $PQ28F = -0.006 + 0.182AHE[28F(-1) + 0.051INV\%S28F$
          $(0.71)$     $(91.25)$         $(3.69)$

$\bar{R}^2 = 0.86$; standard error $= 0.00357$; Durbin-Watson statistic $= 2.01$; $\rho = 0.90$.

(16)   $PM28F = -0.18 + 1.33JFRB28F - 2.76PQ28F$
          $(-4.01)$  $(5.94)$       $(-2.40)$

        $+ 1.2652AHE[28F$
          $(1.46)$

$\bar{R}^2 = 0.76$; standard error $= 0.0352$; Durbin-Watson statistic $= 1.92$; $\rho = 0.60$.

where

$INV\%S28F$ = four-quarter rate of change in the ratio of inventories to shipments in SIC 28; and

$JFRB28F$ = four-quarter rate of change in the FRB index of production for chemicals.

*Rubber (SIC 30)*

(17)     $PQ30F = -0.008 + 0.715AHE[30FWA + 1.36PIN30F(-4)$
            $(-0.55)$    $(2.07)$                              $(4.11)$

$\bar{R}^2 = 0.79$; standard error $= 0.01542$; Durbin-Watson statistic $= 1.83$;
$\rho_1 = 0.9$; $\rho_2 = -0.2$.

(18)     $PM30F = -0.250 + 1.72JFRB30F - 5.62PIN30F$
            $(-4.96)$    $(6.77)$                  $(-3.83)$

            $+ 2.14AHE[30F(-1)$
            $(1.94)$

$\bar{R}^2 = 0.66$; standard error $= 0.1086$; Durbin-Watson statistic $= 1.42$; $\rho = 0.25$.

where

$AHE[30FWA = 0.4AHE[30F + 0.3AHE[30F(-1) + 0.2AHE[30F(-2)$
$+ 0.1AHE[30F(-3)$;

$PIN30F$ = index of input prices for rubber; and

$JFRB30F$ = four-quarter rate of change in the FRB index of production for rubber.

*Stone, Clay, and Glass (SIC 32)*

(19)     $PQ32F = -0.021 + 0.915AHE[32FWA$
            $(-2.15)$    $(4.05)$

$\bar{R}^2 = 0.69$; standard error $= 0.01066$; Durbin-Watson statistic $= 2.10$;
$\rho_1 = 1.25$; $\rho_2 = -0.65$.

(20)     $PM32F = -0.102 + 2.29JFRB32F$
            $(-3.18)$    $(4.74)$

$\bar{R}^2 = 0.44$; standard error $= 0.1442$; Durbin-Watson statistic $= 1.99$; $\rho = 0.30$.

where

$$AHE[32FWA = 0.4AHE[32F + 0.3AHE[32F(-1) + 0.2AHE[32F(-2)$$
$$+ 0.1AHE[32F(-3); \text{ and}$$

$JFRB32F$ = four-quarter rate of change in the FRB index of production for stone, clay, and glass.

*Ferrous Metals (SIC 331)*

(21)  $PQ331F = 0.231PIN331F$
             (2.70)

$\bar{R}^2 = 0.96$; standard error $= 0.004618$; Durbin-Watson statistic $= 1.77$;
$\rho_1 = 1.21$; $\rho_2 = -0.20$.

(22)  $PM331F = 0.074 + 1.50JFRB331F - 4.46AHE[331F(-4)$
             (0.75)    (4.67)               (-1.94)

$\bar{R}^2 = 0.59$; standard error $= 0.230$; Durbin-Watson statistic $= 1.49$; $\rho = 0.39$.

where

$PIN331F$ = four-quarter rate of change in the input price index for ferrous metals;

$JFRB331F$ = four-quarter rate of change in the FRB index of production for ferrous metals; and

$AHE[331F$ = four-quarter rate of change in average hourly earnings, including overtime, in ferrous metals.

*Nonferrous Metals (SIC 333)*

(23)  $PQ333F = 0.002 - 0.083INV\%SC333F + 0.915AHE[33FWA(-2)$
             (0.08)    (1.59)                    (1.86)

$\bar{R}^2 = 0.86$; standard error $= 0.02252$; Durbin-Watson statistic $= 1.97$;
$\rho_1 = 1.4$; $\rho_2 = -0.7$.

(24)  $PM333F = -0.067 + 1.58JFRB333F + 1.37PQ333F$
             (-1.60)    (7.99)              (4.10)

$$- 1.809AHE[33FWA$$
$$(-1.50)$$

$\bar{R}^2 = 0.73$; standard error $= 0.1059$; Durbin-Watson statistic $= 1.95$; $\rho = 0.30$.

where

$INV\%SC333F$ = four-quarter rate of change in the ratio of inventories to sales in nonferrous metals;

$AHE[33FWA = 0.4AHE[33F + 0.3AHE[33F(-1) + 0.2AHE[33F(-2) + 0.1AHE[33F(-3);$

$AHE[33F$ = four-quarter rate of change in average hourly earnings, excluding overtime, in primary metals; and

$JFRB333F$ = four-quarter rate of change in the FRB index of production for nonferrous metals.


*Fabricated Metals and Instruments (SIC 34 and 38)*

(25)   $PQ348F = -0.002 + 0.022INV\%SC348F + 0.387AHE[348FWA$
          (1.05)        (1.74)                        (5.44)

          $+ 0.453PIN348F$
             (8.17)

$\bar{R}^2 = 0.97$; standard error $= 0.00283$; Durbin-Watson statistic $= 1.72$;
$\rho_1 = 0.80; \rho_2 = -0.40.$

(26)   $PM348F = -0.078 + 2.24JFRB348F$
          (-2.52)    (7.68)

$\bar{R}^2 = 0.79$; standard error $= 0.0703$; Durbin-Watson statistic $= 1.78; \rho = 0.65.$

where

$$AHE[348F = \frac{AHE[348 - AHE[348(-4)}{AHE[348(-4)};$$

$$AHE[348 = \frac{EP34AHE[34 + EP38AHE[38}{EP34 + EP38};$$

$EP34$ = employment of production workers in fabricated metal products (SIC 34);

$EP38$ = employment of production workers in instruments and related products (SIC 38);

$PIN348F$ = four-quarter rate of change in the input price index for fabricated metals and instruments;

$INV\%SC348F$ = four-quarter rate of change in the sales-weighted ratio of inventories to sales for fabricated metals (SIC 34) and instruments (SIC 38);

$AHE{348FWA} = 0.4AHE{348F} + 0.3AHE{348F}(-1)$
$\qquad\qquad + 0.2AHE{348F}(-2) - 0.1AHE{348F}(-3);$ and

$JFRB348F =$ four-quarter rate of change in the output weighted FRB index of production for fabricated metals (SIC 34) and instruments (SIC 38).

### Nonelectrical Machinery (SIC 35)

(27)    $PQ35F = 0.005 + 0.253AHE{35FWA} + 0.439PIN35FWA$
$\qquad\quad$ (0.75)    (1.62)                    (4.26)

$\bar{R}^2 = 0.97$; standard error $= 0.00272$; Durbin-Watson statistic $= 1.79$; $\rho = 0.9$.

(28)    $PM35F = -0.057 + 1.01JFRB35F$
$\qquad\quad$ (−1.97)    (3.13)

$\bar{R}^2 = 0.72$; standard error $= 0.07454$; Durbin-Watson statistic $= 2.05$;
$\qquad\qquad\qquad \rho_1 = 0.85; \rho_2 = -0.29$.

where

$AHE{35FWA} = 0.4AHE{35F} + 0.3AHE{35F}(-1) + 0.2AHE{35F}(-2)$
$\qquad\qquad + 0.1AHE{35F}(-3);$
$PIN35FWA = 0.4PIN35F + 0.3PIN35F(-1) + 0.2PIN35F(-2)$
$\qquad\qquad + 0.1PIN35F(-3);$

$PIN35F =$ four-quarter rate of change in the input price index for nonelectrical machinery; and

$JFRB35F =$ four-quarter rate of change in the FRB index of production for nonelectrical machinery.

### Electrical Machinery (SIC 36)

(29)    $PQ36F = 0.002 - 0.133UCAPFRB36F$
$\qquad\quad$ (0.41)    (−2.97)

$\bar{R}^2 = 0.90$; standard error $= 0.0076$; Durbin-Watson statistic $= 2.09$;
$\qquad\qquad\qquad \rho_1 = 1.4; \rho_2 = -0.6$.

(30)    $PM36F = -0.061 + 1.54JFRB36F - 0.400DP36F$
$\qquad\quad$ (−1.19)    (4.61)                (−1.89)

$\bar{R}^2 = 0.64$; standard error $= 0.0849$; Durbin-Watson statistic $= 2.02$; $\rho = 0.70$.

where

*UCAPFRB36F* = four-quarter rate of change in the FRB index of capacity
utilization for electrical machinery;

*JFRB36F* = four-quarter rate of change in the FRB index of industrial production for electrical machinery; and

*DP36F* = four-quarter rate of change of depreciation for electrical
machinery.

*Motor Vehicles (SIC 371)*

(31)   $PQ371F = -0.005 + 0.935PIN371FWA$
              $(-1.29)$   $(5.59)$

   $\bar{R}^2 = 0.83$; standard error $= 0.00827$; Durbin-Watson statistic $= 1.95$;
                     $\rho_1 = 0.85$; $\rho_2 = -0.25$.

(32)   $PM371F = -0.068 + 1.95JFRB371F - 0.848RMAAAF$
              $(-1.15)$   $(7.68)$              $(-1.47)$

   $\bar{R}^2 = 0.64$; standard error $= 0.2217$; Durbin-Watson statistic $= 2.06$; $\rho = 0.33$.

where

*PIN371FWA* = $0.4PIN371F + 0.3PIN371F(-1) + 0.2PIN371F(-2)$
              $+ 0.1PIN371F(-3)$;

*PIN371F* = four-quarter rate of change in input prices for motor
vehicles;

*JFRB371F* = four-quarter rate of change in the FRB index of industrial
production for motor vehicles; and

*RMAAAF* = four-quarter rate of change in Moody's Aaa corporate
bond rate.

# X

# Performance of Other Industries during Controls

Despite limitations of data that circumscribe the analysis, this chapter examines price behavior in the major part of the U.S. economy.[1] The performance of two major manufacturing industries not included in Chapter 9, leather and petroleum, merit attention.[2] The service industries must be analyzed in detail and a summary provided for construction, mining, fuel and utilities, and interest and dividends. A discussion of the wholesale and retail sectors, which encompass a large amount of diversified economic activity, concludes the chapter. The price movements in mining, fuel, and utilities also are dominated by a number of other, extramarket influences. In general, the review of each sector is limited to the relevant policy aspects and to a simple description of price movements, as shown by selected indicators.

## The Leather Industry

During Phase II, leather and leather products represented a major problem. The price of hides had begun to rise prior to the freeze. The wholesale price index for hides rose at an annual rate of 19.3 percent from December 1970 to August 1971, largely because of Argentina's reduction in cattle hide exports to 3.4 million in 1971 from 7.5 million in 1970,[3] and in 1972 that nation completely stopped the export of hides. Coupled with the worldwide economic boom, this led to an increase in

1. The importance of manufacturing often is exaggerated, in part because of the greater availability of data. Yet manufacturing accounts for about the same percentage of national income as services plus wholesale and retail trade—27 to 28 percent in 1973.
2. The remaining manufacturing industries, which are not discussed, are ordnance and miscellaneous.
3. U.S. Department of Commerce, Bureau of Domestic Commerce, Consumer Products Division, tabulation (March 1972).

Table 10-1. *Change in Hide, Leather, and Footwear Components of the Wholesale and Consumer Price Indexes, Various Periods, 1962–72*

Average annual rate in percent

| Index and component | 1962–65 | 1965–68 | 1968–70 | December 1970– August 1971 | Phases I and II, August 1971– December 1972 |
|---|---|---|---|---|---|
| | | *Wholesale price index* | | | |
| Cattle hides | n.a. | n.a. | n.a. | 29.7 | 98.8 |
| All hides | 1.5 | −3.5 | −0.8 | 19.3 | 82.3 |
| Tanned leather | −0.1 | 1.4 | 2.7 | 10.1 | 29.9 |
| Leather footwear | 0.7 | 4.9 | 3.8 | 4.2 | 7.3 |
| | | *Consumer price index* | | | |
| Nonrubber footwear | 0.6 | 5.5 | 5.8 | 2.2 | 4.4 |

Sources: U.S. Bureau of Labor Statistics, *Handbook of Labor Statistics, 1972;* BLS, *Wholesale Prices and Price Indexes,* various issues; BLS, *The Consumer Price Index,* various issues; and unpublished data from the BLS.

n.a. Not available.

the price of cattle hides of some 100 percent between August 1971 and the end of Phase II.

In mid-1972, the Price Commission placed all leather manufacturers on a dollar-for-dollar pass-through of increases in leather costs.[4] Although the retail markup on shoes generally averages more than 80 percent of the wholesale price, the commission did not require a dollar-for-dollar pass-through for retailers; instead, it permitted continued use of the customary initial percentage markup.

Table 10-1 summarizes some historical and controls-period movements in various leather, hide, and footwear price indexes. The doubling of cattle-hide prices from mid-1971 to December 1972 resulted in an 82 percent increase in the price index for all hides, a 30 percent increase in the leather index, and a 7 percent increase in the wholesale price index for leather footwear, whereas the consumer price index component for footwear rose less than 4.5 percent over the period of controls (all annual rates of increase).

4. Price Commission Order 6, in *Federal Register,* vol. 37 (June 28, 1972), p. 12756.

How effective was the dollar-for-dollar regulation for leather producers? The analysis of price movements for leather suggests that the effectiveness of the Price Commission surpassed the letter of its regulations.

The timing of cost increases and production lag time is crucial in estimating the consequences of such huge price increases.[5] To supply retail stores during the period from July through November, the tanner normally buys and accepts delivery of hides from January through May. For hides bought in January, delivery of leather to shoe manufacturers begins in mid-April. Prices have been set by the manufacturers with exhibitions by late March. The production for the fall line begins about May 1 and continues through mid-September. Deliveries to retail outlets arrive about the end of June for mid-July sales. Thus, in assessing the effectiveness of the dollar-for-dollar ruling of July 1972, the average cost increases during the first half of the year should be compared with retail price increases during the second half.

During the first half of 1972 the cost of cattle hides increased 50 percent over the freeze-level price.[6] Table 10-2 illustrates the theoretical dollar-for-dollar pass-through of a 93 percent increase in green (uncured) hides. The 93 percent is equivalent to a 50 percent increase in cured and fleshed hides, assuming that 1965 cost levels for all other cost factors are unchanged.

The CPI components most nearly comparable are men's street oxfords and men's work shoes. From June 1972 to December 1972, their respective rates of increase were 3.0 and 5.1 percent. Both figures are lower than the implied price increase at the retail level with a constant margin. On the other hand, over the full period of controls, the weighted-average price increase granted to tier I shoe manufacturers was 3.8 percent,[7] whereas the comparable WPI indexes increased by 7.3 percent.

Thus, although there may have been some violation of the Price Commission's authorized price increases (which, however, could be the

5. The following is based upon a study by John W. Thompson, "Marketing Spreads for Leather Products," in U.S. Department of Agriculture, Economic Research Service, *Marketing and Transportation Situation*, MTS-156 (February 1965), pp. 28–29, and in consultation with industry representatives.

6. Average of the indexes for January through June 1972 over the November 1971 index. Source: U.S. Bureau of Labor Statistics, *Wholesale Prices and Price Indexes*, various issues.

7. Price Commission data.

Table 10-2. *Hypothetical Dollar-for-Dollar Pass-Through of a 93 Percent Increase in Green Hides, by Stages of Shoe Production and Consumption*

| | Percentage pass-through | |
|---|---|---|
| Stage | All-leather shoe[a] | Shoe with leather upper[b] |
| Packers' green hides | 93 | 93 |
| Tanners' cured and fleshed hides | 50 | 50 |
| Shoe manufacturers' leather | 23 | 24 |
| Retailers' shoes | 16 | 6.5 |
| Consumers' shoe purchases | | |
|     Constant percentage retail markup | 16 | 6.5 |
|     Dollar-for-dollar retail markup | 9 | 3.8 |

Sources: Derived from data in John W. Thompson, "Marketing Spreads for Leather Products," in U.S. Department of Agriculture, Economic Research Service, *Marketing and Transportation Situation*, MTS-156 (February 1965), pp. 28–29; and data from shoe industry representatives.

a. Based upon an assumed price increase in green hides from 8.66 cents per pound of enough hide to make one pair of shoes, and the assumption that the other costs are unchanged at 1965 levels.

b. The same increase as in note *a* in the cost of enough leather to make only the upper portion of a pair of shoes.

result of statistical difficulties), it appears that the level of price increases in shoes at retail was less than the regulations would have permitted, including all stages of production from tanning to retailing. One explanation could be that the widespread ethic to hold down price increases permeated all pricing decisions for leather products; another, that market conditions precluded greater increases.

## The Petroleum Industry

The situation of petroleum controls were—and are—complicated by their being intertwined with a number of national issues such as conservation, clean air, import quotas, special tax subsidies, and the shortage of electrical energy. Without examining all the related issues in detail, however, an analysis of the price movements in petroleum illustrates the effects of jawboning.

The commission was quite successful at holding down price increases for refined petroleum products until about the middle of 1972. It continued its policy throughout the remainder of 1972, but in the second half of the year several petroleum price increases were instituted that had not been approved by the commission.

Virtually all of the price approvals granted to the petroleum-refining industry were term limit pricing agreements, averaging less than 2 percent. But the total applicable sales for all price approvals was only slightly more than $11 billion, or about one-seventh of total corporate sales for the petroleum industry in 1972. At several points, oil companies approached the Price Commission about price increases, but the program operations chief for that division intimated that these requests would be turned down. After further meetings between oil company representatives and higher executives of the Price Commission staff, the oil companies' insistence on filing for price increases was countered with an informal notice that any such requests would bring about public hearings, which would unavoidably focus national attention not only on prices but also on such other features of the oil industry as depletion allowances and import quotas.

This approach appeared to be effective, at least through June 1972; wholesale prices of refined petroleum products increased by only 1.1 percent over their level in August 1971. After June, the policy apparently continued to work well, and as late as December 21, 1972, the Price Commission was still contemplating public hearings before granting price increases on any petroleum products (although by that date the issue had shifted to heating fuel).[8] Nevertheless, over the last six months of Phase II controls, refined petroleum products prices rose another 3.23 percent, bringing the total increase for the control period to 4.4 percent, as against the granted increases of less than 2.0 percent on one-seventh of industry sales.[9]

The muscle of the Price Commission apparently began to weaken about the same time the Cost of Living Council made it clear that no substantive changes should be made before the November presidential election. That the fate of the Price Commission and Pay Board also was determined at that time is pure speculation. Nonetheless, the effectiveness of the commission's jawboning on petroleum prices clearly deteriorated and, in general, the commission's credibility was weakened.

Petroleum firms also argued that controls were distorting the output mix of refined petroleum products. During 1972, several firms requested

8. See, for example, the account in *Journal of Commerce*, December 21, 1972.

9. Whether this increase measured by the WPI is the implicit increased price claimed by retail service stations from changes in base arrangements is indeterminable. Given the nature of the collection of data, the WPI probably is measuring actual price increases rather than implicit ones.

volatility treatment for fuel oil. Their claim was based on the argument that the mild winter of 1970 caused the price of fuel oil to be artificially low, and that with profits being greater for gasoline and other refined products, they would shift away from fuel oil. But holding to a literal interpretation of the volatility rule, the commission denied the request.

There appears to have been some merit to the argument offered by petroleum firms. Over the entire controls period, the *Survey of Current Business* data showed the demand for distillate fuel oil relative to demand for gasoline to be 0.46, slightly above the 1968–70 average relative demand of 0.44:

|  | | *Ratio of distillate fuel oil to gasoline* | |
|  | *Demand* | *Production, domestic* | *Stocks, end of period* |
|---|---|---|---|
| 1968–70 | 0.44 | 0.43 | 0.84 |
| 1971:4 | 0.47 | 0.40 | 0.85 |
| 1972:1 | 0.64 | 0.43 | 0.42 |
| 1972:2 | 0.37 | 0.42 | 0.63 |
| 1972:3 | 0.30 | 0.39 | 0.93 |
| 1972:4 | 0.54 | 0.43 | 0.71 |
| 1971:4–1972:4 | 0.46 | 0.41 | 0.71 |

Production, on the other hand, was 0.41, slightly below the 1968–70 average of 0.43. This combination resulted in a drawdown of distillate fuel oil stocks relative to gasoline to 0.71, in contrast to the 1968–70 average of 0.84. This, of course, represents only a simple examination of the claims, which require a fuller analysis that would incorporate a number of other factors.

## Service Industries

All services except those for health care were subject to the same regulations as were manufacturing firms. But productivity information, readily obtainable for the manufacturing sector, is not available for service industries. Consequently, all service firms were required to calculate their own productivity offsets throughout Phase II. When serious consideration was given to tightening the price regulations early in 1972, one proposal would have placed a flat 3 percent ceiling on all service price increases above the freeze level (except for those services already under special provisions). This proposal actually was adopted by the commission, but for a number of reasons it was never implemented.

First, although the total relative importance of service firms in the consumer price index was 37.41 percent at that time, the special provisions for rent, utilities, and health care and the exemptions for services such as custom tailoring reduced the relative importance of remaining services in the CPI to 14.17 percent.[10] The exemption for small firms, those with 60 or fewer employees, issued by the Cost of Living Council, especially when coupled with prior exemptions, thus eliminated most service firms from the program. The Price Commission staff estimated that the small-firm exemption would eliminate about 80 percent of the remaining sales, leaving under controls about 2.5 percent of the CPI associated with services.

Second, because the service component of the CPI in May 1972 was only 4.1 percent higher than a year before, the rule would have had little aggregate effect. Third, any such effect would be accompanied by a number of inequities and exception requests. The logic of the 3 percent ceiling was a 5.5 percent allowance for wage increases, a 1.0 percent increase in productivity, and a 2.5 percent increase in nonlabor costs. The service sector, however, is extremely heterogeneous, with wide variations in labor intensity, productivity, and amount of nonlabor cost increases incurred by particular companies. Fourth, because service-sector prices were behaving rather well, there was little staff support for tightening the regulations for that sector if comparable restrictions were not placed on other sectors under controls.

As shown in Table 10-3, most service indexes increased at a lower rate during Phase II than prior to controls, with some exceptions. There also were marked reductions, particularly in medical-care services. Legal services, as shown in the consumer price index, suggest limited compliance with either the freeze or Phase II. Unfortunately, the CPI measures only the fees charged for a short-form will, so it is not clear whether this yardstick is truly representative of all legal service fees. Nonetheless, this bulging index prompted the commission to adopt and implement a 2.5 percent ceiling for legal fees of major law firms on September 6, 1972. The 2.5 percent figure was chosen to equalize the regulation for lawyers with those for doctors and dentists. Yet considerable doubt remained within the commission about both the enforceability of, and the compliance with, that regulation.

10. Price Commission estimate.

Table 10-3. *Rates of Change in Selected Components of the Services Consumer Price Index, Various Periods, 1962–72*
Average annual rate in percent

| Services index | 1962–65[a] | 1965–68[a] | 1968–70[a] | December 1970– August 1971[b] | Phase I[b] | Phase II[b] | Phases I and II[b] |
|---|---|---|---|---|---|---|---|
| All services | 2.0 | 4.5 | 7.5 | 4.6 | 3.1 | 3.5 | 3.5 |
| Rent | 1.0 | 1.9 | 3.7 | 4.3 | 2.8 | 3.5 | 3.3 |
| Services, excluding rent[c] | 2.3 | 4.9 | 8.2 | 4.6 | 3.1 | 3.5 | 3.4 |
| Household | 1.9 | 4.8 | 9.4 | 2.3 | 5.5 | 4.4 | 4.6 |
| Transportation | 2.4 | 3.8 | 8.8 | 7.9 | −0.3 | 1.7 | 1.3 |
| Apparel (drycleaning) | 1.8 | 4.0 | 4.4 | 2.6 | 0.7 | 1.4 | 1.3 |
| Medical care[c] | 2.9 | 7.1 | 7.6 | 7.8 | −0.9 | 3.9 | 3.0 |
| Physicians' fees | 2.8 | 6.1 | 7.2 | 6.6 | 2.5 | 2.4 | 2.4 |
| Dentists' fees | 2.9 | 4.6 | 6.4 | 7.1 | 6.1 | 2.8 | 3.4 |
| Semiprivate hospital rooms | 5.1 | 14.4 | 13.1 | 11.9 | 2.9 | 5.1 | 4.7 |
| Personal care | 2.6 | 4.8 | 5.0 | 2.9 | 2.0 | 3.0 | 2.8 |
| Recreation | 3.4[d] | 5.2 | 5.4 | 5.1 | 1.6 | 2.0 | 1.9 |
| Legal (short-form will) | 5.6[d] | 4.0 | 9.5 | 1.8 | 20.2 | 8.4 | 10.5 |

Sources: U.S. Bureau of Labor Statistics, *Handbook of Labor Statistics, 1972*; and BLS, *The Consumer Price Index*, various issues.
a. Ending yearly average over beginning yearly average.
b. Ending month over beginning month; Phase I covers August–November 1971, Phase II, November 1971–December 1972.
c. Includes items not shown separately.
d. Available from 1964 only.

The Pay Board approved sizable increases to longshoremen, from 9.8 to 14.9 percent in wages and fringe benefits. Such increases in costs for highly labor-intensive stevedoring operations could in no way be covered under the Price Commission's allowable limit of 5.5 percent. Moreover, the increases were granted before the commission had developed the loss and low-profit provision for service firms. A solution of sorts was reached when the Cost of Living Council exempted stevedores from the commission's 5.5 percent limitation on labor-cost pass-through, and the commission continued to rule on price increases on a company-by-company basis. A similar exemption from the allowable labor-cost limit was approved by the CLC for firms in building cleaning and maintenance, a field in which wages historically have had a tandem relation to wages of maintenance personnel hired directly by the building owners, personnel not subject to commission regulations.

The television broadcasting industry, which typically prices on the basis of the popularity of the television program, had considerable difficulty with the concept of allowable-cost increase. Accordingly, on April 4, 1972, the broadcasting industry was granted a zero TLP agreement for television programs whereby firms were free to raise and lower particular rates without limit as long as the weighted average of all such changes was less than or equal to zero. Although few data are available to quantify the effect of this ruling, this tactic is believed to have been successful.

In terms of the overall reduction in the rate of change in service prices, a monthly forecasting model (similar to that presented in Chapter 8 but with separate equations for commodities and services), when simulated with and without controls, predicted the average annualized monthly rate of change in the service component of the CPI would have been 2.0 percentage points higher in Phase II without controls. The following tabulation shows the actual annual rate of change for services and predictions by the model for Phases I and II:

|                                       |         | Prediction        |                   |
| ------------------------------------- | ------- | ----------------- | ----------------- |
|                                       | Actual  | With controls     | Without controls  |
| Phase I (August–November 1971)        | 3.1     | 2.9               | 5.5               |
| Phase II (November 1971–December 1972)| 3.5     | 4.0               | 6.0               |
| Phases I and II                       | 3.5     | 3.8               | 6.0               |

## Construction

Considerable difficulty occurred also in the construction industry, much of which was never completely resolved. The Construction Industry Stabilization Committee (CISC) had been the first agency created under the Economic Stabilization Act of 1970. During 1970 construction wages and benefits averaged 19.6 percent for first-year increases and 15.6 percent for the life of the contract.[11] After failing to achieve any significant moderation, the President in February 1971 suspended the Davis-Bacon Act, which sets wage standards for federally funded, assisted, or insured construction. It was reinstated, however, on March 29, 1971, when the CISC was created through cooperation of labor and industry leaders. The freeze of August 1971 brought the CISC under the supervision of the Pay Board, but it was allowed some degree of independence.

The attitude of the CISC was to realign relative wages, which meant that a number of trade unions were allowed wage increases significantly in excess of the 5.5 percent guideline. Early in January 1972 the CISC reached an agreement with the Pay Board to continue its policy, assuring that the weighted average of all increases would be 5.5 percent or less. But no agreement was reached with the Price Commission. Many contractors requiring a mix of trades for a particular job had been granted wage increases far in excess of the 5.5 percent guideline; they simply could not comply with the commission's 5.5 percent limitation. A loss or low-profit provision for those services under which construction contractors were classified would have mitigated the problem.

Accordingly, effective on March 13, 1972, the Price Commission added a section to its regulations whereby construction became a custom product or service. Basically, for custom products and services, the commission required a constant profit margin, thus effectively permitting allowable labor-cost increases in excess of 5.5 percent. To improve the enforceability of this regulation, two steps were taken. First, the Cost of Living Council reclassified construction firms with over $50 million in revenue as tier I and firms with $25 million to $50 million as tier II. Second, it eliminated the option by which the profit-margin violation was the lesser either of the amount in excess of the profit-margin limitation or of the revenues from the price increases; the violation became simply

11. *Economic Report of the President, January 1972*, p. 74.

the excess over the profit margin. This ruling, however, was never published, for reasons that are not clear.

Although the annual price deflators from the national income accounts obscure the acceleration and deceleration in construction costs,
this phenomenon is captured by various other monthly measures. For
example, the weekly *Engineering News Record* index for construction
costs advanced at an annual rate of 18.1 percent during the eight months
before the freeze. Although the different indexes give conflicting reports
for what transpired during the freeze, all show a substantial reduction
relative to the eight preceding months.

Given the competitive nature of construction contracting and the
resulting limitations on the Price Commission's regulation of contract
construction, this is yet another case in which success for a price-control
program depended upon generating an attitude that controls indeed
could reduce the rate of inflation.

## Mining, Fuel, and Utilities

The direct effects of the Price Commission clearly were minimal in
the mining, fuel, and utilities sectors of the economy. The indirect effects
may have been more substantial, however, because the commission engaged in a good deal of rhetoric on highly publicized issues relating to
these areas.

First, the early decision on the coal contract marked a major declara-
tion of independence by the commission. Most coal production, however, either is part of an integrated manufacturing process, as in the
case of steel, or is produced under long-term contracts, fifteen years or
more in some instances; both of these situations preclude any direct
repercussions from the regulations. The total applicable sales for price-
increase requests for bituminous and lignite mining was less than $1.5
billion, compared with approximate sales in 1971 of $5.5 billion.[12] Most
other mining, such as that of bauxite, iron, lead, and zinc ores, also is
part of an integrated process that would come under the manufacturing
regulations.

Natural gas and electric power, the remaining fuels not discussed
under petroleum, generally were not controlled by the commission;
instead, supervision of those industries was returned to their respective

12. *Survey of Current Business*, vol. 53 (May 1973), pp. S-34, S-35.

Table 10-4. *Rates of Change in Selected Fuel and Power Components of the Wholesale Price Index, Various Periods, 1962–72*

Average annual rate in percent

| Period | All fuels[a] | Coal | Coke | Gas | Electric power |
|---|---|---|---|---|---|
| 1962–65 | −0.4 | −0.1 | 1.2 | 1.3 | −0.7 |
| 1965–68 | 1.2 | 3.5 | 2.6 | * | 0.3 |
| 1968–70 | 3.5 | 20.3 | 10.9 | 5.6 | 1.9 |
| December 1970–August 1971 | 2.7 | 6.1 | 4.8 | −0.4 | 9.2 |
| Phase I, August–November 1971 | −0.3 | 0.0 | 0.0 | 6.1 | 3.2 |
| Phase II, November 1971– December 1972 | 5.8 | 11.4 | 5.8 | 8.8 | 5.3 |
| Phases I and II | 4.6 | 9.1 | 4.6 | 8.3 | 4.9 |

Sources: U.S. Bureau of Labor Statistics, *Handbook of Labor Statistics, 1972;* and BLS, *Wholesale Prices and Price Indexes,* various issues.

a. Includes items not shown separately.

* Less than 0.05.

regulatory agencies. Nonetheless, the commission ordered a freeze on utility increases during part of Phase II and attempted to influence the granting of price increases through the certification of other regulatory agencies.[13]

Table 10-4 summarizes the movements of fuel and power components of the wholesale price index from 1962 to 1972, rounding out the discussion of price movements during the controls experiment. Without a detailed investigation of matters outside the scope of this work, little more can be written about the effect of the regulations. The influences of the general energy crisis and such conservation measures as the clean-air regulations dominate the price movements, historically and over the period of controls. Therefore, any quantifiable measure of the effect of Phase II requires a separate, in-depth analysis.

## Interest Rates and Dividends

Interest rates and dividends were exempted from controls during the freeze and Phase II. Both were under the purview of the Committee on Interest and Dividends (CID),[14] which issued voluntary guidelines on

13. See the discussion of the utilities' regulations in Chapter 3.

14. The committee comprised the chairmen of the Federal Reserve Board, the Federal Deposit Insurance Corporation, and the Federal Home Loan Bank Board and the secretaries of the treasury, commerce, and housing and urban development.

dividends and jawboned banks during the latter days of Phase II about the undesirable aspects of raising interest rates.

The guidelines promulgated by the CID and monitored by a subcommittee from the Department of Commerce limited cash dividend increases to 4 percent above the highest payout in the three years prior to controls. Firms expected to comply were those with more than $1 million in assets, more than 500 owners of common stock, and those subject to the reporting requirements of the SEC—some 7,000 firms in all.

A number of exceptions to the 4 percent ceiling also were allowed. For example, companies that distributed no or very low dividends in previous years were permitted to make 1972 dividend payouts of up to 25 percent (initially 15 percent) of net earnings in 1971.

The Department of Commerce staff spotted only eighteen violations through the first half of 1972; in each case a letter to the firm resulted in a promise of future reductions to bring the firm into compliance with the voluntary guidelines. Judging by the typical movements in corporate dividends, this policy restrained the growth in dividends, as shown below:

|  | Average annual growth in corporate dividends (percent) | |
| --- | --- | --- |
|  | One-quarter rate of change | Four-quarter rate of change |
| 1949–71:2 | 6.5 | 5.9 |
| 1960–65 | 8.4 | 7.9 |
| 1966–68 | 5.7 | 6.1 |
| 1969–71:2 | 1.6 | 2.3 |
| 1971:3–72 | 3.6 | 3.1 |

The long-term average annual growth in dividends is about 6 percent. During periods of rapid increases in profits, dividends follow suit, but to a lesser extent.[15] Dividends grew an average of 8 percent during the period 1960–65, but only an average of about 2 percent during the period 1969–1971:2 because profits declined for seven of those ten

15. The simple regression between overlapping four-quarter rates of change for the period 1949–1971:2 is $DDF = 4.935 + 0.2211\ DZF$ ($\overline{R}^2 = 0.40$; Durbin-Watson statistic $= 0.93$; standard error $= 5.08$), where $DDF$ is the four-quarter rate of change in corporate dividends and $DZF$ is the four-quarter rate of change in after-tax corporate profits. But the high standard error and low Durbin-Watson statistic preclude the use of this equation for analysis of the controls period.

Table 10-5. *Levels of Selected Interest Rates, Various Dates, 1971–72*

| Interest item | August 1971 | April 1972 | December 1972 |
|---|---|---|---|
| Moody's Aaa bonds | 7.59 | 7.30 | 7.08 |
| Residential mortgages[a] | | | |
|   Existing homes | 7.58 | 7.30 | 7.45 |
|   New homes | 7.60 | 7.38 | 7.51 |
| Prime rate charged by banks | 6.00 | 4.97[b] | 5.75 |

Source: *Federal Reserve Bulletin*, various issues.
a. Contract rate on conventional first mortgages.
b. Rate changed from 4.75 to 5.00 percent on April 5.

quarters. The stage would seem to have been set for a rapid growth in dividends, but it did not materialize. Thus, the rate of growth in dividends was lower than the guideline of 4 percent because after-tax profits grew at an average rate of 25 percent over the six quarters of controls.

Interest rates, as published in the *Federal Reserve Bulletin,* generally declined over Phases I and II until about mid-1972, after which they began to rise, though by December they were still at a lower level than in August 1971 (see Table 10-5).

## Wholesale and Retail Trade

A significant retardation in the rate of inflation apparently occurred during Phase II in the trade sector, despite the fact that this sector was subjected to relatively complicated and often ill-fitting and expensive compliance requirements. First, with the available data, the reduction in the overall rate of inflation as shown by the various aggregate wage-price models—and particularly the difference between the rates of increase in the WPI and the CPI—cannot be ascribed entirely to the service sector. Second, the regulations created substantial conflicts with customary business practices, partly because of a determined effort by the Internal Revenue Service to enforce the regulations in a literal fashion in an area in which public visibility was the greatest—a reflection of the IRS tradition on tax matters.[16]

The reduction in the inflation rate in the trade sector can be inferred from two sources. First, the different rates of increase in the wholesale and consumer price indexes suggest that the spread between wholesale

16. See Chapter 5.

and retail prices was narrowed during Phase II relative to precontrols periods. For example, the simple historical model developed in Chapter 8,[17] which takes the rate of change in the WPI as exogenous, predicts that the CPI would have risen at an annual rate of 5.4 percent without controls, whereas its average rate of increase during the controls period actually was 3.2 percent. Similar conclusions follow from a simple comparison between the seasonally adjusted annual rates of change in the price of consumer finished goods and the CPI for commodities less food:

|  | Wholesale price index: consumer-finished goods (excluding food) | Consumer price index: nonfood commodities (excluding used cars) |
|---|---|---|
| 1962–65 | 0.4 | 0.8 |
| 1965–68 | 2.0 | 3.0 |
| 1968–70 | 3.4 | 4.7 |
| December 1970– August 1971 | 2.2 | 2.6 |
| Phase I | −0.4 | 1.0 |
| Phases I and II | 1.9 | 2.2 |

Historically, the annual rate of change of the CPI has exceeded that of the WPI for comparable nonfood items by about 1.0 percentage point. For the entire controls program, however, the difference was only 0.3 percentage point.

Second, a comparison of specific price changes for the eighty-seven nonfood items that are in both the WPI and the CPI for the year August 1971–August 1972 indicates the overall effect to be a reduction of retail profit margins of 1.0 percent (see Table 10-6), which is surprisingly close to the implications of the immediately preceding comparisons.

The highly competitive nature of retailing and wholesaling operations and the relative ease of entry and exit into and out of the field suggest that the effects on inflation stemmed basically from a voluntary restraint by firms in this sector. This is supported by the fact that although a number of audits of retail-wholesale firms were undertaken by the Internal Revenue Service, the fraction of total firms audited was insignificant, and each audit—even one made merely to determine whether the firm priced on an item-by-item or category markup basis—was extremely time consuming.

17. Chapter 8, p. 114, and section D of the appendix to Chapter 8, pp. 136–37.

Table 10-6. *Effect on Retail Profit Margins of Differential Price Changes for Nonfood Commodities in the Consumer and Wholesale Price Indexes, by Type of Change, August 1971–August 1972*

| | Change in profit margin | | | |
| Item | Reduction | Increase | No effect | All commodities |
|---|---|---|---|---|
| Number of nonfood commodities | 38 | 33 | 16 | 87 |
| Weight in nonfood commodity index | 0.678 | 0.196 | 0.126 | 1.000 |
| Percent price change | | | | |
|   Consumer price index | 1.1 | 2.0 | 1.0 | 1.3 |
|   Wholesale price index | 3.4 | −0.8 | 1.0 | 2.3 |
| Difference (percentage points)[a] | −2.3 | 2.8 | 0.00 | −1.0 |
| Effect on profit margin (percent) | −1.55 | +0.55 | 0.00 | −1.00 |

Source: Price Commission Report DPA No. R-487.
a. Row 3 minus row 4.

Competitive theory would suggest further that although a willingness and a desire to comply may have existed on the part of firms, a sufficient expansion in volume and spreading of fixed costs also would have had to occur to permit such a marked difference in the rates of increase in the WPI and the CPI. The year 1972 was one of extraordinary sales growth and a year in which the A&P grocery chain switched to full-scale discount pricing, touching off (at least in some areas) a significant discount price war in food retailing.

This view is neither refuted nor overwhelmingly supported by the available summary data below (from various issues of *Survey of Current Business*):

| | Average annual rate of change (percent) | |
| | Retail trade | Wholesale trade |
|---|---|---|
| 1962–65 | 6.4 | 7.1 |
| 1965–68 | 6.4 | 5.5 |
| 1968–70 | 4.9 | 6.0 |
| December 1970– August 1971 | 14.0 | 14.0 |
| Phases I and II | 10.1 | 14.1 |

The average annual rate of growth in retail sales during the controls period was 10.1 percent, 68 percent greater than the average from 1962 to 1970 but less than the 14 percent rate in the eight months prior to

Table 10-7. *Ratios of Inventory to Sales and of Full-Time Employee Equivalents to Sales in Retail and Wholesale Trade, Various Periods, 1960–72*

| | Ratios | | | |
|---|---|---|---|---|
| | Inventory to sales | | Full-time employee equivalents to sales | |
| Period | Retail trade | Wholesale trade | Retail trade | Wholesale trade |
| 1960–65 | 1.41 | 1.17 | 0.36 | 0.22 |
| 1966–68 | 1.44 | 1.18 | 0.32 | 0.19 |
| 1969–70[a] | ... | ... | 0.30 | 0.18 |
| December 1970–August 1971 | 1.46 | 1.24 | ... | ... |
| 1971[a] | ... | ... | 0.28 | 0.16 |
| 1972[a] | ... | ... | 0.26 | 0.15 |
| Phases I and II, August 1971– December 1972 | 1.42 | 1.22 | ... | ... |

Source: *Survey of Current Business*, various issues.
a. Available annually only.

controls. The volume of wholesale trade increased at an annual rate of 14.1 percent during the sixteen months of controls, more than double the 1962–70 averages and equal to the eight-month prefreeze rate.

Possible sources of productivity gains in wholesale and retail trade are reductions in the ratio of inventory to sales and in the ratio of employment to sales. The data in Table 10-7 show no significant reduction in inventory to sales in Phases I and II relative to the eight months before controls, and show controls levels that are above the 1960–65 averages. The ratio of full-time equivalent employees to sales also declined for both 1971 and 1972. Employment data are available only annually, however, and attempts to form an adequate regression relation between the change in employment and the change in sales and time proved unsatisfactory and indicated no significant deviation from past trends.

Thus, the slowing of inflation at the retail level may have resulted from competition at the retail level, but an analysis of price-reduction orders issued by the commission suggests that controls may have been a limiting factor as well. By November 30, 1972, 102 price-reduction orders had been issued, of which 40 were sent to retail firms and 8 to firms involved in a combination of wholesale and retail activities.[18] In

18. Price Commission Paper M-549, December 12, 1972.

other words, nearly 50 percent of violations resulting in price-reduction orders were in retail trade. Of the 48 firms so ordered, 22 were in violation only of the profit-margin limitation, which suggests that the profit-margin constraint may have been more limiting than the customary initial percentage markup rule. Controls on the retail sector also may have had an indirect effect on prices. Discussions with retailers by the commission staff suggest retailers may have exerted some pressure on manufacturing suppliers to limit price increases. This cannot be substantiated with evidence, but the staff interpretation was that, to some extent, manufacturers may have been deterred in fully implementing approved price increases.

## Conclusion

In summary, the data reviewed in this chapter are consistent with the conclusions drawn in Chapter 8 about the effectiveness of price controls. The evidence indicates a modest reduction in the rate of change in prices in manufactures of leather products, petroleum refining, the service industries, construction, and wholesale and retail trade.

# XI

# Costs and Benefits of Price Controls

A complete assessment of U.S. wage and price controls requires a comparison of the total social costs and the total social benefits associated with the program. Unfortunately, many of the data necessary to satisfy a rigorous definition of proper costs and benefits simply do not exist. Even if such data were available, their use would require value judgments about aggregation and comparison. But although the calculation cannot be made unambiguously, some approximations can be made of the order of magnitude of the social costs and benefits of Phase II.

In a pure economic sense, social costs and benefits of price controls are related directly to the social costs and benefits of inflation.[1] Although debatable in both a quantitative and qualitative sense, the costs of inflation include cruel and capricious income-redistribution effects, reduction in liquidity, problems in international competitive conditions and balance of payments, loss of information from unstable prices, and diversion of resources for hedging or in other attempts to beat the "inflation game."

The economic benefits of inflation are ambiguous. Based on the work of A. W. Phillips[2] and others following him, one alleged benefit of inflation has been the reduction in unemployment and the associated increase in real output: that is, increased inflation lowers the level of unemployment.[3] This position has been challenged by some neoclassical economists,

1. For a general discussion of the latter, see Edward Foster, *Costs and Benefits of Inflation,* Studies in Monetary Economics (Federal Reserve Bank of Minneapolis, Research Department, March 1972). Some empirical analyses include Maurice Allais, "Growth and Inflation," *Journal of Money, Credit and Banking,* vol. 1 (August 1969), pp. 355–426; Prakash Lohani and Earl A. Thompson, "The Optimal Rate of Secular Inflation," *Journal of Political Economy,* vol. 79 (September/October 1971), pp. 962–82; and William D. Nordhaus, "The Effects of Inflation on the Distribution of Economic Welfare," *Journal of Money, Credit and Banking,* vol. 5 (February 1973), pp. 465–504.

2. A. W. Phillips, "The Relation between Unemployment and the Rate of Change of Money Wage Rates in the United Kingdom, 1861–1957," *Economica,* vol. 25, n.s. (November 1958), pp. 283–99.

3. The current form of the Phillips curve is based on the work of George L. Perry; see his *Unemployment, Money Wage Rates, and Inflation* (M.I.T. Press, 1966). A form of the Phillips relation also is embodied in each of the aggregate models discussed in Chapter 8.

who argue that the trade-off of more inflation for less unemployment represents a short-run phenomenon that eventually will be offset by long-run adjustments in the economic system.[4]

Neither theoretical position makes any explicit predictions of the effects of wage-price controls attributable to institutional changes in the wage-price mechanism, particularly the attenuation of inflationary expectations. For example, if the Phillips relation is operative, a lower rate of inflation than that which would have occurred does not necessarily imply a higher rate of unemployment. Controls can alter expectations and thus shift the Phillips curve closer to the origin—that is, make feasible both a lower rate of inflation and a lower rate of unemployment.

## Output, Employment, Productivity, and Profits during Phase II

The controls program was conducted under the generally favorable conditions of an expanding economy, increased production, gains in output per man-hour, and attendant reduced pressure on prices. The recovery began before the institution of controls and generally continued throughout the controls period at slightly higher rates than in the precontrols period (see Table 11-1).

The growth in real gross national product (1958 dollars) during the controls period averaged 6.4 percent, compared with an average of 6.0 during the first two quarters of 1971. Likewise, the private economy and the private nonfarm sector averaged slightly higher rates of growth in output over the controls period relative to the first half of 1971. The rate

4. See Milton Friedman, "The Role of Monetary Policy," *American Economic Review*, vol. 58 (March 1968), pp. 1–17; the collection of papers by Edmund S. Phelps and others, *Microeconomic Foundations of Employment and Inflation Theory* (Norton, 1970); or Karl Brunner and Allan H. Meltzer, "Money, Debt, and Economic Activity," *Journal of Political Economy*, vol. 80 (September/October 1972), pp. 951–77. Theoretical models that support a long-run Phillips relation include Charles C. Holt, "Job Search, Phillips' Wage Relation, and Union Influence: Theory and Evidence," in Phelps and others, *Microeconomic Foundations;* George A. Akerlof, "Relative Wages and the Rate of Inflation," *Quarterly Journal of Economics*, vol. 83 (August 1969), pp. 353–74; Stephen A. Ross and Michael L. Wachter, "Wage Determination, Inflation, and the Industrial Structure," *American Economic Review*, vol. 63 (September 1973), pp. 675–92; and Arthur M. Okun, "Upward Mobility in a High-pressure Economy," *Brookings Papers on Economic Activity* (1:1973), pp. 207–52.

Table 11-1. *Rates of Change in Selected Output and Employment Indicators, Various Periods, 1961–72*

Seasonally adjusted average quarterly percent changes at annual rates

| Indicator | 1961–65 | 1966–68 | 1969–70 | First half of 1971 | Controls period, August 1971– December 1972 |
|---|---|---|---|---|---|
| *Gross national product* | | | | | |
| Current dollars | 7.2 | 7.9 | 5.6 | 11.5 | 9.5 |
| 1958 dollars | 5.7 | 4.0 | 0.2 | 6.0 | 6.4 |
| *Indexes of gross national product* | | | | | |
| Private economy | 5.9 | 4.0 | 0.2 | 6.5 | 6.8 |
| Private nonfarm economy | 6.2 | 4.1 | 0.1 | 6.7 | 7.2 |
| Manufacturing | 7.8 | 4.5 | −2.6 | 14.6 | 8.5 |
| *Productivity gains* | | | | | |
| Private economy | 4.3 | 2.6 | 0.4 | 5.5 | 4.7 |
| Private nonfarm economy | 3.9 | 2.3 | 0.3 | 5.7 | 4.5 |
| Manufacturing | 4.5 | 2.3 | 1.8 | 13.4 | 4.5 |
| *Labor force* | | | | | |
| Employment | 1.8 | 2.1 | 1.3 | 0.6 | 3.2 |
| Unemployment rate, total | 5.5 | 3.7 | 4.2 | 5.9 | 5.7[a] |
| Females | 6.3 | 4.9 | 5.3 | 7.0 | 6.7[a] |
| Males | 5.1 | 3.0 | 3.6 | 5.3 | 5.1[a] |
| Married men | 3.3 | 1.8 | 2.1 | 3.2 | 2.9[a] |
| Teenagers | 16.0 | 12.7 | 13.7 | 16.9 | 16.5[a] |

Sources: Gross national product, U.S. Office of Business Economics, *The National Income and Product Accounts of the United States, 1929–1965: Statistical Tables* (1966), and *Survey of Current Business*, various issues; other data, U.S. Bureau of Labor Statistics, *Employment and Earnings*, various issues.
a. Average rate of unemployment for all categories, August 1971 to December 1972.

of growth in manufacturing was high over the controls period but substantially less than the average of 14.6 percent in the first half of 1971. Average productivity gains slowed from the levels attained at the beginning of the recovery; the rate of increase in the manufacturing sector dropped from 13.4 percent to 4.5 percent.

The economic expansion over the controls period included an average quarterly gain (annualized) in employment of 3.2 percent, but because of the expanded labor force, the average level of unemployment remained relatively high, 5.7 percent, over the six quarters of controls. Although the aggregate civilian unemployment rate increased to 6.1 percent in August 1971, by the end of controls in December 1972 the rate was down to 5.1 percent.

Table 11-2. *Estimated Effect of Phase II Controls on Selected Private Nonfarm Economic Indicators, Alternative Models*

Percentage points per quarter at annual rate

| Model | Real outputᵃ | Unemploy- ment rateᵇ | Output per man-hourᶜ | Profitsᶜ | Unit labor costsᵈ |
|---|---|---|---|---|---|
| EB | +1.74 | −0.21 | +1.05 | −5.8 | −0.58 |
| G | +2.34 | −0.27 | +1.39 | +1.6 | −2.67 |
| SZ | +1.76 | −0.21 | +1.05 | −1.6 | −1.09 |

Source: Derived using models described in Chapter 8.

a. Equal to the negative of the effect on the private nonfarm gross national product price deflator—average quarterly percentage change (annualized) predicted with controls less that predicted without controls.

b. Actual quarterly average of the aggregate civilian unemployment rate minus the unemployment rate predicted without controls.

c. Actual average quarterly percentage change (annualized) less average quarterly change predicted without controls.

d. Impact on wages (see Chapter 8) minus the effect on productivity.

Interesting and informative as these data may be, they fail to indicate the extent to which they were affected by controls, directly or indirectly. If real GNP were fixed—that is, unaffected by the controls program—there would be no effect on the data in Table 11-1. On the other hand, if nominal GNP were unaltered by the controls, it could be argued that there would be a boost to real output, depending upon the elasticity of aggregate supply and demand. The aggregate models presented in Chapter 8 can be used to estimate generalized effects of controls. If each model is solved under the assumption of a price-control elasticity of real output equal to 1, it simultaneously estimates what these other variables would have been without controls.[5]

Table 11-2 contains estimates generated by the simulations of the three models under the stated assumptions. Each model estimates a positive stimulus on real output, between 1.7 and 2.3 percentage points (equal to the negative of the retardation in the rate of inflation as measured by the private nonfarm deflator). Because private nonfarm sector output makes up roughly 85 percent of the GNP (assuming no change in real

5. The method used assumed that nominal gross national product would have been the same with or without controls. The difference lies in the distribution of the percentage gain in GNP between the growth in real output and the rate of inflation. The second assumption is a variant of Okun's law that links the stimulus of real output to productivity and employment. The effect on employment, coupled with an assumed unaffected labor force, produces an estimate of the rate of unemployment in the absence of controls. The consequences for profits then may be ascertained by assuming, first, that the impact on value added per unit of output equals the effect on the rate of inflation; and, second, that the controls did not alter the level of net interest.

Table 11-3. *Average Percentage Change in Unit Labor Costs and Private Nonfarm Deflator, Various Periods, 1947–72*
Average quarterly percent changes at annual rates

| Economic indicator | 1947–72 | 1955–60 | 1961–65 | 1966–67 | 1968–70 | First half of 1971 | Controls period, August 1971–December 1972 |
|---|---|---|---|---|---|---|---|
| Unit labor costs | 2.6 | 2.6 | 0.3 | 3.9 | 6.2 | 1.9 | 2.1 |
| Private nonfarm deflator | 2.6 | 2.2 | 1.0 | 3.2 | 4.5 | 4.3 | 2.0 |

Sources: Calculated from official U.S. Bureau of Labor Statistics and U.S. Bureau of Economic Analysis data.

growth of the remaining sectors), the average real rate of growth in the GNP would have been between 6.6 and 7.2 percent (instead of 8.6) over the six quarters of controls.

The three models are quite close in their respective estimates of the effect on unemployment (between 0.2 and 0.3 percentage point lower with controls) and in the rate of growth in output per man-hour in the private nonfarm sector (productivity being an estimated 1.0 to 1.4 percentage points higher on average over the controls period). The three models give significantly different estimates, however, for the rate of change in unit labor costs, ranging from an average of 0.6 percentage point (annual rate) per quarter to more than 2.5 percentage points.

Over the long run, prices normally move in accordance with changes in unit labor costs,[6] but there are significant short-run variations to this rule of thumb. A comparison of the relative effect on prices and the effect on unit labor costs might be used as a measure of the relative effectiveness of the wage and price controls. Table 11-3 shows the actual changes in unit labor costs and prices for the controls period and selected historical periods.[7]

6. For example, from 1947 to 1972 the average quarterly percentage change (annualized) in unit labor costs was 2.60 percent and in the private nonfarm deflator, 2.62 percent. On a quarterly basis, however, this relation is not so unique.
7. Models EB and SZ estimated that price changes would have substantially exceeded changes in unit labor costs had controls not been in effect, much the same as the relation between the two variables during the first half of 1971. These two models thus estimate that the primary effects were on prices. Model G predicts that changes in unit labor costs would have exceeded price changes in the absence of a structural shift in the economy, implying that the major effect was on unit labor costs.

The estimated effects on profits from the models are consistent with the estimates of the change in unit labor costs, but the models give conflicting estimates in comparison with one another.[8]

The above estimates using the aggregate models rest on special assumptions. Nonetheless, the altered models, incorporating the assumption that real output was higher than it would have been without controls, are consistent with the regression equation that shows profits following a normal cyclical response over the period of controls. If, on the other hand, real output were not higher than it would have been, given the greater effect on prices than on wages, profits would have been squeezed during Phases I and II.

## Costs of the Controls Program

The only accurate available cost figures are the direct outlays by the federal government for the Economic Stabilization Program, shown below (in millions of dollars):

|  | Fiscal 1972 | Fiscal 1973 | Total |
|---|---|---|---|
| Cost of Living Council ⎫ | | | |
| Price Commission ⎬ | 20.5 | 26.0 | 46.5 |
| Pay Board ⎭ | | | |
| Internal Revenue Service | 34.5 | 40.3 | 74.8 |
| Department of Justice | 1.3 | 2.5 | 3.8 |
| Total | 56.3 | 68.8 | 125.1 |

8. Model G estimates that profits grew an average of 1.6 percentage points more each quarter (annualized rate) than they would have without controls (Table 11-2). Model EB estimates the growth in corporate profits was nearly 6 percentage points less than it would have been. Considering the statistical qualities of the models, the most reasonable conclusion would be "no effect" or "an ambiguous effect" on profits. Several regressions relating pretax corporate profits to GNP were run; the following, for the period 1955:1–1972:4, is the best-fitting equation that includes dummy variables for the period of the guideposts and the period of controls:

$$ZB = -5.08 + 5.19GNP - 0.56T + 0.06GPD + 0.19ESP$$
$$(-5.42)\ (13.0)\qquad (-2.64)\quad (0.06)\qquad (0.12)$$

$(\bar{R}^2 = 0.71$; Durbin-Watson statistic $= 1.76$; standard error $= 3.14)$,

where $ZB$ is the quarterly percentage change in pretax corporate profits; $GNP$ is the quarterly percentage change in nominal gross national product; $T$ is a time dummy

The total expenditure for fiscal 1972 and 1973 was $125.1 million.[9] Assuming all outlays were in Phases I and II (part of which was spent for Phase III), the cost is $20.85 million per quarter, or a rate of $83.4 million per year.

Other federal agencies, as well as Congress and the White House, also incurred expenditures that were directly and indirectly related to the price-control program. Many agencies were called upon for assistance; some employees remained at their respective agencies, and others were detailed to the Price Commission, Pay Board, and other agencies in the Economic Stabilization Program. The total "other" governmental costs, including salaries and overhead expenses, is estimated to be less than $2 million for the full period of controls.

No reliable data are available for direct expenditures by firms and unions, but several different approaches, including a casual sampling of the firms' representatives for costs incurred in complying with the program, produced an estimate of three man-years for tier I and two man-years for tier II manufacturing firms. These figures clearly are not maximums, especially for firms engaged in litigation over the regulations. In addition, the expenses of retailing firms that had to comply with posting requirements probably were higher on average. Assuming that salaries, overhead, and other expenses were $50,000 per man-year, the approximately 470 tier II firms and 1,112 tier I firms (excluding food and general-merchandise firms) expended approximately $200 million.[10]

The main compliance cost in retailing was for posting, which fell principally upon food and general merchandise retailers. On the basis of cost estimates supplied by industry associations, compliance costs are assumed to have averaged 0.5 percent per dollar of sales, which the authors believe to be a high average. Firms with more than sixty employees account for about 71 percent of industry sales in general merchandising and 49 percent in food retailing. On the basis of average sales over the period of

with a value of 1 in 1955:1; GPD is a guidepost-era dummy variable; and ESP is a controls-period dummy. (The numbers in parentheses are t-statistics.) The coefficients for both the guidepost and controls-period dummy variables are not significant. In addition, the regression equation predicts an average annual rate of increase in corporate profits of 18.8 percent for the controls period, which is just equal to the average of the actual changes in corporate profits over the period.

9. The Budget of the United States Government, Fiscal Year 1974, p. 183; and The Budget of the United States Government, Fiscal Year 1975, p. 164; and data provided by Ernest Salisbury, Office of Administration, CLC.

10. Source: Price Commission data.

controls, these estimates would imply about $500 million (annual rate) expended directly to comply with the controls program. Thus, the direct expenditures for both the federal government and firms totaled about $800 million annually.[11]

The social costs of controls also include the "indirect social costs" incurred because the regulations created inefficiencies.[12] From the available evidence, in few actual cases did firms incur socially unproductive expenses.

The major problem areas encountered during Phase II were in lumber and hides. In lumber, the reported major evasion tactic was multiple wholesaling, involving mostly paper transactions (filling out an invoice requires effort, but the magnitude involved was probably insignificant). On the basis of the information gathered by the Price Commission, no cases were confirmed in which lumber was actually shipped out of the country and then imported—or some similar ruse that used up a sizable amount of resources. This does not mean that attempts to circumvent the regulations were minor, but rather that the associated wasted resources were of a small order of magnitude.

Hides became a problem essentially because a worldwide demand in excess of the available supply was bidding up prices, thus increasing normal export levels. Shoe manufacturers and other leather processors were required to pass through such cost increases on a dollar-for-dollar basis. But even fewer reports than in regard to lumber were received of any type of added costs being incurred to avoid the regulations. Indeed, costs for shoe manufacturers were rising too fast as it was, and domestic shoe manufacturers in general were irate that the federal government was doing nothing to hold down the rising price of hides. It is also quite doubtful that shoe or other apparel styles were changed and more expensive resources utilized in items that otherwise would have been fabricated

11. In February 1974, the CLC estimated costs of compliance to range between $700 million and $2.0 billion annually. See testimony of John T. Dunlop in *Oversight on Economic Stabilization,* Hearings before the Subcommittee on Production and Stabilization of the Senate Committee on Banking, Housing, and Urban Affairs (1974), Appendix P.

12. To be an added social cost in the sense used here, however, the term "distortion" must be limited to those expenditures of real resources which without controls would have been unnecessary for the same level of real output. In other words, the term "indirect social cost" refers to added costs of resource utilization and not to changes in the distribution of income, or the lack thereof, which, in the opinion of some, may add to social welfare. The former is not necessarily more important than the latter, but it is much less ambiguous.

out of leather. Just at this time, shoes with more leather, as well as higher-legged boots and leather clothing, were climbing in fashion appeal. (No doubt this was spurred along, in Veblenesque fashion, by the very factors of rising prices and scarcity.)

Other apparent problems arose because some price increases were considered by the public to be inconsistent with the promulgated goals of the program, or because the permitted price increases created a two-tier (or multitier) pricing system. Such consequences were inequitable but were not problem areas in the sense that massive expenditures of resources were incurred. Some prices simply must be permitted to rise more than the target if demand pressures are strong or supplies inadequate.

This is not to deny that some inefficiencies resulted from the program. On the basis of available evidence—which, of course, may mount with the passage of time—their magnitude apparently was small. Considering the sales levels in the problem areas and the reported actions undertaken by those involved, a rough estimate of the added social costs would appear to be about $500 million annually. This brings the total direct and indirect social costs of the controls program, by both firms and the government, to $1.3 billion.[13]

## Indirect Benefits and Costs

The longer-term economic consequences of the controls program represent an important consideration. If, for example, the entire economy is competitive in the long run and if the policies of Phase II squeezed normal competitive returns, reduced prices and stimulated output would give way in the future to higher-than-normal prices and concomitant reductions in real output, thus reducing the estimated short-run benefits.[14] Another major consideration is whether the policies of the controls program, if permanent, could have continued to have the same effectiveness for an

13. The range of estimated boost to real output, under the assumption of a fixed level of nominal GNP, would suggest a short-run economic "benefit-cost" ratio of (11.7–17.5) to 1. If it is assumed that real GNP were unaffected by the burden of controls, there are no benefits from increased real output. Because the benefits from reduced inflation are ambiguous, so is the benefit-cost ratio.

14. Thus, the benefits would be reduced to a fraction of the above estimate (equal only to an appropriate rate of interest times the benefits over the control period), whereas the economic costs would be unaffected or perhaps augmented by future expeditures.

indefinitely extended period into the future.[15] The latter days of Phase II were accompanied by an increasing burden of paperwork and pressures against the regulations, prompting a commission official to observe, "The system is about to crack." It is also clear that the economic conditions under which Phase II began were changing drastically, from one of excess capacity to one of shortage and demand pressures. Thus, the policies and specific regulations were in need of revision in any event, a circumstance that the commission recognized and to which it wished to respond. Whether these revised policies would have improved the program's effectiveness is debatable because the major stabilization forces lay outside the controls regulations; that is, more of the reduction in inflation emanated from the competitive, or unorganized, sectors rather than from those directly controlled.

The controls program may have had social values in several other areas. For example, the foregoing estimates ascribed no economic value or benefit to the attenuation in the general inflationary psychology, to the economic value arising from greater stability in international monetary arrangements, or to a number of similar favorable effects.

Perhaps the most significant and longest-lasting economic benefits from the controls program lay in the educational area—in what was learned about the economics of controls—and in the disclosure of the perverse impact of various governmental policies on price-stabilization objectives. Acreage diversion, import quotas, export subsidies, and direct price supports have had few, if any, redeeming economic qualities and have been long overdue for revision. The Price Commission often pointed out to other administration agencies, to Congress, and to the public that special-interest legislation often entails a social cost in institutional rigidities that prevent productivity gains and add to price pressures. Particularly noteworthy in this regard is such congressional legislation as the Davis-Bacon Act, regulation of the trucking industry that promotes inefficient routing, and minimum-wage legislation. Aside from the desirable or undesirable features of minimum-wage legislation in income redistribution, such legislation tends to increase costs—both directly and indirectly through the maintance of relative wages—that are passed along in the form of higher prices. Consequently, the Price Commission prepared estimates of the inflationary consequences of a proposed increase in the minimum wage and supplied these estimates on request to various members of Congress. In

---

15. The price explosion during Phase III raises still other questions in this regard.

such ways, the Price Commission often was able to focus national attention on the macroeconomic price ramifications of such legislation that by and large had gone unpublicized before.[16]

Productivity is another area in which the Price Commission and its regulations may have had significant educational value. At first, firms were required to calculate their own productivity gains. This was a new experience for many firms, one that gave them added information about unit costs of production that they had not had before. It also caused management to focus attention on the role of productivity in the cost-price relation and eventually may have led to gains in productivity that otherwise would not have been achieved (at least as quickly). Productivity was part of the initial stabilization arithmetic, and the commissioners, the commission staff, and other governmental officials often spoke about the importance of productivity in relation to wage gains and inflation. Finally, the Price Commission's attempts to obtain useful data on productivity confirmed the virtual uselessness of the National Commission on Productivity and contributed to its reorganization and redirection.

A variety of other more subjective costs and benefits should be noted. Their merit may be debatable, but they may be of importance to decisionmakers. To some persons, the primary objective of an incomes policy should be a more nearly equal distribution of income. The controls program certainly affected the distribution of income, particularly in specific cases, even though this was neither a specific charge nor an objective of the commission or of the Pay Board. But the movement of relative shares over the controls period indicates that any such effect was minimal.[17]

Some persons also might wish to add to the benefit side of the controls ledger an amount greater than the pure economic value of the reduction of unemployment. Ethics, such as the work ethic, always have been and will continue to be of utmost value to any society, but it is highly debatable whether the fortification or dilution of such social decorums should be considered in the evaluation of wage-price controls.

The most important social cost of controls from the Phase II decisionmakers' points of view probably was the cost of the very act of instituting

16. This does not mean cost-increasing actions are necessarily undesirable, but the consequences are another legitimate factor that should be included in the process of decisionmaking about public policy.

17. For estimates of the distribution of income by functional shares, see the annual July issues of the *Survey of Current Business*, Table 1.10.

controls. The dramatic manner in which Phase II was shifted into Phase III suggests that such considerations far outweighed the pure economic aspects of controls. Despite the importance of the economic considerations, only limited rigorous inquiry into the economics of the controls program apparently was undertaken before the decision was made, in effect, to lift controls, under the label of Phase III. The political ramifications of what generally had been perceived in the press to be a successful Phase II program may be significant for future policy actions.

## Conclusions

In retrospect, political considerations appear to have played a more significant role than did pure economic considerations in both the institution of the freeze and the dismantling of the wage-price controls program. Over time, the apparent success of Phase II increasingly became a source of economic embarrassment to administration officials, who had been driven to adopt direct controls out of political pressures but who opposed this approach on ideological grounds as well as from a sincere conviction that such measures are inherently counterproductive in efficient economic processes. Meetings in the latter part of 1972 between the price commissioners and administration officials to discuss modifications of Phase II regulations were little more than a perfunctory review of what had been learned from the experiment and how the regulations might be made even more effective as an instrument of economic policy.[18] From an inside perspective, therefore, it appeared that with the presidential elections out of the way, it remained only to prepare a quiet grave for the controls apparatus. It is in this context that the costs and benefits of the program ultimately must be evaluated.

18. The Council of Economic Advisers assessed the costs of controls in its January 1973 report to the President, stating: "An impressionistic review suggests that these costs were probably not large in 1972, relative to the role that the system played in the national economy, but that they were growing as the year progressed. . . . A case could therefore be made for continuing the anti-inflationary influence of controls in 1973. But the experience of 1972 also suggested a number of dangers to be avoided. . . . These dangers and difficulties did not mean that continuation of controls was impossible or undesirable. They did mean that even temporary continuation would require modification of the program. *They reinforced the idea that controls should not be a permanent part of the American economic system*." *Economic Report of the President, January 1973*, pp. 66, 69, 70 (emphasis added).

# XII

# Some Lessons of Phase II

It may be rash to presume that much can be learned from the recent U.S. experiment with wage and price controls, given the relatively short span of time between November 14, 1971, and the present. Certainly, a definitive evaluation of the overall impact of controls on output and employment, as well as on the rate of inflation, will look different from a more distant perspective. But if only to add to the dialogue about future steps in U.S. controls policy, it will be useful to identify some lessons that have emerged from Phase II.

## Principal Problems of Controls

The experience during Phase II suggests that the effectiveness of controls depends on the resolution of two major problems: acceptance of the controls policy on the part of the public and the degree of autonomy afforded the controls agency.

### Creating a Stabilization Ethic

It was stated earlier that Phase II had everything going for it: a propitious economic atmosphere in which the economy was recovering from recession; the presence of underused capacity; a prospect of large gains in productivity; and the competitive market forces characteristic of this stage of the business cycle. All these were present in good measure, but equally significant was the sympathetic receptivity of business, labor, and the public generally to the development of an anti-inflation policy.

In the summer of 1971 the various constituencies of the U.S. economy apparently were ready—indeed, eager—to support a program that would use direct price and wage restraints. Phase II had the kind of widespread acceptance that historically has characterized wartime patriotism and peacetime income tax compliance. The consequent favorable results generated an air of success in meeting anti-inflationary goals.

197

Whether the effectiveness associated with Phase II controls could have been maintained depends upon answers to other questions that have been raised and discussed in this study. What are the fundamental causes of inflation? How do controls alter this process at both the microeconomic and macroeconomic levels? How do the economic conditions prevailing at any particular time affect the answers to these questions? More theory and empirical research clearly are needed to work toward definitive answers, but a few observations can be made with respect to Phase II.

Near the end of 1972 there were indications that general cooperation with the controls program was deteriorating, at least in particular sectors of the economy. Two qualifications to this observation are relevant. First, there is reason to believe that political pressures, based primarily upon ideology, may have led to a deterioration in the support for controls during the fall of 1972. The Cost of Living Council also was partly responsible for the growing dissatisfaction, because it blocked several constructive changes in the regulations proposed by the Price Commission. Second, if the hypothesis that a stabilization ethic had been established correctly explains the effectiveness of Phase II, the consequences of the manner in which Phase III was announced and promulgated would be precisely to reverse or dampen this ethic altogether.

The major change in Phase III was the shift from a system of specific rules requiring cost justification and prior approval to one that was governed largely by vague and self-administered standards. One provision, for example, allowed price increases over and above those justified by cost "as necessary for efficient allocation of resources or to maintain adequate levels of supply."[1] More detrimental still were the differing interpretations given by administration officials of what the standards meant. This policy shift was followed by a 12.5 percent annual rate of increase in the prices of wholesale industrial commodities and of 4.3 percent in prices of consumer goods and services other than food from December 1972 to June 1973.

Phase II officials had successfully overseen development of a stabilization ethic that had worked during its brief span, but it proved entirely too fragile to withstand the sudden and confusing shift, or "dash back to market," represented by Phase III. It is clear from this experience that abrupt shifts in policy can easily undermine the willingness of business and labor to accept the constraints of a controls program.

---

1. *Code of Federal Regulations,* Title 6 (February 1, 1974), sec. 130.13, p. 23.

## The Control of Controls

In Phase II the issue of control of policy was first raised by prospective labor appointees to the Pay Board and resolved in favor of autonomy for that body. But no similar issue was raised by the Price Commission. Political considerations were largely ignored after the initial action of August 1971 and during Phase II, but they influenced the commission's efforts at certain critical stages, especially the attempt by the Cost of Living Council in November 1971 to delay the effective date of certain price regulations, discussed earlier in regard to the birth of the 72-hour rule; the neutralization of the Price Commission as an effective policymaking body after the food-crisis memorandum of June 1972; and the intervention by the White House in the automobile price decision in August 1972.

The purpose of detailing these intrusions on the autonomy of the commission is not to censure the CLC for doing what it perceived to be its job, but rather to raise the question as to whether a controls agency (or agencies) should be autonomous—that is, largely free from political influence on its policies and actions. Given a decision to institute wage and price controls or a review board of some type, which is to be preferred: a quasi-autonomous unit or units such as the Pay Board and Price Commission of Phase II; a Cost of Living Council alone such as existed in Phases III and IV and was directly responsible to the President or his deputy or some other alternative?

There is much to be said for centralizing all economic policymaking in the executive branch, thus making the President fully responsible and accountable for policy development and economic results. On the other hand, rationale for the so-called independent agencies (Federal Reserve Board, Federal Trade Commission, Interstate Commerce Commission, and others) is based on the logic of the checks and balances between executive appointment, Senate confirmation, and judicial review of actions consistent with congressional mandates.

Basically, the answer to the question of control of controls requires a decision as to whether society is better off under a coordinated system of economic policy, with the responsibility vested solely and directly in the executive branch, or whether an independent agency functioning under a system of checks and balances will be better able to promote desired social ends. If the United States should turn again to direct control of prices and wages, the issue of control of controls must be resolved before the form of controls is decided.

## Basic Requirements of Controls

If fiscal policy were more responsive and responsible and if more were known about the leads and lags associated with monetary policy, perhaps wage-price controls would not be necessary. Practical realities, however, may preclude the optimal application of monetary and fiscal policy, and a second-best mix of policies may require controls as a supplement. Several basic requirements for a controls program, if it is ever tried again, emerge from this study.

First, realistic national goals for wages and prices, coupled with appropriate exceptions and exemptions, are essential to create an atmosphere of receptivity for controls. The experience during Phase II suggests that the contribution of controls to reducing the rate of inflation may be small, but the contribution to higher real output and employment may be significant. Experience also suggests that setting goals may be difficult—given the low reliability of forecasts (which probably could be improved with intensive research efforts)—as well as politically unpalatable at times.

Second, the regulations need to be flexible to meet changing economic conditions and should be applicable to conditions in particular markets without an excessive amount of interpretation. This creates several problems that may be difficult, if not impossible, to overcome, including those associated with obtaining accurate, unbiased, detailed data; with various legal-constitutional requirements such as due process, public disclosure, and nondiscrimination; and with the pervasive and nebulous idea of equity. As discussed in Chapter 6, the ability to cope with these problems was not well developed in the control mechanism of Phase II. The principal drawbacks, which should be rectified in future controls agencies, were a lack of economic expertise among senior staff members, the political pressures exerted by the executive branch, and the part-time status of the official decisionmakers.

Third, understanding the difference between inflation and relative changes in wages and prices is a difficult problem of public education. The public, firms, unions, and media tend to view any price increase as inflationary and any constant or falling price as noninflationary, thereby totally ignoring the function of relative wages and prices in the process of allocation and distribution. The reason is the simplicity and concreteness of the concept of a general increase in the price level compared with the

complex notion of a change in relative prices—a distinction that is sufficiently difficult to evaluate in a purely competitive, private economy, let
alone in a mixed-market, public-private economy as huge as that of the
United States. This problem may not be insurmountable, but it adds to the
difficulty of administration and public relations.

Fourth, direct controls should not be arbitrary and should not be used
arbitrarily. In other words, policy must be grounded firmly in economic
theory and empirical verification and aimed toward promoting the general well-being of society, with substantially equal sacrifice by all sectors
of the economy. This does not imply universal coverage: controls should
be applied where they are needed and should not disrupt the allocative
function of the price system.

Business can live with a set of internally consistent regulations that are
respected by its administrators. Accordingly, when firms qualify for price
relief under the regulations, special ad hoc standards should not be invoked for political reasons. This occurred in the automobile price case in
1972. The automobile manufacturers provided all information requested
by the commission and waited through weeks of review. After the companies formulated their requests for price relief to cover only the costs of
government-ordered emission systems, belts, and buzzers, the commission
reached a consensus that such increases should be approved (all were between $50 and $100), subject to the profit-margin rule. At this juncture,
Cost of Living Director Donald Rumsfeld summoned automobile company presidents to the White House, where they were asked by Rumsfeld
and Treasury Secretary George Shultz to reduce or withdraw their requests
for increases.[2] The director of the CLC chose to exert pressure outside the
normal channels of regulations and enforcement, even though the sharply
curtailed price requests were below the amounts justified under the regulations. Such actions tend to discredit controls. In this sense, then, the more
apolitical the controls, the more likely it is that such controls will elicit
national support.

Fifth, good relations with firms, unions, and the public are critical to
the success of the program. Consistent policy closely controlled by full-

2. In a press release of August 16, 1972, Lynn A. Townsend, chairman of Chrysler Corporation, stated: "This meeting was for the purpose of asking us to reduce or
withdraw our requests for a price increase to cover the cost of added government
safety and emission control requirements. I want to state categorically that I consider this request by Mr. Rumsfeld to be arbitrary and discriminatory against the
automobile industry."

time decisionmakers is therefore paramount. Also, maintaining candid and open relations with the press is necessary to provide the public with explanations of the nature and implications of alternative policies. An inquisitive and probing press can serve as a healthy check and review of public policy and administrative decisions.

Sixth, Phase II did much to educate all segments of society, especially various agencies of the federal government, about the interrelated nature of specific decisions—and particularly about their price ramifications. As noted in Chapter 11, this aspect may be one of the greater benefits of a controls or quasi-controls program whose primary objective is to curb inflation. Before Phase II rarely had such national attention been paid to the inflationary consequences of agricultural policy, import-tariff legislation, minimum wage legislation, and similar long-accepted dogmas. Certainly, this public awakening resulted in part from improved communications and the increasing number of special-interest groups, such as the consumer movement, that keep track of developments in Washington for their constituencies. But an agency that could keep continually abreast of the inflationary consequences of the multitude of changes in policy, both actual and contemplated, would add greatly to the font of public information about these matters.

Seventh, the timing and extent of decontrol remains a vexing problem, except for those persons who advocate immediate and complete elimination of controls regardless of the consequences. The precise operational criteria to trigger decontrol are vague. Should decontrol be keyed to the intensity of demand and cost-push pressures, to the stage of the business cycle, to the effectiveness of competition in different sectors, or to specific price performance? It may be that the rules will have to be arbitrary, but they should be stipulated in advance, made as definite as possible, and carried out consistently.

## The Outlook and Conclusions

European evidence indicates that controls become unmanageable and are soon discarded.[3] In the United States the impending onerousness of Phase II controls led to their termination before economic conditions worsened. Despite this experience, close examination of the results of

3. See Lloyd Ulman and Robert J. Flanagan, *Wage Restraint: A Study of Incomes Policies in Western Europe* (University of California Press, 1971).

Phase II and subsequent developments leads to the conclusion that some form of controls or at least prior review of price and wage increases are likely to become a permanent feature of U.S. economic policy. Controls may evolve into a form much different from that of Phase II or subsequent phases. But a mechanism will be established to keep a watchful eye on prices and wages. The agency charged with this responsibility will have a formidable role in the determination of economic policy, either directly or through interaction with other agencies of the federal government.

In this regard, two steps might be taken: first, the Employment Act of 1946 might be amended to include price stability as an explicit national goal; and, second, a stabilization board might be created with a fixed number of members appointed by the President, with Senate confirmation, for terms comparable in duration to those of members of the federal regulatory commissions. The function of the board would be to monitor price and wage movements in critical sectors of the economy. After holding public hearings, it would be empowered to limit prospective or actual price and wage increases on the basis of predetermined norms or guidelines. Concomitantly, such an agency would be expected to assess the price ramification of various governmental and private actions, thereby bringing into the public debate the inflationary consequences of such decisions. Earlier discussion has made clear that inflationary price or wage movements are not to be confused with relative price or wage changes that improve the allocation of resources. Such a board may well find certain proposed price increases necessary to assure adequate long-run supply, as in the cases of lumber in Phase II and petroleum in Phase III.

The fundamental disadvantages of such an approach are, first, a loss of control by the executive branch; second, the inability of a single individual or office to coordinate economic policy; and, third, the creation of another bureaucracy with all the undesirable consequences—more red tape, federal intervention in price decisions, and the tendency of controls agencies to become the pawns of the industries they are intended to control. The disadvantages cannot be overlooked, but the current evidence on the Phase II experience suggests that the advantages outweigh the disadvantages.

Finally, Phase II and all the diverse assessments it has generated, including this one, will not settle the fundamental issue concerning the appropriateness and economic efficacy of direct controls. The difficulties, complexities, and side effects no doubt will reinforce the arguments of opponents of controls, who contend that the economy is not a tinker toy whose elements can be twisted from one weird shape to another. At the same time, the recurring inability of traditional economic policies to maintain durable price stability—for whatever reason—is a continual reminder that the economy is a complex machine that cannot be regulated by general fiscal and monetary policies alone. Somewhere in between must lie a path to rational and effective economic policy. The policies initiated on August 15, 1971, marked the beginning of a new effort to find such a policy.

# Index

Ackley, Gardner, 30n
Agricultural products: control after first sale, 63; rising prices of, 57, 58, 61–62; volatility and, 71–72, 141
Agriculture, Department of, crop restrictions, 20, 64–65, 194
Akerlof, George A., 186n
Aliber, Robert Z., 28n
Allais, Maurice, 185n
Allowable costs, pass through of, 15, 25, 32–35, 48, 66, 69–70, 81–82; dollar-for-dollar, 88, 97, 169; fractional, 90; of labor, 12, 13, 16, 31, 34, 38; leather, 168; rules for, 35, 88–91; unnecessary costs, 89. *See also* Nonallowable cost increases
Aluminum industry, 46
Argentina, hide exports, 167
Automotive industry: cost pass through by, 69–70; mandated costs, 69–70; price increases in, 74
Averch, Harvey, 84n

Baking industry, effect on, 74
Base period: defined, 73; initial, 53; profit constraints, 32–40, 54, 66–67, 73; rules for selection of, 35, 67. *See also* Profit margin limitations
Base price: concept, 31, 35, 66–69; defined, 67–68, 141
Baumol, William J., 84n
Beef prices, monitoring of, 63–64
Benefits of controls, 185, 194
Black, S. W., 157n
Borts, George H., 84n
Bosworth, Barry, 8n, 15n, 112
Bowles, Chester, 29
Brinner, Roger, 104. *See also* Eckstein-Brinner aggregate model
Broadcasting. *See* Television broadcasting
Bronfenbrenner, Martin, 80n
Brunner, Karl, 80n, 186n
Bureau of Labor Statistics, productivity data, 35
Burns, Arthur F., 18, 30n, 50
Business investment, return on, 75–76
Butz, Earl L., 20

Category pricing, 51, 53, 54
Ceiling prices, 28, 52, 67
Cement industry, 74–75
Certified Public Accountants Advisory Committee, 28n, 80
CIPM. *See* Customary initial percentage markup
CLC. *See* Cost of Living Council
Coal industry, 12, 38, 39, 82, 177
Coleman, William T., Jr., 10
Collective bargaining, 5
Committee on Health Services Industry, 9, 19, 32, 36–37, 173
Committee on Interest and Dividends, function of, 9, 18, 178–80. *See also* Dividends; Interest
Congress: control advocacy and, 7; Price Commission and, 22
Connally, John B., 13–14, 60
Construction: allowed profit margin, 176; costs, index of, 177; wage increases in *1970,* 176
Construction Industry Stabilization Committee, 9, 176–77
Consumer price index (CPI), 28n, 98–100, 113, 182; effect of controls on, 110–114, 127–37; effect of trade sector on, 180–81; food component, changes in, 57–60, 64; leather index, changes in, 168–69; *1960–65* 3; *1965–68,* 98; *1968–70,* 98; *1970–71,* 5; *1971–72* 98; *1972–73,* 198; service component, changes in, 173–75
Container industry, control of, 70
Controls: administration of, 27, 199; classification system of, 11, 30, 32–33; requirements of, 200–02; social costs of, 185, 193
Corn crop, 20, 59, 64
Cost justification, 51, 66, 143
Cost of Living Council (CLC), establishment of, 9; Price Commission and, 11–15, 68, 198–99; White House and, 61–63
Council of Economic Advisers, 6, 13, 18, 196n
CPI. *See* Consumer price index

205